THE NEUROLINGUISTICS OF BILINGUALISM

The Neurolinguistics of Bilingualism

An Introduction

Franco Fabbro

University of Trieste and
Research Hospital 'Eugenio Medea', Bosisio-Parini (Lecco), Italy

Psychology Press
a member of the Taylor & Francis group

B.S

Psychology Press Ltd, Publishers
27 Church Road
Hove
East Sussex, BN3 2FA
UK

British Library Cataloguing in Publication Data

A catalogue record for this book is available from the British Library

ISBN 0-86377-755-4

Typeset by DP Photosetting, Aylesbury, Bucks
Printed and bound in the UK by Biddles Ltd, Guildford and King's Lynn

11/21/02

Contents

Acknowledgements

Thanks are due to all colleagues who have read the manuscript and proposed modifications, in particular Salvatore Aglioti, Barbara Alberti, Anna Fini, Yvan Lebrun, Amir Muzur and Michel Paradis, to Guido DeLuca and Lorenza Vorano for allowing me to study many of their patients, and to Alessandro Fantin for the figures in the book. My gratitude goes to the Italian National Research Council for the scholarship to Canada I was granted that has allowed me to work on this project.

Lastly, my wife Valeria deserves special thanks not only for her affectionate support and her thorough editing of the manuscript, but also for her valuable suggestions on the issue of bilingualism and polyglossia.

Introduction

Bilingual individuals are all those people who use two or more languages or dialects in their everyday lives. In the past, only those speaking two or more *major* languages (such as English, French, or German) were considered to be bilinguals, but this idea turned out to be a mere cultural bias. It can be stated that the distinction between "language" and "dialect" is only political and it is of no relevance to linguistic or neurolinguistic research and practice. Another deep-rooted bias has been the idea of considering as bilingual only those people who knew two or more languages "perfectly". This has probably been dictated by a monolinguistic view of the phenomenon of bilingualism. For this reason, some scholars felt the need to point out that bilingual individuals are not two monolinguals in one person, but rather speakers using different languages in different domains or situations, for different purposes, and with different interlocutors. Once this premise has been accepted, an important insight has been provided, which might also be of interest to those involved in clinical neurolinguistics, namely that more than half the world population is actually bilingual.

On the basis of these considerations, one can easily deduce that more than half of the patients diagnosed with aphasic disorders, i.e. specific disorders of language, in fact show "bilingual aphasia". Despite this, clinical literature does not reflect such a large amount of bilingual cases. In the last century bilingual aphasia has been considered a sort of rarity, and unfortunately not much has changed since then. In the literature concerning aphasia, one can find a few hundred papers on bilingual aphasics as against several thousands of cases of (presumed) monolinguals aphasics. Until rather recently clinicians have often superficially supposed that their patients could only speak the language(s) commonly used in their own surroundings, such as the hospital where they were treated. As a consequence, most individuals whose cases have been described in the specialized literature "coincidentally" spoke only the language used by their clinicians! This situation is gradually improving, as more and more clinicians and researchers have become aware of the fact that they should at least consider the probability that their patients with aphasic disorders may know more than just one language and that a "pure" monolingual is an exception rather than the rule.

Another fundamental issue of the neurolinguistics of bilingualism is whether the cerebral representation of language in bilinguals differs from that of unilinguals, and if so, in what specific way. This is also a basic question for most psychological and neurological disciplines devoted to the study of the linguistic, psychological, and neural substrates related to education in general, and to the acquisition/learning of languages in particular. In addition, such a question reveals the need to identify and differentiate all the levels involved in the cerebral representation of language(s), i.e. the biochemical, anatomical, neurofunctional, psychological, and linguistic levels, and probably others. Actually, the representation of languages in the brain may differ for some but not all of these levels (e.g. at neurofunctional, but not at biochemical or neuroanatomical level). A large series of neurolinguistic studies seem to suggest that specific factors such as age and manner of acquisition/learning of a language and use of it (implicit linguistic competence versus explicit metalinguistic knowledge) may affect its cerebral representation.

A cerebral lesion in a bilingual aphasic can thus determine differences in symptomatology between the two known languages. This discrepancy may depend on several factors: on a different neuroanatomical representation of some components of the two respective languages (e.g. of syntax, of the lexicon, etc.), or on a selective disactivation or inhibition of some neurofunctional subsystems accounting for one of the two languages or some components of it. Also, as is often the case, where both languages show similar impairment, it is very useful to compare between the two languages the severity of specific aphasic symptoms (e.g. grammar errors). These cross-language studies in one particular patient have shed more light on the various linguistic manifestations of one and the same aphasic syndrome in two different languages. The simplistic opinion, according to which a specific aphasic syndrome (e.g. Broca's aphasia) presents the same types of errors in *each* of the languages known by an individual (e.g. "only" omissions of free grammatical morphemes), has gradually changed.

A series of linguistic symptoms that were considered typical of bilingual aphasics, such as mixing, switching, spontaneous translation, paradoxical translation, and translation without comprehension, deserve particular attention. Researchers have also tried to distinguish pathological mixing and switching from the normal habit of individuals belonging to certain bilingual cultures or social groups to switch from one language to the other and mix the two languages during normal communication with interlocutors who understand both. The study of these "specific" symptoms and of language disorders in bilingual aphasics more generally has been successfully used in order to formulate psycholinguistic and neuropsychological models of the bilingual brain.

Recovery patterns are also an important aspect in the study of bilingual aphasics. After an acute cerebral lesion, bilingual individuals may present a parallel recovery of both languages, or they may only recover one language (e.g. the first language, or else the second, the most used language, the more automatized, or the less automatized, etc.). Recovery may be influenced by several factors, such as neuropsychological, sociolinguistic, and rehabilitation factors. Because aphasic symptomatology and recovery patterns may differ across languages, before starting a rehabilitation program for a bilingual aphasic patient, an assessment of his/her residual linguistic abilities in all languages known before onset has to be made. The decision whether to rehabilitate only one specific language known by the patient depends on the neurolinguistic assessment as well as on clinical and sociolinguistic factors, which the therapeutical staff have to consider and also discuss with the patients and their families.

In 1994, 100 years after the publication of the first scientific paper on bilingual aphasia by Jean-Albert Pitres, an international symposium was held in his city, Bordeaux, in order to take stock of the state of the art on the bilingual brain. The book published after that symposium (*Aspects of bilingual aphasia,* edited by Michel Paradis, 1995), containing the results of the studies and discussions led by the most active researchers in this specific field, ends with the following statement: "Given what we now know, it is no longer ethically acceptable to assess aphasic patients on the basis of the examination of only one of their languages" (p. 219). If, thus, it is no longer ethical to evaluate only one of the languages known by bilingual aphasic patients, it is wrong for the staff involved in the diagnosis and therapy of language disorders to ignore the basic principles of bilingual aphasia. The failure to recognize these principles would only be trivial if the bilingual population were a minority, but it becomes a serious mistake if one considers that about half the world population is bilingual. This book is an attempt at bridging this gap.

My decision to write a book on the organization of the bi- or multilingual brain stems from the realization that neither in Italy nor in other countries is a comprehensive work available that is scientifically sound and, at the same time, easy to read and thus directed at a large audience. Of course, there are several excellent books and a large number of interesting articles, but they are only accessible to experts in the field. Thus, I have endeavored to write a book dealing as exhaustively as possible with the issue of bi- and multilingualism, a book which addresses a target readership with secondary or college education. It is my belief that knowledge of the brain can be useful not only to physicians, psychologists, and speech and language therapists, but also to teachers in general, irrespective of the level they teach. After all, every day they have to deal with one of the most typical features of the human brain, namely the ability to learn. For this reason, I have taken nothing for granted and I have systematically avoided resorting to technical expressions or jargon. On the other hand, neurolinguistics—like any other scientific discipline—has obviously developed a terminology of its own. Therefore, each time I have used a technical term or expression, I have also provided a brief but clear explanation.

The bilingual brain has been studied using several different approaches. In this book I have given more importance to the contributions derived from studies of clinical neurolinguistics. Although the study of brain-damaged populations raises a series of problems as to its real "power" of revealing brain functioning, I believe that, given the present state of the art of neuropsychological research, this method is still one that yields an enormous amount of reliable data. Part of these data is also important for the clinical management of multilingual aphasic patients. A further methodological aspect that should not be underestimated is that the existing literature on "bilingual aphasia" practically only deals with speakers of European languages, thus revealing an important gap that will, one hopes, be closed in the medium term.

This book consists of two main parts. The first 10 chapters introduce basic concepts concerning the cerebral organization of language, and the remaining chapters deal with the neurolinguistics of bilingualism proper. In the first part, therefore, the reader becomes familiar with the main topics of neurolinguistics in general, without reference to bi- and multilingualism. Those who already have a sound knowledge of this discipline may therefore simply start reading from Chapter 11 onwards. Chapters 1–3 focus on basic concepts of linguistics, acoustics, and the neurophysiology of vocalizations, respectively. They are too simple for experts in the field and, at the same time, quite demanding for readers approaching these topics for the first time; these readers should focus on the general interest raised by these chapters and not be concerned with understanding the fine detail.

All the chapters are rather short. They are always preceded by a summary outline, which may be useful to look back on. Besides the presentation and discussion of scientific aspects and data, most chapters also contain the clinical histories of several patients, as I believe that reporting real and

personal experiences, rather than data alone, is necessary for the development of a science of the brain.

F.F.
Milan, March 1998

CHAPTER ONE

What is language?

This chapter attempts to answer the general question: "What is language?".
One of the most obvious remarks that can be made on human language is that
it exists in the form of a variety of different languages. At present, more than
6000 spoken languages are used in the world and the features they bear in
common are referred to as "language". They all show two main characteristics: (1) They make use of the vocal-auditory channel (to produce and perceive sounds), and (2) they are organized according to the principle of double
articulation or duality of patterning: that implies a level of words, which bear
meaning, and a level of sounds (phonemes), which are limited in number.
Phonemes combine to form all the words of a given language. Language is the
subject matter of linguistics, a relatively recent discipline comprising several
branches, among which phonology, morphology, syntax, and semantics are
the ones most studied.

One of the first and most obvious remarks made by those approaching the
study of human verbal communication is that language does not exist *per se*
but in the form of several different languages. At present, there are more
than 6000 spoken languages all over the world, each one representing a
specimen of that typically human phenomenon called "language". There is
no evidence of human groups who do not speak at least one language.
Generally, children can learn any language in infancy, unless they have
phoniatric or neurological impairments or learning disabilities. Stress is to
be laid on the difference between *language* and *communication* (Hinde, 1972;
Miller, 1951, 1981). To this effect, linguists have defined language as a
verbal communication tool based on double articulation.

Two main features differentiate a human spoken language from any other form of communication: the use of the vocal-auditory channel and the principle of double articulation. All spoken languages use the *vocal-auditory channel*: they are spoken and can be understood because speakers produce particular sounds that are perceived and comprehended by listeners. A language also utilizes other communication modalities, such as writing and fingerspelling, but they derive from the spoken language. In addition, languages are always organized according to the principle of *double* articulation, that is, at two levels. The first level—also called first articulation—refers to *words*, i.e. the smallest units of meaning, that can combine to form an almost infinite number of sentences. The second level, or second articulation, refers to sounds peculiar to a given language. They are limited in number and meaningless. They are called *phonemes* and can combine to form all the words of a given language. This duality in the structure of any language allows the speaker to produce an infinite number of sentences, utterances, and texts by using a relatively small and fixed number of sounds and words.

In deaf communities sign languages are used; these languages have many structural features in common with spoken languages, but they do not use the vocal-auditory channel. In addition, the great majority of signers acquire and use in their everyday life both the minority language (sign language) and the majority language (Woll & Kyle, 1994).

LINGUISTICS AND THE STUDY OF LANGUAGE

Linguistics is the science that studies language. It is generally subdivided into four main branches (Akmajian, Demers, & Harnish, 1979; Asher, 1994; Fromkin & Rodman, 1993):

1. Phonology studies phonemes, i.e. the sounds peculiar to every single language, and also deals with sounds as acoustic phenomena; it is thus sometimes further defined as "phonetics". For example, /f/ and /v/ are two phonemes of the English language because they mark the only difference between the two words "fine" and "vine". Although the letters of the alphabet have been invented as a way to represent phonemes graphically, they do not correspond on a one-to-one basis to the different phonemes of a language.
2. Syntax studies the rules governing the combination of words within sentences. For example, a syntactic rule of English is that the article must always precede the noun and not vice versa.
3. Morphology studies the rules governing the internal structure of words, i.e. rules of concordance between adjective and noun, or gender, or number, etc., as well as word inflection and derivation. The

systematic addition of an "s" to form the third person singular of verbs in the present tense (e.g. "he works") is an example of a morphological rule in English.
4. Semantics studies the relationship between words and their meaning. Words carry pieces of infomation, called semantic properties; some words may have more semantic properties in common than other words have (e.g. girl and woman as opposed to stone and apple).

Phonetics and phonology

When a linguist approaches a formally unknown language for the first time, his duty is to find out the precise number of *phonemes* of this language. This operation is called phonemic analysis and implies the detection and description of every single phoneme of a language. Linguists have developed a special method to transcribe these sounds objectively onto paper, namely the International Phonetic Alphabet (IPA), which makes it possible to note down every phoneme of all languages that have been identified and formally studied so far. Phonemic analysis basically depends on the idea of word segmentation, which, in turn, derives from the invention of alphabetic writing.

A phoneme is the minimal sound distinguishing two words of a given language that would otherwise be identical. A phoneme is thus the smallest distinctive segment of sound between two similar sound sequences. For example, *bat* and *pat* are two different English words with different meaning and they only differ in the starting sound /b/ as opposed to /p/. Therefore, /p/ and /b/ are two separate phonemes in English. By similarly comparing and contrasting a large number of words in order to define "minimal pairs"—an operation that is called commutation test—a linguist is able to identify all the phonemes necessary and sufficient to describe the phonemic repertoire of a language. When carrying out a commutation test, a linguist substitutes one sound segment with another and asks a native speaker (an informant) if the substitution implies a change in meaning. The procedure continues until all phonemes of a language have been detected.

It is likely that the limited capacity of motor, perceptive, and mnestic skills in humans has implicitly set a limit on the number of possible phonemes of any given language. None of the languages that have been studied so far have more than 150 phonemes (70% of all languages spoken in the world have on average 20–37 phonemes). This may be due to the fact that the human brain cannot deal effectively with a larger number of separate sounds.

It should be noted, however, that the concept of the phoneme is an abstract entity and has been invented by modern linguistics. At the level of physics and acoustic engineering, researchers have not yet succeeded in identifying and strictly marking the physical boundaries of a consonantic phoneme within the context of a sound sequence forming a word. This is mainly due to the fact that, as experts in acoustics have found out, a given phoneme is never articulated in exactly the same manner either by one speaker as opposed to other speakers, or by one and the same speaker within different linguistic contexts (e.g. the phoneme /t/ in the words *study* and *stool*), or even by the same speaker within the same linguistic contexts but under different emotional circumstances.

The different forms of articulation of a phoneme are called *allophones*. Although they have slightly different acoustic properties, a listener perceives and classifies them as one and the same phoneme of a given language. As underlined by Malberg (1974), the phoneme is represented both in the brain of the speaker and the listener, whereas allophones are "formed" in the phonatory organs and are found in the sound waves. When listeners want to decode a vocal message, it is in the sound waves that they find the implementation of the same phonemes the speakers intended to produce when they planned their messages. If listeners do not make this kind of phonemic identification, they will not be able to interpret the message correctly. Therefore, when an Italian monolingual listens to the English word *black* [blæk], he will probably have the impression of having heard [blek] or [blak], because the phoneme /æ/ does not exist in Italian. He will thus classify the English phoneme /æ/ as an allophone of the Italian /e/ or /a/.

After proposing the concept of phoneme, linguists found that phonemes had to be broken down further into smaller units if they were to be described in detail. These smaller units are called *distinctive features*, each of them corresponding to the smallest difference existing between two different phonemes. A phoneme is thus made of several concurrent distinctive features—partly shared by other phonemes, yet never exactly the same in two separate phonemes. Some linguists chose to describe phonemes according to their acoustical properties, others still according to the way they are articulated. Both types of classification use distinctive features, and both present pros and cons. I personally believe that the classification based on articulation is simpler and, at the same time, more useful for the purpose of describing specific language disorders. By definition, according to the principle of the so-called *dual opposition*, a distinctive articulatory feature may be present or absent in a given phoneme. Distinctive features are abstract entities which provide a description of a series of muscle movements the speaker has to perform in order to shape his vocal tract (i.e. the system producing the sounds of language) into a given configuration.

A list of the main distinctive features used to describe the phonemes of most Indo-European languages follows. These features apply to languages like Italian, English, French, Spanish, etc.

Consonants may be classified according to place and manner of articulation on the basis of the following distinctive features (see Table 1.1):

1. *Voiced* consonants: If a linguistic sound to be produced requires the vibration of the vocal folds, this sound is called "voiced", otherwise it is "voiceless". In the latter case, the vocal folds remain open as in normal breathing. Voiced consonants comprise: b, d, g, v, z, m, n, and l. Vowels are all voiced sounds.

2. *Plosives* (stops) are the simplest to be produced and the clearest in perception. During phonation of a plosive, air is temporarily blocked in some parts of the vocal tract, e.g. by the lips (b, p), near the teeth (d, t), or in the region of the soft palate (*velum*) (/k/ as in "*c*at", /g/, as in "*g*ap"). In this case, some linguists make a further distinction between labial, alveolar, and velar consonants, respectively.

3. *Fricatives*, also called constrictive consonants, are characterized by a narrowing of some parts of the vocal tract; air escapes through a small passage, e.g. between the lips and the teeth (labio-dental consonants /v/, as "*v*at", and /f/, as "*f*at"), between the teeth (interdental consonants /θ/, as "*th*in"; /đ/, as "*th*en"), in the alveolar region (/z/, /s/), in the larynx (/h/, as in "*h*at"), or in the palato-alveolar region (/ʃ/, as in "fi*sh*"; /ʒ/, as in "a*z*ure"). This narrowing creates friction and attrition between air and some anatomical structures of the phonatory organs, thus making the hissing sound typical of this group of consonants.

4. In *affricates*, the effect of an occlusion is followed by that of a friction, e.g. /tʃ/ as in "ri*ch*", or /dʒ/ as in "*j*u*dg*e". They are produced at palato-alveolar level.

5. *Nasals* are produced when air flows through the nasal passages because the soft palate is raised in the upper position; at the same time, there is an occlusion either of the lips (/m/, as in "s*m*ack"), or in the alveolar region (/n/, as in "*n*ick"), or in the palate (/ŋ/, as in "si*ng*").

6. *Liquid* consonants imply a partial narrowing of the vocal tract so that the air flow is not completely blocked. Examples of liquid consonants are /l/, as in "ca*ll*" and /r/, as in "singe*r*".

Vowels are classified according to the position of the tongue within the oral cavity: anterior versus posterior, high versus low, central, etc. For example, /a:/ is a central low vowel, /u:/ is a posterior high vowel, etc.

The analysis and description of the phonemes and their distinctive features belong to a specific branch of theoretical and applied linguistics. However, the use of modern computerized devices and of *automatic speech recognition techniques* has highlighted that all the classification methods proposed by phonologists and phoneticians only partially reflect the real sound production process. It is hoped that in the near future computers will perceive and understand these sounds and thus contribute to the "translation" of oral language into written language.

TABLE 1.1

Classification of English consonant phonemes according to their place and manner of articulation (adapted from Aitchison, 1992).

Manner of articulation	Place of articulation							
	Bilabial	Labio-dental	Dental	Alveolar	Palato-alveolar	Palatal	Velar	Glottal
Stop (oral)								
Voiceless	p			t			k	
Voiced	b			d			g	
Nasal (stop)	m			n			ŋ	
Fricative								
Voiceless		f	θ	s	ʃ			h
Voiced		v	ð	z	ʒ			
Affricate								
Voiceless					tʃ			
Voiced					dʒ			
Liquid				lr				
Semivowels	(w)					j	w	

One of the major difficulties researchers working on automatic speech recognition are still facing is the fact that all the sounds forming the words of an oral message are linked together in an uninterrupted sequence. The monitoring—by means of special cameras (cineradiographs)—of the articulatory movements performed by a speaker during the production of words has shown that the various phonemes cannot be separated. It has also shown that some phonemes are produced concurrently and consequently, which is due to the fact that the supralaryngeal vocal tract can be engaged in the *coarticulation* of several phonemes at the same time (Perkell, 1969).

Syntax

The word syntax derives from the Greek *syntaxis*, literally meaning "combination" or "putting together". It traditionally refers to that branch of linguistics that deals with the way in which words are linked together in order to construct sentences that convey intentional meanings. One of the major goals of syntax is to identify constant, i.e. "universal", grammatical rules applicable to all languages in the world. One of the main debated issues in the field concerns the segmentation of the minimal units of discourse. As early as in the second half of the 19th century, the English neurologist John Hughlings Jackson, on the basis of his clinical findings, suggested that the smallest linguistic unit was the *sentence*. In his opinion, to talk means to produce sentences, in his words "to propositionize" (Jackson, 1874/1958). At present, several linguists agree on the idea that the sentence is indeed a constant feature of the syntax of all known languages. North-American linguist Philip Lieberman proposed a biological explanation for the presence of the "sentence" unit in all languages. He claims that the slight lowering of the voice pitch caused by the natural exhaustion of expiratory air during phonation is perceived by listeners as a sign that the sentence is coming to a close. At the end of a sentence, speakers have no air left in their lungs, thus they have to pause briefly and breathe in again before uttering a new sentence (Lieberman, 1967, 1975). However, it must be noted that individuals can produce sentences of indefinite length, independently of the amount of air flow through their lungs. In addition, the sentence is an abstract grammatical concept based on a linguistic theory.

The identification of constant syntactic rules across languages turned out to be difficult. North-American linguist Edward Sapir highlighted the numerous differences in the syntactic organization of the various languages. Sapir classified languages on the basis of their main syntactic features and distinguished *analytical languages*, i.e. with a fixed and precise word order within the sentence, from *synthetic languages*, i.e. the word order is less fixed. Consider the following four Latin sentences: "*Hominem femina videt*"; "*Femina hominem videt*"; "*Hominem videt femina*"; "*Videt femina homi-*

nem". They all mean "The woman sees the man" with slightly rhetorical and stylistic differences. As word order in Latin does not affect meaning, it follows that Latin is a synthetic language. In contrast, English is an analytical language, because a change in the word order implies a change in meaning. Consider the following sentences: "*The man ate the chicken*" and "*The chicken ate the man*". The two sentences have different meanings determined by their word order. An analytical language is a language that either does not combine concepts into single words (e.g. Chinese), or it does so in a very economical way (e.g. French, English). In an analytical language the sentence is always of primary importance, whereas the word is less important. On the other hand, in a synthetic language (e.g. Latin, Arabic, Finnish), concepts are densely grouped within words that thus turn out to be more "meaningful". However, there is a general tendency to limit the number of different meanings that a single word may have (Sapir, 1921).

French linguist André Martinet underlined the importance of social structure in the evolution of the syntax of a given language. In small communities, everybody knows everybody, thus one knows what to expect from the neighbors. In large cities, however, where the division of labor is extreme and the population is mobile and changes rapidly, individuals have to face many unknown and unexpected events. For example, if John is known to be an aggressive, brutal man, whereas Peter is known to be weak and fearful, it is not necessary to specify who has beaten whom. On the other hand, if John and Peter are two strangers whom we have met by chance or just heard of, then more information as to who did what to whom is needed. As Martinet (1985) points out, one can live an isolated life within one's own family with a very restricted set of friends even in New York or, conversely, have an active life, full of unforeseen events, even in a small village. Statistically, however, the reverse applies. A change in the social structure of a linguistic community may affect the frequency with which its members feel the necessity to specify further the functions of each single word within a context and hence the degree of automaticity of such specifications.

Noam Chomsky is among those linguists who have tried to describe syntax as a set of logical rules (Chomsky, 1977, 1980). Together with his co-workers, Chomsky mainly focused on English syntax and suggested that certain universals are applicable to all other languages as well (Jackendoff, 1994; Pinker 1994). Although Chomsky made valuable contributions to linguistics in general—and nowadays many linguistic departments in North America are run by Chomsky's pupils—his studies and theories have found a very limited use in the study of individuals with language disorders. Indeed, there is no data suggesting that the human brain organizes syntax according to rules (Marshall, 1983; McCawley, 1983). Therefore, the idea that syntax is governed by a set of rules should rather be considered as a temporary approach to this unsolved problem.

Morphology

This branch of linguistics deals with the internal structure of words, i.e. with the way they are formed. A "morpheme" is the smallest linguistic unit bearing meaning. Each word is made of one or more morphemes. Speakers are said to have a "mental lexicon" containing all possible information on the words of the language they speak; they know how to pronounce and write words, what they mean, and what functions they have within the discourse (e.g. they may function as nouns, verbs, prepositions, etc.). A language has a limited number of *closed class words*, also called function words (e.g. articles, pronouns, prepositions, conjunctions), and a large number of *open class words*, also called content words (i.e. nouns, verbs, adjectives, adverbs). Some words consist of a single morpheme that can stand alone (*free morpheme*), as is the case with English prepositions or articles; other words are formed by more than one morpheme, generally a lexical morpheme (e.g. *go*) plus a *bound morpheme* (e.g. *-ing* as in going). English has more free morphemes than Italian, a language with many bound morphemes because pronouns, adjectives, and nouns must agree in number and gender, and verbs must agree in person and tense.

Semantics

Semantics studies the meaning of words and sentences. Within this branch of linguistics, the study of the lexicon concerns the features of words and morphemes. They are described in terms of "semantic properties". For example, the following semantic properties define the word "girl": female, human, young; certainly, the same word cannot be described as male, inanimate, old. More recently, the focus of attention has shifted to the meaning of sentences and texts, which depends both on the meaning of single words and on their place within sentences or texts.

CHAPTER TWO

How language sounds are produced and perceived

Three different systems are involved in the production of speech sounds in humans: the lungs, supplying energy for the vocal signal during expiration; the vocal folds, representing the source of vocalization; and the supralaryngeal vocal tract, modeling the signal coming from the vocal folds and thus producing the typical sounds of a language. The acoustic analysis of a sound belonging to a language system, e.g. a vowel, allows the identification of several components of the sound, namely the fundamental frequency (fo), i.e. the frequency of vibration of the vocal folds, and the formants, i.e. the vocal tract resonances defined as F1, F2, F3. The vocal tract must be shaped into different configurations in order to produce the various vowels of a given language. Speakers unconsciously know what configuration their vocal tract is to be shaped into in order to produce a specific sound. At the acoustic level this configuration corresponds to the production of the formant frequencies characterizing the sound. During sound perception the inner ear and related brain structures detect the formant frequencies of a sound and classify it as a given phoneme of a (known) language. In infancy children implicitly learn what configuration their vocal tracts must be shaped into so as to produce the sounds of their mother tongue; at the same time, they also develop the systems accounting for the recognition and classification of these sounds. Adults learning a second language must resort to a larger extent to conscious strategies in order to produce and perceive the phonemes of the foreign language.

PHYSIOLOGY OF SPEECH PRODUCTION

In all human spoken languages the vocal-auditory channel is the primary means of linguistic communication. Communication requires that individuals activate their vocal systems and produce vibrations that are transmitted by air; the information carried by the vibrations reaches the auditory systems of other individuals who then decode it. Sounds that do not present the double articulation pattern are defined as vocalizations. A large number of vertebrates produce vocalizations in order to communicate with others of the same species. Starting from the frog—philogenetically the oldest species capable of vocalizing—up to man, all animals capable of vocalizing use the same systems to produce vocal sounds. These systems are: (a) the *lungs* supplying the energy necessary for vocalizing during air expiration; (b) the *larynx* functioning as source of the vocal signal; and (c) the *supralaryngeal vocal tract* acting as a filter and determining the final characteristics of the vocal signal (Borden & Harris, 1984; Denes & Pisoni, 1973; Fant, 1970) (cf. Figure 2.1).

The system that produces speech sounds is formed by the lungs, which supply the initial energy, the larynx where the vocal signal originates, and the vocal tract consisting of the pharynx, the mouth, and the nasal cavity. The vocal tract filters and modulates all subtle variations of speech sounds. Vocal signals are produced during expiration. In humans, during a normal respiration cycle (quiet breathing), inspiration takes approximately the same time as expiration, whereas during verbal production expiration can increase to approximately 90% of the entire cycle.

When an amphibian, a mammal, or a human starts vocalizing, the laryngeal nerve causes the vocal folds to close. At the same time, the exhalation phase begins. During the expiration phase and the concurrent closure of the vocal folds—the latter being determined by nerve impulses—pressure in the

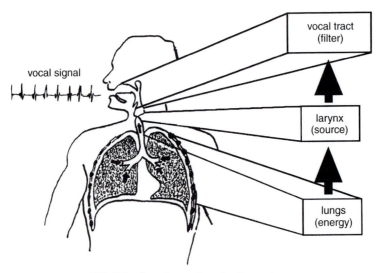

FIG. 2.1.   Speech sound production systems.

subglottal areas (situated below the larynx) increases in such a way that the vocal folds will suddenly open and will close again as soon as air has rapidly flowed through them. The vocal folds continue vibrating, i.e. opening and closing very quickly, until the impulses from the central nervous system reach the laryngeal nerve and cause their closure and the concurrent exhalation of the remaining air from the lungs. The frequency of vibration corresponds to the number of opening and closing movements of the vocal folds in 1 second; it is called *fundamental frequency* (fo) and is measured in Hertz (Hz), or cycles per second. For example, a frog can produce 400 cycles of closure and opening of its vocal folds (fo = 400Hz) in 1 second, whereas a cat's vocal folds can vibrate at a frequency of 800–1000Hz. Primates like macaques may reach a fo of 1200Hz. With regard to humans, children present the highest frequency of vibration (up to 600Hz) and indeed their voice is perceived as "higher" than that of women or men, the latter usually having the lowest fundamental frequency. At language perception level, fundamental frequency corresponds to what is generally known as voice *pitch*. The male voice is generally perceived as lower than the female voice because in the former case vocal folds vibrate at a lower fo. The frequency of vibration can be determined by both the pressure of the subglottal air and the tension of the vocal folds, the latter being controlled by a branch of the vagal nerve. These modulations are crucial for prosody and singing. For example, in some Indo-European languages, questions are also marked at the acoustic level, as an increase in fundamental frequency determines a higher voice pitch. In Sino-Tibetan languages (e.g. Mandarin and Cantonese) and Austro-Asiatic languages (Vietnamese, Thai, etc.) phonemes differ in their frequencies of vibration. For example, in Chinese [i] marked by a constant frequency of vibration and [i] marked by a decreasing frequency of vibration are two separate phonemes and mark the difference between two words that would otherwise be identical (Lieberman & Blumstein, 1988).

A small microphone situated near the vocal folds during the production of vowels would always record the same sound, a buzzing. What perceptively distinguishes vowel from vowel is the vocal tract (pharynx, mouth, and nasal cavity) acting as a filter of the laryngeal signal. Discrete or constant modifications in the configuration of pharynx, mouth, and soft velum depend on the activity of numerous muscles that are controlled by cranial nerves (the trigeminal, the facial, the glossopharyngeal, the vagal, and the hypoglossal). For example, head and neck X-rays show that the vocal tract shapes into a specific configuration during the production of vowels. With regard to Italian, the production of the vowel [a] requires that speakers control their muscles so that the configuration of their vocal tract is the same in all speakers.

The capacity to perform fine movements at vocal tract level seems to distinguish humans from all other primates and vertebrates capable of vocalizing. Generally, except for humans and a few songbird species, animals can shape their vocal tracts into only a few configurations. Because the shape of the vocal tract determines the final characteristics of the sounds to be produced, almost all species capable of vocalizing can only produce a very limited number of sounds. On the other hand, the peculiar configuration of the vocal tract in humans allows a wide range of fine movements (Kuypers, 1958). Therefore, humans can produce all the different phonemes of the language they are exposed to as well as a considerable number of sequences of movements leading to the production of words.

Indeed, the production of a word depends on the subjects' learning and correct execution of these sequences of movements, which are unconsciously and automatically stored (Kuehn, Lemme, & Baumgartner, 1989; Mac-Neilage & Ladefoged, 1976). An example of acquired vocalizations in Italian is provided by the production of the vowel /a/. When producing this vowel speakers expire, concurrently causing the vocal folds to vibrate and shaping their vocal tracts into a specific configuration. Speakers unconsciously know how to move their lips and their tongue in order to produce the vowel as well as what configuration the vocal tract is to be shaped into in order to produce the vowels and consonants of their mother tongue. Special devices are used to study the features of the glottal signal during the production of a vowel (cf. Fig. 2.2). It is a complex sound, which can be broken down into smaller units by means of a particular mathematical technique (Fourier's analysis) in order to analyze its harmonic frequencies, which are graphically represented in the *spectrum* of the glottal signal. The first frequency of this spectrum is the fundamental frequency (fo), namely the number of vibrations of the vocal folds per second. The anatomical shape of the vocal tract during the production of a vowel or a consonant filters the glottal signal, thus increasing the energy of some harmonics and reducing the energy of others. Each shape of the vocal tract acts as a particular filter for the flow and amplification of some harmonics of the glottal signal, while at the same time it obstructs the flow and amplification of others. The filter function of the vocal tract depends on its shape. Therefore, it continuously changes during the production of the separate phonemes of a language, staying the same shape for each single phoneme.

Harmonics receiving more energy from the filter are known as *formants* of the acoustic signal. A given vowel is defined by two or more formants (F1, F2). All speakers of a language, when producing the same vowel, filter the glottal signal in the same manner: the sound thus produced presents the (two) formants that characterize the vowel. What changes during the production of the same vowel is the fundamental frequency, namely the voice pitch, which is higher in children and women as opposed to men. Even though men have a fundamental frequency that is lower than that of women during the production of a given speech sound, e.g. [a], the vocal tract in both men and women is

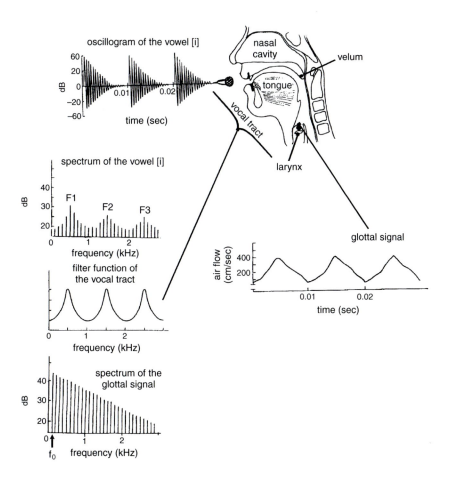

FIG. 2.2. Different modalities of acoustic analysis of a vowel.

shaped into the same configuration and produces two sounds with the same features, i.e. similar formants F1, F2, and F3. What makes the difference to listeners, who will clearly distinguish the male voice from the female voice, is the typical fundamental frequency of the two speakers: about 100Hz in men and 300Hz in women. The more the vocal folds vibrate in one second, the higher the fundamental frequency and hence the voice pitch of the speaker.

ACOUSTIC ANALYSIS OF SPEECH

In the 1940s, American researchers developed an instrument called a *spectrograph*, which visually shows the formants of speech sounds by marking them on paper. The original idea behind this instrument was to give

deaf people the possibility of "seeing" words (*visible speech*), but it turned
out that it was rather difficult for them to interpret a spectrogram. On the
other hand, this device became extremely useful for the acoustic analysis of
oral speech. The production of speech sounds into a microphone connected
to a spectrograph permits one to visualize in real time the formants of a
sound and hence the formants of phonemes (Liberman, 1996). The formants
are plotted on a spectrogram and appear like vertical lines of different
lengths (cf. Fig. 2.3, showing the formants of the vowels [i], [a], and [u]).
When a speaker pronounces these vowels one after the other, as in the word
"miaow", the analysis of the formants will result in a graph showing the
transitions of the formants from sound to sound (cf. Fig. 2.3). As each vowel
is characterized by specific formants, central and peripheral (i.e. inner ear)
auditory structures isolate formants so as to detect and decode each single
vowel even when embedded in a sequence of speech sounds (Handel, 1989).

There are several ways to represent speech sounds, particularly vowels,
graphically. The top part of Figure 2.4 shows an oscillogram of the syllable
[da]; the same syllable is reproduced in the middle of the figure in a three-
dimensional spectrogram, in which the three formants of the vowel [a] are
clearly shown (F1 = 800Hz, F2 = 1000Hz, F3 = 2500Hz); the lower part
of the figure presents a schematic illustration of the cochlea, a basic structure of the auditory apparatus. The formants of the sound [a] provoke an
excitation of different sites of the cochlear basilar membrane, apparently
one of the anatomical structures crucial for speech sound decoding (Békésy,
1960).

The use of the spectrograph led to the identification of all the formants of
a language's vowels. A practical way to plot language-specific vowel systems
consists in setting up graphs in which the first formant (F1) is on the
abscissa and the second formant (F2) on the ordinate (cf. Fig. 2.5). This
graph shows the "vowel space" of each single vowel, namely the extension
of the formants that were experimentally recorded from a large sample of

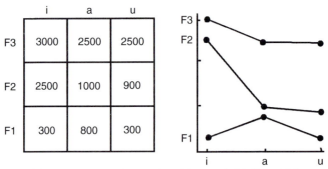

FIG. 2.3.   Formant frequencies of the vowels [a], [i], and [u].

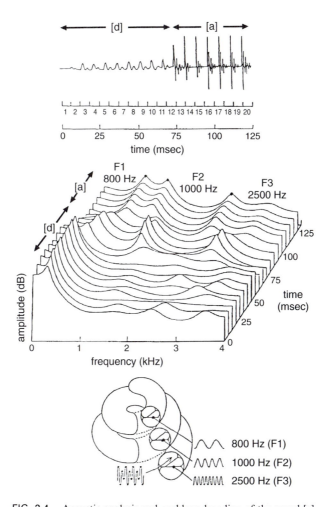

FIG. 2.4.   Acoustic analysis and cochlear decoding of the vowel [a].

native speakers. For example, in the graph at the top, the vowel space of [a] in Italian is larger than that of all other vowels, which means that in Italian [a] can be pronounced in many more different acoustic variants than any other vowel and yet it can still be recognized as [a]. In addition, the graph shows the vowels that—from an acoustic point of view—can be more easily recognized, namely, those that are more distant from each other. The graph also compares the Italian vowel system (top) and the American English vowel system, which is definitely "richer" (bottom). In both systems, the vowels that differ most from each other can be found at the three vertices of a fictitious triangle, the so-called *fundamental vocalic triangle* ([i], [a], [u]).

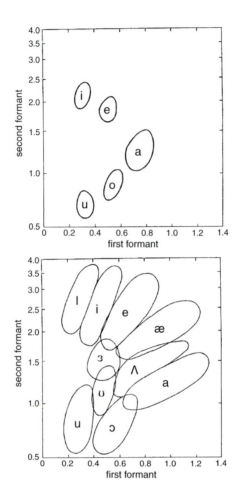

FIG. 2.5.   Vowel space of Italian (top) and American English (bottom) vowels.

Usually, these are also the most frequent vowels in all human languages, probably because their acoustic features differ completely and they are thus easier to perceive and recognize.

In languages with a large number of vowels, as is the case with American English, the spaces vowels occupy are much closer and sometimes even overlap. Unlike non-native speakers, native speakers do not have difficulties in distinguishing vowel from vowel, even though they are similar. Generally, speakers whose mother tongue is richer in vowels have less difficulties in distinguishing sounds of a foreign language with fewer vowels than do speakers whose native language has a simpler vocalic system. The hypothesis is that native speakers of languages rich in vowels naturally develop an enhanced ability to detect and classify complex sounds, including those that do not belong to their own language. For example, an American English native speaker cannot easily distinguish [ø:] from [oe], two vowels of Swedish, a language with even more vowels than American English. An Italian speaker, however, would have even more difficulties. Surprisingly enough, however, experiments on newborn babies have shown that the ability to discriminate similar vowels is the same, irrespective of the language of exposure. By measuring the heartbeat of English and Swedish babies, researchers found out that both groups reacted in the same way to vowel-recognition tasks in both languages. It follows that the ability to distinguish and classify all the different complex sounds of a language depends on the preservation of the ability to activate specific cerebral structures that are only stimulated with early and prolonged exposure to the sounds of that particular language in infancy. If children are not exposed to certain sounds, e.g. because they do not exist in their own native language, some neurofunctional structures used for the decoding of sounds are not activated. Within their first year of life humans have the potential ability to discriminate any given speech sound and thus to acquire the phonology of any language, and also of more than one language at the same time, but over time this ability decreases (Bates, Thal, & Janowsky, 1992; Kuhl, 1994; Stager & Werker, 1997).

PRODUCTION AND PERCEPTION OF VOWELS AND CONSONANTS

The simplest and one of the oldest methods used to classify speech sounds draws a major distinction between *vowels* and *consonants*. Vowels are produced by opening one's mouth (in French they are called *ouvreuses*, i.e. "openers") and generally last longer than consonants (about 100–150 milliseconds); they form the so-called "nucleus" of the syllables. On the other hand, consonants are produced with a rapid occlusion in some part of the supralaryngeal vocal tract (in French *fermeuses*, from *fermer*, to close), and usually last less than 100 milliseconds. Linguist Roman Jakobson explained the role played by vowels and consonants in conveying meaning via speech sounds through a vivid metaphor (Jakobson & Waugh, 1987). From an acoustic point of view, vowels are to speakers what a marble block is to a sculptor, a "nucleus" of stone from which the artist removes bits and pieces in order to shape the statue according to his project; consonants correspond to the skilled modeling of the raw material. In the spectrographic shape of a syllable, consonants mark the boundaries of vowels and determine the final shape of the syllable. In ancient times, the defining character of consonants was already known. For example, the Sanskrit word for consonant is *vyanjana*, which literally means "revealing". Moreover, in numerous writing systems, such as in Hebrew and Arabic, vowels are generally omitted because they are less relevant to the definition of words. The Greek alphabet was the first phonetic writing system that introduced signs representing vowels (De Kerckhove & Lumsden, 1988). The acoustic analysis of consonants has revealed that they correspond to rapid modifications, i.e. "transitions", of the formant frequencies of the vowels preceding and following them. Therefore, each single consonant is acoustically different from any other in that it characteristically modifies the margins of adjacent vowels. The auditory recognition of vowels and consonants is probably based on a system of acoustic decoding that isolates the formants (in order to recognize vowels) and the transitions of the formants (in order to recognize consonants) from the different speech sounds (cf. Fig. 2.4).

CHAPTER THREE

How the brain controls vocalizations

This chapter describes the main cerebral structures subserving the production of animal and human vocalizations. There can be innate or learnt vocal utterances. Neural structures controlling learnt vocalizations, such as human language, parrots' imitating calls, chaffinches' and canaries' songs, are located in the higher cerebral areas. Lower cerebral areas control innate vocal utterances, such as man's crying, dogs' barking calls, cats' meowing calls, and fowls' crowing. Some passeriform species (chaffinches, nightingales, canaries) have learnt vocal communication forms that show many similarities with human languages.

BASIC CONCEPTS OF BRAIN ANATOMY AND PHYSIOLOGY

The human brain contains billions of neural cells, the so-called *neurons*, whose exact number is still to be defined: some researchers claim that neurons number 10 billion; others go even further, claiming there are 1000 billion. One neuron can influence 1000–10,000 other neurons and, in turn, can be influenced by other neural cells, irrespective of their distance. Neurons continuously exchange information by electrical signals through extensions of single cells, namely *axons*, whose length can exceed 1 meter. In the proximity of the contact points (*synapses*) between the neural cells, electrical signals release chemical substances that modify the electrical activity of the post-synaptic neuron. Modern neuroscientific studies have widely shown that human behavior reflects the integrated activity of cerebral neural cells.

The human central nervous system (CNS) consists of four main parts (cf. Fig. 3.1):

1. The *spinal cord* receives information from the skin, the joints, and the muscular tissue of limbs and trunk, and controls the reflexes and the voluntary activity of the muscles of the limbs and trunk.
2. The *brainstem*, consisting of the medulla oblongata, the pons, and the midbrain (mesencephalon), is of crucial importance, e.g. for the automatic control of respiration and sleep. Furthermore, the brainstem structures contain sensory-motor nuclei controlling facial movements and sensitivity. In this structure there are small bundles of neural fibers carrying information to both cerebral hemispheres, and motor fibers connecting the cerebral hemispheres to motor neurons controlling movement.
3. The *diencephalon* comprises two extremely important structures: the thalamus and the hypothalamus. The thalamus is a fundamental

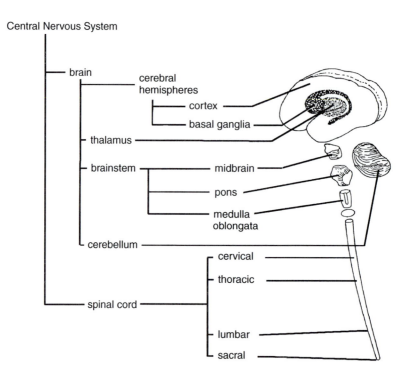

FIG. 3.1.   Main components of the central nervous system (adapted from DeMyer 1988).

station of sensory information controlling sleep and attentive and mnestic functions. The hypothalamus is crucial for the control of several functions that are essential for survival, such as the regulation of body temperature, sexual behavior, and hunger and thirst.

4. The *cerebral hemispheres* comprise the basal ganglia and the cerebral cortex. The cerebral hemispheres are involved in the organization of typically human cognitive functions such as emotions, language, writing, reading, music, arithmetic, and visual imagination. The cerebral hemispheres are connected through the *corpus callosum*, a bundle of more than 2 billion neural fibers.

The first experimental study proving that neurons communicate through electrical signal propagation was carried out in 1870 by two German physiologists, Gustav Fritsch and Eduard Hitzig (Kandel, Schwartz, & Jessell, 1991). By electrically stimulating different sections of a dog's cerebral cortex, they succeeded in eliciting single movements of its limbs. These movements were exclusively determined by electrical stimulation of the cortex and were contralateral to the hemisphere to be stimulated: if it was the motor cortex of the left hemisphere which had been stimulated, the dog moved its right limbs and, conversely, if the right hemisphere cortex was stimulated, the dog moved its left limbs. This is due to the fact that sensory-motor pathways connecting the neural centers to the various parts of the body are crossed in the brain. The right hemisphere receives stimuli from the left side of the body and controls it, the left hemisphere receives stimuli from the right side of the body and controls it. Subsequently, numerous neurophysiological studies substantiated and further explained the electrical nature of neural transmission.

During the 1950s renowned Canadian neurosurgeon Wilder Penfield carried out many electro-cortical stimulation studies in conscious patients who were to undergo neurosurgical operations under local anesthesia (Penfield & Roberts, 1976). Because the brain does not have pain receptors, operations on the brain can be performed without general anesthesia. Local anesthesia of some outer parts of the head (scalp, skull, etc.) is sufficient. By electrically stimulating the various cerebral areas, Penfield identified the cerebral area that had to be removed in order to cure the patient. During these operations Penfield electrically stimulated some structures of the motor cortex and thus elicited movements in the contralateral side of the patient's body, in the arms, legs, tongue, face, etc. Conversely, by electrically stimulating sensory cortical areas, patients reported they had been touched on one hand, on their face, or on one leg on the side of the body that was contralateral to the hemisphere that had been stimulated. Penfield not only proved that information between neural cells was exchanged through nerve impulse transmission, but also that the sensory-motor representation of the cerebral cortex does not correspond to the size of the organs, but rather to their functional importance. Hands and face occupy three-quarters of the sensory-motor areas of the brain, whereas arms, trunk, legs, feet, and genitals occupy only 25%, which means that in the human brain most of the cortical neurons control the sensory-motor functions of hands, mouth, and face. For this reason, humans succeed in performing very fine movements with their hands so as to make and use tools, and with their vocal tract structures so as to produce speech sounds.

Two methods are most widely used to study the organization of the cerebral functions accounting for behavior: the analysis of behavior during the *electrical stimulation* of neural structures and the study of behavior in *brain-damaged patients* or in animals whose cerebral tissue has only partially been removed. Other techniques have also been developed: (i) the *monitoring of the electrical activity of single neural cells* during perceptive, motor or cognitive tasks, which is mainly used in the study of animal brain but also in specific cases in man, for example during neurosurgical operations; (ii) electroencephalogram (EEG) and mapping EEG; (iii) evoked potentials and event-related potentials (ERPs; cf. Chapter 7, pp. 62–63) and (iv) techniques of visualization of the nervous system structures during the execution of complex perceptive, cognitive, or motor tasks (Positron Emission Tomography, PET; functional Magnetic Resonance Imaging, fRMI; cf. Chapter 7, pp. 63–64).

NEURAL CENTERS CONTROLLING VOCALIZATIONS

Animal vocalizations are usually divided into innate and learnt vocalizations. The former, namely, dogs' barking calls, cats' meowing calls, fowls' crows or man's crying, persist even after the removal of a whole section of the midbrain, whereas learnt vocalizations, specifically, the song of some passeriform species (canaries, chaffinches, nightingales, etc.), parrots' imitating calls, and human language cannot be reproduced after the midbrain has been dissected. This is due to the fact that after the dissection of the midbrain the impulses for motor sequences subserving the production of songs in passeriforms and words in humans can no longer reach the neural centers of pons and medulla that account for these functions. In humans, "memory" of sensory-motor sequences subserving speech is organized in cerebral structures lying above the midbrain, namely the cerebral hemispheres. If sensory-motor pathways are interrupted, the impulses produced by the cerebral hemispheres no longer reach the sensory-motor centers (situated under the midbrain) that "execute" these impulses.

Over the past 30 years a number of studies on the neural organization of vocalizations in many vertebrate species (frogs, lizards, cats, birds, and primates) have been carried out (Jürgens, 1979; Newman, 1988; Sutton, Larson, & Lindeman, 1974). These studies relied on various neurological, neuroanatomic, and neurophysiological techniques and contributed to the description of the role played by some centers of the nervous system in the production of vocalizations, both in animals and humans (cf. Fig. 3.2). A brief review of the most important centers follows.

1. The *mesencephalic periaqueductal gray matter*. The destruction of this neural structure, which lies in the high part of the brainstem, destroys all species-specific vocalizations, from frog to man. In humans, a vascular or traumatic lesion to the periaqueductal gray matter causes mutism (Botez & Barbeau, 1971). The electrical stimulation of this neural structure elicits

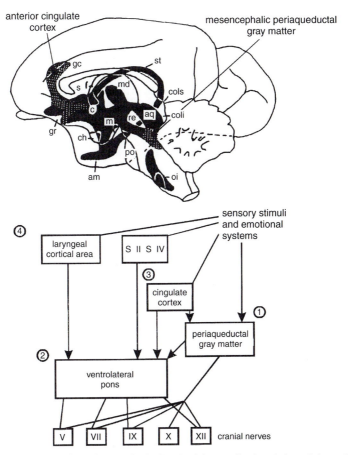

FIG. 3.2. Structures of a primate's brain involved in vocalization (adapted from Jürgens, 1979).

vocalizations in all vertebrate species capable of vocalizing. The studies that have been carried out have led to the conclusion that this area is the oldest center of vocalization. The periaqueductal gray matter is closely linked to other neural structures involved in the control of sensitivity to pain (LeDoux, 1996). This might explain why in several animals painful stimulation provokes reflex vocalization. The periaqueductal gray matter receives information (afferences) from various neural structures (hypothalamus, amygdala, the anterior cortex of the cingulate, and the somato-sensory areas of the cortex); it transmits information to the ventrolateral pons and coordinates the activity of the nuclei of the cranial nerves that are involved in the production of vocalizations.

2. The *ventrolateral pons*. The destruction of this nucleus of neural cells considerably affects the capacity to vocalize, whereas the electrical stimulation of this area elicits vocalizations. This center receives information from the periaqueductal gray matter, the anterior cingulate cortex, the laryngeal cortical area, and the somato-sensory areas of the cerebral hemispheres, whereas it transmits information to the thalamus, the cerebellum, and some nuclei of the cranial nerves.

3. The *anterior cingulate cortex*. In rhesus monkeys the complete destruction of this structure eliminates the capacity to produce voluntary vocalizations. Cases of bilateral lesions to the cingulate cortex in humans revealed the temporary loss of the capacity to speak, while comprehension was preserved. Fortunately, mutism was temporary. Indeed, after a few months patients recovered their ability to speak (Jürgens & von Carmon, 1982). Electrophysiological studies on nonhuman primates have shown that the anterior cingulate cortex activates half a second before the animal starts vocalizing. As the cingulate cortical areas are crucial for the control of emotions, it was suggested that they mediate between the impulse to vocalize and its execution. North-American linguist John Lamendella proposed that they are differently involved in the production of the mother tongue as against foreign languages, because these structures subserve both the organization of emotions and the production of vocalizations and speech. In particular, Lamendella claimed that a language learnt during adult age through grammatical rules probably does not involve emotional structures and thus requires an ongoing process of translation from the mother tongue to the foreign language before the latter is spoken (Lamendella, 1977a, b).

4. The *laryngeal cortical area*. Studies on primates have underlined that the electrical stimulation of the area accounting for the motor representation of the larynx, which lies in the inferior precentral cortex, elicits single closures (adduction) of the vocal folds. Because phonation always starts with a closing movement of the vocal folds, the activation of this cortical area is necessary for verbal expression. The cortical laryngeal area receives information from the anterior cingulate cortex and is involved in the control

of neural activity of the periaqueductal gray matter structures and of the ventrolateral pons structures.

5. The *hypothalamus*. The electrical stimulation of some areas of the hypothalamus (the preoptic region and the ventromedial area) elicits vocalizations in cats resembling those of spontaneous meowing.

6. Lastly, stimulation of the *supplementary motor area*—an area lying in the frontal lobe—elicits vocalizations in man and in other primates, too.

ANALOGIES BETWEEN HUMAN LANGUAGES AND BIRDSONG

The most direct example of vocal communication resembling human language is provided by some bird species, even though these animals are phylogenetically very distant from man (Marler, 1981; Nottebohm, 1970). Many passeriform species show forms of *learnt vocal communication* that are similar to human languages. The vocal production of chaffinches, canaries, and some sparrow species from the United States are called *songs*. The songs are formed by notes—comparable to phonemes of human languages—which combine to form sequences known as "syllables"—comparable to words. Syllables, in turn, combine to form sentences according to specific "syntactic rules". Another analogy between birdsongs and human languages is the fact that birds belonging to the same species do not sing one language only: there are geographically isolated groups that sing different "languages" or "dialects". Groups belonging to the same species (chaffinches) living in different environments sing languages with different syllables and with different rules of syllabic combination. This is made possible by the fact that passerine chicks can learn the language or the dialect of their parents. This type of behavior is one of the most interesting forms of animal "culture" (Bonner, 1980). However, the analogy between passeriform birdsongs and human languages is restricted to the phonological and syntactical level—as far as our knowledge goes—and does not involve the semantic level. Human languages use sounds and word combination rules to convey meaning (semantic level), whereas passeriform languages do not have this peculiar feature, because at most they convey important, yet stereotyped, meaning aimed at delimiting territory and at coupling.

Yet another analogy between human languages and passeriform songs concerns neural structures subserving song and language. As in humans, in these birds there is a direct neural pathway linking the more complex structures of the telencephalon with the motor cells that control anatomic structures subserving phonation (syrinx and tongue). Furthermore, even more surprisingly, in these species—like in man—neural centers accounting for song asymmetrically lie in one side of the brain only, namely the left (Konishi, 1985).

CHAPTER FOUR

Language areas in the brain

This chapter describes the first studies on cerebral organization of language in monolinguals. In the first half of the 19th century Pierre Paul Broca, a French physician, was the first to identify the center accounting for articulated language (localized in the left frontal lobe). Furthermore, Broca discovered that language centers lie in the left side of the brain. For this reason, he stated that we speak with our left cerebral hemisphere. In 1874 Carl Wernicke, a German neurologist, described a language disorder marked by the incapability to understand words (sensory aphasia), which led him to identify a second language center (localized in the left temporal lobe) accounting for comprehension of phonemes and words. Wernicke also proposed the first model of cerebral language representation.

PIONEERING STUDIES

The oldest document reporting a loss of the ability to speak following a disease affecting the brain is an Egyptian papyrus dating back to 1700 BC. As early as in the 6th century BC Hebrew cultural circles were apparently aware of the relation between the loss of linguistic ability and a right-sided paralysis—two pathologies caused by a left hemisphere lesion (Fabbro, 1994). Psalm 137, 5–6 reads as follows: "If I forget you, o Jerusalem, let my right hand wither! Let my tongue cleave to the roof of my mouth, if I do not remember you, if I do not set Jerusalem above my highest joy!". Hippocrates, in the 5th century BC, seemed to be aware of the relationship between brain and language too, as he reported cases of

29

temporary loss of the ability to speak after convulsive crises resulting in a paralysis of the tongue and of the right side of the body. Furthermore, at an empirical level Hippocrates knew that sensory and motor functions are crossed in the brain. He explained that right hemisphere lesions provoked spasms in the left side of the body and, conversely, left hemisphere lesions provoked spasms in the right side of the body. What is unclear is the level of awareness of these authors. Probably they only described associations of symptoms, rather than ask themselves questions and thus reflect on the cerebral representation of language (Fabbro, 1995a; O'Neill, 1980). This kind of cognitive awareness would be achieved by Pierre Paul Broca only in the second half of the 19th century.

In the first half of the 19th century, in France, a physician of German origin called Franz Joseph Gall focused on the organization of higher cerebral functions in humans. In his experiments he showed that the brain is the seat of the mind. Furthermore, unlike his predecessors from Aristotle to Descartes, Gall claimed that the mind is not a single system, but a system consisting of many organs that are specific and independent of each other, namely a system of faculties. Gall also suggested that each faculty is localized in a specific area of the cerebral cortex. He distinguished about 30 faculties (ideality, constructive attitude, benevolence, hope, greed, caution, secrecy, destructiveness, self-respect, vitality, etc.) and suggested that the wider cortical extension of some faculties determined the prevalence of specific aspects of an individual's temperament. The faculties of articulated language and of memory were localized by Gall in the orbital region of the frontal lobe of both cerebral hemispheres.

Gall's theories met with support by progressives and anti-clericals. Yet, they were opposed by scientists and intellectuals, who were mainly of a Catholic and conservative background. Gall's fiercest opponent was French physiologist Pierre Flourens, who carried out many experiments of partial brain ablation in birds and drew the conclusion that cerebral functions presupposed a unitary nervous system (Harrington, 1987).

THE LOCATION OF ARTICULATED LANGUAGE

In the second half of the 19th century, at the Anthropological Society of Paris, a heated debate on Gall's theories took place, especially with regard to the issue of cerebral organization of linguistic functions. These discussions were followed with great interest by a young surgeon, Pierre Paul Broca, secretary of the Society, who became renowned as the father of the theory of left hemisphere lateralization of language (Benton, 1981; Whitaker, 1998). In 1861 Broca visited a patient at the Bicêtre Infirmary in Paris. The patient, 51 years of age, named Leborgne, suffered from a severe gangrene to his right leg. Broca noticed that the patient could only utter a monosyllabic word ("tan"), even though he understood perfectly well what Broca was saying. Broca became interested in this case and decided he would draw up a detailed medical history of the patient. He found out that even as a young man, Leborgne had suffered from epileptic fits, but this had not prevented him for learning the shoemaker's trade.

When Leborgne was 30, he lost the ability to speak and after 2–3 months he was admitted to the Bicêtre Hospice. Doctors established that he was in good health and clever and that he had only lost his verbal capacity. He could go in and out of the Hospice as he liked and everyone called him "Tan". Leborgne's verbal comprehension was good, but if he was addressed, he always replied with the monosyllables "tan tan". He tried to express himself through gestures and easily lost his temper. Only in these cases did he succeed in swearing and would say "*Sacré nom de Dieu!*". At the Hospice the patient performed small tasks and, notwith-standing the fact that he was considered vindictive and selfish by the other patients, he was reputed to be sane and with preserved intelligence. Therefore, the patient was never transferred to the psychiatric ward. Ten years after he had lost the ability to speak, "Tan" began to exhibit a gradual weakening of his right arm muscles until he suffered complete paralysis. The paralysis gradually affected his right leg. At this point the patient had to stay in bed. Owing to suppuration of a bedsore a gangrene to his right leg set in and he was delivered to the Infirmary. When Broca visited him, Leborgne's right limbs were completely paralyzed. His general sensitivity was preserved, but the right side of his body was less sensitive than his left side. It was probably for this reason that the patient did not complain much about the pain caused by the gangrene. The voluntary motility of the muscles of his face and his tongue was completely pre-served. His hearing and his calculation ability were unaffected, too. On this basis, Broca suspected that the patient suffered from a progressive left hemisphere lesion.

The patient died of septicemia six days after Broca had seen him for the first time. The autopsy revealed a left frontal lobe lesion (cf. Fig. 5.2). The structure that had been mostly affected by the lesion was the third frontal convolution of the left hemisphere cortex (Broca, 1861; Cabanis, Iba-Zizen, Abelanet, Monod-Broca, & Signoret, 1994). A few hours after-wards, Broca presented his first important findings in a report on Tan's case at the Anthropological Society of Paris, showing the patient's brain and the frontal lobe lesion. His conclusions on this case perfectly fitted the general discussion at the Society in that period. Broca stated that he had for the first time localized a faculty of human mind in the brain and advanced the hypothesis that the faculty of articulated language was independent of both verbal comprehension and nonverbal communication and that it was localized in the third convolution of the frontal lobe.

CEREBRAL LATERALIZATION OF LINGUISTIC FUNCTIONS

Broca's findings caused sensation among experts in the field and intellectuals, not only in France but also in the rest of the world. After the first findings, like any good researcher, Broca continued to carry out autopsies on the brains of patients who had lost the ability to speak. Between 1861 and 1863 Broca studied another eight aphasic patients and found that they all showed a lesion to the third frontal convolution of the left hemisphere. These results perplexed Broca because he knew that all classic theories, from Aristotle onwards, had viewed symmetry as the highest form of organization. The fact that the faculty for language, a defining characteristic of humans—the most important creatures in the universe— was not bilaterally represented in the two cerebral hemispheres was not only unexpected, but it was also hardly accepted even by Broca himself. In his work in 1863 he reiterated his perplexity, stating he did not dare draw conclusions and was waiting for further data. After he had gathered new information that proved the validity of his data, in 1865 Broca presented his second important findings. He proposed what was to become a milestone in the study of cerebral functions, namely the fact that "we speak with our left hemisphere" ("Nous parlons avec l'hémisphère gauche").

His second findings showed that in human beings linguistic functions are not only localized in some cortical areas, but are also lateralized in the left hemisphere. Subsequently, numerous studies on right-handed individuals corroborated this data. In over 95% of right-handed individuals language is lateralized in the left hemisphere. Furthermore, humans show another asymmetry, namely right manual preference. This means that over 90% of individuals prefer to use their right hand when performing fine movements, whereas they use their left hand as support for the actions made by their right hand. The analysis of many works of art depicting scenes of work being carried out with one hand only has shown that the right manual preference has been known since ancient times (at least since 3000 BC) and has been a constant feature until the present day (Coren, 1992; Hécaen, 1984).

Broca was the first to establish that right manual preference and language were both controlled by the left hemisphere. Language acquisition and the dominant use of the right hand, two typical cultural acquisitions, were thus controlled by the hemisphere which—in Broca's opinion—developed earlier in infancy, namely the left hemisphere.

SENSORY APHASIA

The control of voluntary movement according to Wernicke

In 1874 a young German neurologist, Carl Wernicke, published a short monograph entitled: "The aphasic symptomatic complex. A psychological study on an anatomical basis" (Wernicke, 1874/1974). This short book, only 72 pages long, was unusual for the German cultural style of that time, which was characterized by more voluminous neurological works, but it became one of the fundamental texts for the study of language disorders caused by cerebral lesions. The significance of this book lies in the fact that Wernicke not only described new cases of aphasia but also, on the basis of knowledge at that time, attempted to explain the way in which voluntary movement and language—a particular type of movement—were organized in the brain. Nowadays some of his explanations are simplistic and outdated, but certainly some intuitive ideas and the general framework of Wernicke's theories are still valid and useful in the development of experimental and clinical studies on brain functions. Wernicke learnt and developed many of the ideas expressed in his book during his stay in Vienna with Theodor Meynert, a renowned clinical neurologist. In fact, in the preface to his book Wernicke writes that "whatever will be considered of value in the present book is to be ascribed to Meynert". Subsequent neurological studies substantiated Wernicke's acknowledgment. Indeed, most of Wernicke's theories on cerebral organization of language had already been published a few years earlier by Meynert in a medical review in Vienna (Whitaker & Etlinger, 1993; Whitaker, 1998).

Wernicke proposed that the cerebral cortex was organized in a system of very simple psychic functions, for instance in areas accounting for visual perception, in areas accounting for olfactory perception, and in areas accounting for tactile perception. These areas were anatomically connected. In Wernicke's opinion, such an organization could explain *memory*. When two cerebral structures were simultaneously activated, they tended to remain regularly associated. The ongoing activation of a neural circuit involved in a given function, such as listening to a word, reduced the energy necessary for activating the same circuit. The more frequent the repetition of a task, such as piano-playing or listening to a symphony, the more stable the associations between the system of cerebral cortical areas subserving this function. The neural circuits to be activated by very weak nerve excitations or auto-excitations were called by Wernicke "mnestic images" in order to distinguish them from genuine visual, tactile, and acoustic perceptions, as well as from movements. However, he postulated the existence of "mnestic images" for movements in the cerebral cortex, too.

Furthermore, Wernicke proposed a division of the whole cerebral sur-face into two large sectors with different functions: the *frontal brain*, formed by the cerebral structures anterior to the Rolandic fissure, and the *temporo-occipital brain* (cf. Fig. 4.1). In keeping with contemporary knowledge Wernicke ascribed the motor functions to the frontal brain and the sensory functions to the temporo-occipital brain. This scheme is roughly still valid and will be briefly reviewed here. In the case of an impulse (e) reaching the temporo-occipital cortex (o) via (e–o), if the sub-ject wanted to make a voluntary movement, the information sent to the visual cortex was to reach the cortex of the frontal brain (f), because it was believed that this structure controlled voluntary movement. The impulse initiating the movement of an arm was thus sent to the spinal cord (b) via (f–b), where motoneurons responsible for the arm movement were located. Performing a specific movement depended on the mnestic images available to the subject: the more images available, the greater the ability to choose the kind of movement.

The language scheme in the brain

Wernicke considered language to be a particular kind of voluntary move-ment. Therefore, as for voluntary movements, interconnected sensory and motor centers subserving language had to be postulated. Wernicke's scheme of cerebral organization of language will briefly be reviewed here (cf. Fig. 4.1): (a) acoustic pathways connecting the acoustic nerve with the acoustic cortex; (a1) a memory area for the sound images of words (acoustic sensory area localized in the first temporal convolution); (b) a memory area for motor images of words (Broca's area, localized in the third frontal convolution); (a1–b) fibers linking the center for sensory images of words to the center for motor images of words that is respon-sible for the psychic reflex arc.

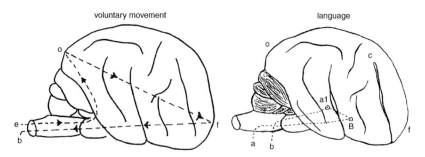

FIG. 4.1.   Centers subserving the organization of voluntary movement and language according to Wernicke's theory.

Because Wernicke viewed language as being organized in various inter-connected centers via specific communication pathways, he necessarily presupposed the existence of various types of aphasia and language disorders, the latter depending on the area where pathways were interrupted.

1. Interruption of pathways from (a) to (a1): such an interruption would provoke deafness without aphasia in adults, whereas in children it would provoke deafness and mutism.

2. Lesion in (a1): a lesion in this area of the temporal lobe cortex would provoke *sensory aphasia*. In these patients hearing would be preserved, whereas sensory images of words would be lost. Patients had a clear memory of the concepts to be expressed, but as they lost the memory of the sound images of words they would no longer be able to perform the naming task correctly. Furthermore, they would not be able to understand words, because sounds would mean nothing to them without a memory of the sound images of words. The situation would be tantamount to listening to a foreign language. Therefore, it might be difficult to distinguish between sensory aphasic patients and subjects suffering from mental confusion. However, an expert psychiatrist would be able to distinguish symptoms of mental confusion (look, care, and nonverbal communication) from this type of aphasia. Associated motor disorders would not be expected, whereas writing disorders (agraphia) and reading disorders (alexia) might arise.

3. Lesion of pathways (a1–b): in this case, sound images would no longer innervate the center for motor images of words. A patient affected by *conduction aphasia* would not be able to repeat words, whereas neither expression nor comprehension would be severely impaired. Word-finding difficulties and the tendency to mix words were expected to be slightly less frequent than in the same disorders caused by a lesion in area (a1). Furthermore, the patient would be aware of his verbal production errors and would probably be frustrated by them. Lastly, associated motor disorders (hemiplegia) might also arise.

4. Destruction of the area subserving motor images of words (Broca's area): in this case the patient would be affected by *motor aphasia*. Comprehension of words would be preserved, whereas verbal production would be limited to only some words to be used in all contexts. Patients would express themselves through gestures and perform verbal orders correctly. This type of aphasia might frequently be accompanied by motor disorders (hemiplegia) and writing disorders (agraphia).

After describing the various types of aphasia on the basis of his scheme of cerebral organization of language, Wernicke reiterated that the existence of motor aphasia could no longer be doubted, as after the first cases reported by Broca many other cases had been published in medical journals, whereas clinical cases of *sensory aphasia* had not yet been reported. For this reason, he described two cases of sensory aphasia, which will be illustrated in the next section.

Clinical cases

First case.   Susanne Adam was a 59-year-old widow who suddenly, on March 1st 1874, showed associated symptoms such as headache, dizziness, and a highly confused verbal expression, without loss of consciousness. She gave absurd answers to all questions and kept on repeating the nonword *begräben*. The following day she was taken to hospital, where a confusional state without sensory or motor disorders was diagnosed. She was therefore transferred to the insanity ward. Some days later Wernicke visited her and noticed that the patient could not understand a word of what she was told. She only understood gestures. At a first glance the patient appeared to be mentally challenged because her answers were irrelevant to questions and she often made sentences full of mistakes, containing meaningless words or words in the wrong position within the sentence. However, Adam's behavior was normal, despite the fact that—from a clinical point of view—confusion should have been accompanied by psychically altered behavior. She correctly pronounced the following sentences: "I ate well today", "I hope I recover", "The doctor gave me two shillings". Very often, when she was excited, she managed to produce other equally correct sentences. In the morning and in the evening she said her prayers without difficulties and managed to intone a Tirolean song correctly, even though she could not pronounce the words of it.

The patient was not confused. Wernicke reported that during the examination he had to be very careful, because—even though she understood nothing of what she was told—she was very skilled at recognizing gestures and contextual situations. For example, if she was asked to show her tongue, she could execute the order because she imitated other patients. But if she was asked to close her eyes first, she showed her tongue. Furthermore, if she was asked to fetch the glass from the table—the verbal order was not accompanied by gestures—the patient became very embarrassed and made several attempts: she closed her eyes, she showed her tongue or her teeth, or she performed orders that had previously been performed by other patients. Finally, she asked embarrassed: "What shall I do? What shall I show you?". Afterwards she would start to cry and exclaim: "Will I ever recover?". In addition, she could no longer read or write. In the following days the patient made considerable progress.

An excerpt of a conversation she had with Wernicke might be useful to understand her verbal production more easily:

Doctor: "Good morning, how are you feeling today?"
S.A.: "Very well, thank you."
Doctor: "How old are you?"
S.A.: "Well, thank you."
Doctor: "How old are you?"
S.A.: "You mean what's my na..., how I am?"
Doctor: "No, I was asking how old you are?"
S.A.: "I don't know what my nime *name* (*she corrects herself*) how I feel name."
The doctor moves a watch close to one of her ears, takes it away and moves it closer again.
S.A.: "Yes, I can hear it, this one, too, this I can no longer hear, now it gets weaker."
She is shown a button.
S.A.: "I know its name, it is a *bottin, a bottan*".
Doctor: "Is this your hair?"
S.A.: "Yes, my watch, my *hoir*, my *hairywatch* (*Haaruhre*)".
At last, after she had cried, the patient would conclude with a correct sentence: "My God, may I become healthy again!"

Over time the patient improved further. Indeed, 40 days after the emergence of the first symptoms, she understood almost everything she was told. In the end, she recovered language almost completely and could identify her own errors. In addition, she recovered reading completely, but recovered writing only partially.

Second case. Susanne Roth, aged 75, was admitted to the hospital where Wernicke worked due to gait difficulties, weakness, dizziness, and loss of sphincter control. After a month the patient suddenly lost the ability to express herself correctly. She gave wrong answers to questions, did not carry out instructions, and—if she did—did it in the wrong manner. Her spontaneous vocabulary was reduced, but not so much as to suggest that she was affected by motor aphasia. She often said: "Thank you very much", "Thank you *clearly*", or "I'm very ill and I'm cold", "You are a good man". Often she tended to repeat these sentences. The very doctor she had previously addressed as "good man" would immediately afterwards be called "my daughter, my son". Her sensitivity and her muscular strength were preserved. Because the patient showed disorders concerning both words and syntactical order, she was diagnosed as having mental confusion accompanied by aphasia. After a month she died owing to a gradual worsening of her physical conditions. The autopsy revealed a lesion in some convolutions of the left temporal lobe (cf. Fig. 5.2), in the brain structures that Wernicke had called a1 (Fig. 4.1). On this basis, Wernicke stated that this led him to suppose that Susanne Adam (the first case) also had a focal disease in the same structures of the left temporal lobe.

Wernicke's contribution to the study of cerebral organization of language was very important. Not only did he propose a scheme of the organization of language in the brain, but he also advanced hypotheses on the various types of aphasia that could be predicted on the basis of his model. In addition, he described one type of aphasia—sensory aphasia—now known as *Wernicke's aphasia*.

CHAPTER FIVE

Aphasia: The undoing of language

The most widespread method of assessing the cerebral organization of language is that of observing patients with language disorders caused by localized cerebral lesions. Depending on the site and the extent of the left cortical lesion, different language disorders can arise, which have been defined in many technical ways (paraphasia, anomia, neologism, agrammatism, paragrammatism, etc.). Moreover, some typical language disruption patterns have been detected and defined as aphasic syndromes (Broca's aphasia, Wernicke's aphasia, conduction aphasia, motor and sensory transcortical aphasia, global aphasia, anomic aphasia). They are particularly useful in the patient's clinical assessment. Recent studies have shown that the right hemisphere is also involved in specific aspects of verbal communication.

BASIC TERMINOLOGY IN APHASIA

The term *aphasia* refers to a loss of linguistic faculty as a consequence of a cerebral lesion. There are various types of lesions causing aphasia (cranial trauma, infection, tumor, cerebral infarction, and hemorrhage). Aphasia is characterized by errors in verbal expression that are known as *paraphasias* (substitution of one element for another), word-finding difficulties (*anomias*), and comprehension disorders. The study of language disorders and the patients' rehabilitation from them is an important branch of medicine and employs many researchers, and the technical terms used need an explanation before we come to a description of the various types of aphasia (Blanken, Dittmann, Grimm, Marshall, & Wallesch, 1993; Lecours and Lhermitte, 1979; Taylor Sarno, 1981).

1. *Phonemic paraphasia* may result in the production of a nonword. This type of error in verbal expression consists in the substitution of one or two phonemes within a word that the patient wanted to produce. Nevertheless, a listener manages to understand the word that the subject wanted to utter (i.e. *wesh* in place of wish, *seep* in place of sheep). *Phonemic paraphasia* may also result in the production of a word. This type of error depends on the substitution of one or two phonemes within a word that the patient wanted to produce, which results in another real word that is irrelevant to the discourse context. It is usually easy to recognize the *target word* that the patient wanted to produce (i.e. "I am hungry and even dirty", "I am hungry and even thirsty").

2. *Semantic paraphasia* produces a word irrelevant to the context, yet semantically linked to the target word. For instance, the patient says: "I use a *spoon* and fork to cut steak" instead of "I use a knife and fork to cut steak".

3. *Verbal paraphasia* consists in the production of a word irrelevant to the discourse context and that is not phonemically similar to or semantically related to the target word (i.e. I have been absent for *cat* instead of I have been absent for long).

4. *A neologism* is a nonword that prevents recognition of the word the patient intended to produce. The phonemic sequences of these nonwords, however, follow the phonological rules of the language in which the patient is expressing himself (i.e. I have seen a *gat* on the *sep*).

5. *Anomia* is the incapability of retrieving a word during naming tasks or during spontaneous verbal expression.

6. *Circumlocution.* When the patient has word-finding difficulties owing to anomia, he often replaces the word he intended to produce with a sentence describing the object to be named or its function. If the patient cannot name the object *watch* he will say: "It is an object with two hands", or in the case of *key* "It is used to open the door".

7. *Echolalia* is the involuntary and uncontrollable tendency on the part of the patient (P) to repeat what the interlocutor (I) has just said, e.g. (I): "What's your name?" (P): "What's your name? My name's John".

8. *Perseveration* implies the involuntary repetition of syllables, words, or syntagms (i.e. "I had soup, then I drank *soup* and lastly I washed *soup* up").

9. *Agrammatism* is generally marked by the tendency to use the simplest inflections, e.g. the infinitive ending in Italian verbs or the basic (nominative) form of adjectives in German with no regard for case inflection. In particular, in Italian, for instance, it consists in the

omission of bound morphemes, which are the smallest lexical units (articles, prepositions, conjunctions, pronouns, auxiliaries, demonstrative and possessive pronouns) of a sentence. A typical production could thus be, for example: "Seen cat garden" instead of "I have seen a cat in my garden". Moreover, agrammatism is characterized by the incorrect use of affixes, which leads to violations in concordance, for instance between article and noun for number (e.g. *a* cars), or between subject and verb (Mark *eat*), etc. (Menn & Obler, 1990).

10. *Paragrammatism* implies any incorrect use of grammatical morphemes and forms that is not included in agrammatism, specifically, the substitution of grammatical words or errors in the selection of tenses, aspects and persons (i.e. "He says they can go *for* get the dishes").

11. *Errors in word order*. Sometimes all words uttered by the patient are correct but the word order is wrong (e.g. "Bath had we").

12. *Closed class words*, also known as "function words", comprise articles, prepositions, conjunctions, demonstrative and possessive adjectives, and personal and possessive pronouns. Their number within a given language is limited. Aphasic patients with lesions in structures anterior to the Rolandic fissure (cf. Fig. 5.1) make a large number of errors in this category of words.

13. *Open class words*, also known as "content words", comprise nouns, adjectives, verbs, and adverbs. They are called open class words because their number can constantly increase. Aphasic patients with a lesion in an area posterior to the Rolandic fissure (cf. Fig. 5.1) generally present an alteration in the use of this category of words.

DIFFERENT TYPES OF APHASIA

Many neurologists have become concerned with the classification and description of the different types of aphasia related to brain lesions. One of the most systematic classifications was proposed in 1885 by German neurologist Ludwig Lichtheim, who extended and worked out the language scheme that had been proposed by Carl Wernicke 11 years earlier (Lichtheim, 1885). Lichtheim presupposed the existence of a center accounting for acoustic images (A) where the acoustic memory for words was located, and a center accounting for motor images (M) where motor memory for coordinated movements for word production was located (cf. Fig. 5.1). From auditory periphery (a) acoustic impressions reached the auditory cortex (A). However, sound comprehension required another link between the acoustic center (A) and the concept center (B). In Lichtheim's opinion, the production of voluntary language started when the center for concepts B sent information to the center accounting for motor images M, which, in turn, sent

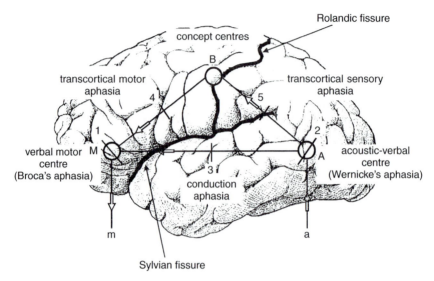

FIG. 5.1   Lichtheim's classification of the various aphasic syndromes.

nerve stimuli to the language areas. Lichtheim's diagram was not a mere cerebral representation of language, but permitted workers to advance hypotheses on the various types of aphasia that might affect a patient.

On the basis of Lichtheim's model the following types of aphasia were forecast:

1. *Broca's aphasia* as a consequence of a lesion localized in Broca's area (M);
2. *Wernicke's aphasia* as a consequence of a lesion in Wernicke's area (A);
3. *Conduction aphasia* as a consequence of a lesion in the connection fibers between Wernicke's area and Broca's area (A-M);
4. *Transcortical motor aphasia* as a consequence of a lesion in the structures between the concept center and Broca's area (B-M);
5. *Transcortical sensory aphasia* as a consequence of a lesion in the structures between the concept center and Wernicke's area (B-A).

This classification of language disorders in a limited number of aphasic syndromes has remained almost unchanged until the present day. During the 1970s, a group of North-American aphasiologists proposed a more updated version (Albert, Goodglass, Helm, Rubens, & Alexander, 1981; Frederiks, 1985). However, this version was essentially similar to Lichtheim's model, which had been widely applied in clinical settings because it is a useful way of communication between doctors. If a neurologist were to transfer an aphasic patient from London to Glasgow for instance, he could immediately exchange information with his colleague in Glasgow and inform him of the type of aphasic syndrome from which the patient suffers. The same holds for exchange of information between neurologists from various nations.

A brief review of one of the most accepted and currently most widespread classifications of aphasia follows. It is an updated version of Lichtheim's classification. Figure 5.2 schematically shows the extension of the cortical lesions causing the various aphasic syndromes (Maruszewski, 1975; Murdoch, 1990).

1. *Broca's aphasia.*   Verbal expression is impeded (not fluent). Spontaneous speech is effortful, poorly articulated, hesitating, and scanty; there is a paucity and simplification of grammatical forms with omissions of closed class words ("telegraphic speech"). Patients' verbal comprehension is good, but they often have difficulty in understanding complex grammatical sentences. Repetition of words or sentences is very limited (cf. Table 5.1). These patients usually present a lesion circumscribed to Broca's area, localized in the left frontal lobe (cf. Fig. 5.2). This aphasic syndrome is frequently accompanied by a right-sided paralysis (right-sided hemiparesis or hemiplegia). Broca's aphasia accounts for 20% of all aphasic syndromes that are usually diagnosed.

2. *Transcortical motor aphasia.*   Spontaneous speech is reduced, not fluent, and quite agrammatic. The patient has no difficulty in naming and comprehending (cf. Table 5.1). The lesion interrupts the pathways between Broca's area and the other frontal structures (anterior marginal areas, supplementary motor area, cf. Fig. 5.2). It is often accompanied by a right-sided paralysis. This form of aphasia is rare (< 5%).

3. *Wernicke's aphasia.*   Verbal expression is fluent, yet characterized by many paraphasias (phonemic paraphasias and neologisms). Naming is severely impaired, as are verbal comprehension and repetition (cf. Table 5.1). The lesion causing this aphasic syndrome generally affects Wernicke's area, which is localized in the left temporal lobe (cf. Fig. 5.2). This form of aphasia is frequently accompanied by blindness of the right visual field (right homonymous hemianopia) and amounts to almost 20% of all cases.

4. *Conduction aphasia.*   Speech is fluent, with phonemic paraphasias. Acoustic comprehension is good, whereas repetition is severely impaired (cf. Table 5.1). The site of the lesion causing this type of aphasia generally comprises fibers of the arcuate fasciculus, which allow communication between frontal areas of language and temporal areas (cf. Fig. 5.2). Conduction aphasia is rather rare and accounts for 5% of all cases.

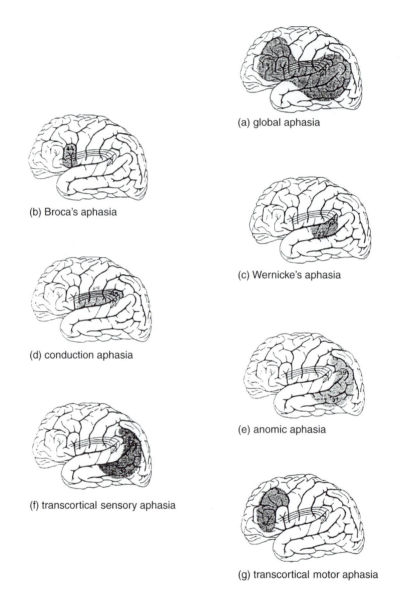

(a) global aphasia

(b) Broca's aphasia

(c) Wernicke's aphasia

(d) conduction aphasia

(e) anomic aphasia

(f) transcortical sensory aphasia

(g) transcortical motor aphasia

FIG. 5.2. Site of the main lesions causing aphasic syndromes.

5. *Transcortical sensory aphasia.*   Speech is fluent, with many para-phasias (phonemic, semantic, and verbal paraphasias) and serious deficits in naming (anomia). Acoustic comprehension is impaired, whereas repetition is relatively preserved (cf. Table 5.1). Lesions causing this form of aphasia are generally diffuse and affect the associated temporo-parieto-occipital areas (cf. Fig. 5.2). This form of aphasia has a frequency lower than 5%.

6. *Anomic aphasia.*   Spontaneous speech is fluent. Comprehension and repetition are generally preserved. Expression is impaired by frequent word-finding difficulties (anomia), which is the most serious disorder the patient suffers from (cf. Table 5.1). The lesion causing this form of aphasia affects the left associated temporo-parieto-occipital areas (cf. Fig. 5.2). The extension of the lesion is generally limited and lower in severity than that of sensory transcortical aphasia. Anomic aphasia accounts for about 5%.

7. *Global aphasia.*   This is the most severe clinical form of disturbance. Speech is highly impeded, even nonexistent. Acoustic comprehension is severely damaged (cf. Table 5.1). The lesion causing this form of aphasia generally affects almost all language areas of the left hemisphere (cf. Fig. 5.2). Aphasia can be accompanied either by a right-sided paralysis or by a loss of the visual capacity of the right field. Global aphasia accounts for around 20%.

8. *Isolation of the speech area syndrome.*   This is a very rare and severe clinical form of disturbance. Spontaneous speech and comprehension are absent; only repetition is preserved (cf. Table 5.1). This particular syndrome is generally caused by severe carbon monoxide poisoning, which destroys the cortical areas surrounding the cortical structures of language.

In assessing language disorders stress is to be laid on the type of cerebral lesion that has affected the brain (infarction, hemorrhage, tumor, or infection) and the lapse of time between the occurrence of the insult and the assessment of the patient's linguistic abilities. Generally, the first systematic assessment takes place a month after insult. Only later can the patient undergo language rehabilitation sessions (*speech and language therapy*). Most patients undergoing language rehabilitation show recovery of their linguistic functions accompanied by milder deficits that sometimes mark the recovery to a less severe aphasic syndrome. For instance, after a year of language rehabilitation Broca's aphasia may regress to transcortical motor aphasia, or Wernicke's aphasia may change to anomic aphasia.

The aforementioned clinical aphasia classification is only one of many alternative approaches. Actually many others have been proposed, including systems typically based on linguistic and cognitive neuropsychological

TABLE 5.1
Main clinical features of aphasic syndromes

Aphasia	Spontaneous Speech	Comprehension	Repetition
Broca's aphasia	Nonfluent	Good	Poor
Transcortical motor aphasia	Nonfluent	Good	Good
Wernicke's aphasia	Fluent	Poor	Poor
Transcortical sensory aphasia	Fluent	Poor	Good
Anomic aphasia	Fluent	Preserved	Preserved
Conduction aphasia	Fluent	Good	Poor
Global aphasia	Nonfluent	Poor	Poor
Isolation of the speech area syndrome	Nonfluent	Poor	Good

insights (see e.g. Lesser, 1978; McCarthy & Warrington, 1990). Apart from these differences, for methodological and therapeutic reasons, neurolinguists dealing with acquired language disorders usually give a detailed description of what patients are able to do and what they cannot do rather than classify them according to a given aphasic syndrome at all costs. The assessment of the patient's residual linguistic abilities, together with the evaluation of the patient's neurological and neuropsychological conditions, allow one to establish when speech therapy should begin and what to assess and, if necessary, to decide a change in the therapeutic program.

THE RIGHT HEMISPHERE AND VERBAL COMMUNICATION

Over the past few years the study of patients with focal lesions in the right hemisphere has led to a better understanding of the role played by the so-called nondominant cerebral hemisphere in the organization of communication. Right hemisphere lesions can considerably compromise some nonlinguistic components of verbal communication, such as prosody, pragmatics (production and comprehension of metaphors, anaphors, indirect linguistic acts, sarcasm, etc.), and some aspects of text use and comprehension. Furthermore, the right hemisphere is involved in the comprehension of high-frequency words, words that can easily be visually imagined, and concrete words (Code, 1987).

Studies comprising the analysis of regional cerebral blood flow (rCBF), a technique used to highlight the most active cortical areas during a cognitive task, show that the right hemisphere is also active during linguistic production (Ingvar, 1983). However, whereas the left hemisphere focally activates in the language areas only, the right hemisphere activates globally and diffusely. It is probable that, during verbal expression, the right hemisphere is involved in tasks such as maintenance of diffuse attention, control of emotions, assessment of nonverbal stimuli with regard to interlocutors, etc. Harry A. Whitaker, a neurolinguist working at the Northern Michigan University, proposed that the most automatized cognitive functions are controlled by limited cortical areas. Hence, according to this hypothesis, the left hemisphere controls the most automatic aspects of language, whereas the right hemisphere, which activates diffusely, processes language non-automatically.

Many clinical data show that the right hemisphere is involved in the control of *affective prosody*, namely voice intonation during verbal expression. For instance, following a focal lesion to the right hemisphere that did not affect language but severely impaired affective prosody, a primary school teacher could no longer teach. The melodic and intonational properties of his verbal expression were so impaired that his young pupils could not cope with it. This clinical case underlines the crucial role played by prosody. It expresses the affective meaning of voice in verbal communication. Furthermore, many patients with right hemisphere lesions cannot understand or effectively summarize complex texts, such as short stories, fables, and parables. They are not able to understand the deep meaning of metaphors and proverbs, they so often merely perform a literal interpretation of what they hear. If, for example, they hear the sentence (in context) "I could inherit a fortune only after my uncle had kicked the bucket" they tend to understand the metaphorical expression literally and imagine somebody hitting a pail or some kind of container with his foot. These disorders sometimes severely compromise communication, even though the patient apparently has no difficulties in verbal expression and comprehension (Chantraine, Joanette, & Cardebat, 1998; Joanette, Goulet, & Hannequin, 1990).

CHAPTER SIX

The assessment of aphasia

This chapter describes the techniques used to assess aphasia. The analysis of an acquired language disorder can be carried out quite easily during a clinical examination by assessing the patient's spontaneous speech and by asking him/her to perform verbal orders of increasing syntactic complexity. Tests for the objective assessment of the linguistic abilities of aphasic monolingual and bilingual patients have been developed. With regard to monolinguals, the most frequently used language test in Europe is the Aachener Aphasie Test (AAT) developed by neurologists and linguists of the University of Aachen. The most frequently used test for the assessment of bilingual aphasia is the Bilingual Aphasia Test (BAT) developed by a neurolinguist at McGill University, Montreal. This test is currently available in more than 50 languages and allows the analysis of the linguistic history of the patients (Part A), their linguistic performance in the various linguistic components in each of their languages (Part B) and their capacity to translate from language to language (Part C).

CLINICAL CRITERIA

It is legitimate to suspect aphasia in adults when they lose the ability to express themselves and/or comprehend language, or when they suddenly begin to make many errors while speaking. Generally, these people exhibit other associated neurological problems, such as single or repeated episodes of loss of consciousness, motor problems (right-sided hemiparesis or hemiplegia), or sensory problems (loss of the visual capacity of the right visual field).

The clinical assessment of a patient's linguistic disorders requires the evaluation of spontaneous speech first. The clinician will make patients speak about simple and everyday things, such as their job prior to insult, hobbies, and family. Through an informal dialogue the clinician can understand whether the aphasic patient speaks fluently or nonfluently. In addition, the clinician can detect errors in expression, such as word-finding difficulties (anomia) or substitution of a word for another word belonging to a similar semantic field (semantic paraphasia), or for words not directly linked to the target word (verbal paraphasia). If the patient speaks fluently he is likely to have difficulties in understanding verbal orders or questions. Furthermore, he is likely to make many errors, such as substituting one or two phonemes within a word (phonemic paraphasia) or producing completely invented words (neologisms). If the patient does not speak much and only with difficulty, errors in word articulation, errors in phoneme substitution (substitution of voiced phonemes for voiceless phonemes, e.g. *pook* instead of *book*), and errors in the grammatical construction of sentences are normally to be looked for. After a first meeting an experienced clinician or a neurolinguist is able to establish whether the patient is aphasic and, if so, classify the aphasic syndrome and advance hypotheses on which area of the brain has probably been affected by the lesion.

During a rapid clinical assessment of the patient's abilities a set of tools may contribute to a better understanding of the language disorders involved. The clinician can thus always be equipped with a few common objects such as a key, a pen, a coin, a pencil, a rubber, etc., in order to evaluate the patient's naming abilities by showing him the objects one at a time, and assessing whether there is anomia or semantic, verbal, or phonemic paraphasia. After this stage, the clinician will ask the patient to recognize and point to the various objects which he will name, so as to assess the patient's ability to discriminate between sounds and words. After the object-recognition task the patient will be asked to perform orders of increasing syntactical complexity, such as "Point to the key and the pencil", "Put the rubber in front of the pencil", "Put the pencil on the key", "After turning the coin, touch the rubber with the key". These tasks aim to study the grammatical and mnestic abilities of the patient.

If aphasic patients are bilingual, the clinical assessment of their languages ought to be carried out separately (i.e. on two consecutive days). Assessment of spontaneous speech in the first language (L1), apart from the typical disorders accompanying aphasia in monolinguals, requires detection of possible symptoms typical of aphasia in bilinguals. Patients might have completely lost spontaneous speech in one language only (cf. Chapters 12 and 13), or might involuntarily switch back to the second language (L2), if experiencing word-finding difficulties in L1 (mixing phenomena, cf. Chapter 17). Sometimes patients do not understand a verbal order and thus do not perform it, but paradoxically can automatically translate the sentence that has just been heard (translation without comprehension, cf. Chapter 24, pp. 200–201). At other times, patients involuntarily translate what they have just said in all the languages they know (spontaneous translation, cf. Chapter 24, pp. 199–200). In assessing spontaneous speech in aphasic bilingual patients, daily or weekly, variations in their verbal capacity have to be taken into consideration. Cases have been reported in which patients spoke only L1 on a given day, whereas the day after the reverse applied (alternating antagonism, cf. Chapter 18). Besides the interview, the naming tasks, pointing and syntactic comprehension in L1 and L2, aphasic bilingual patients can be administered tasks aimed at assessing their ability to translate words and sentences, so as to detect possible disorders in both directions of translation. Sometimes patients can translate in one direction only (i.e. from L1 to L2, but not conversely from L2 to L1). Translation disorders can be constant or can vary over time (paradoxical translation, cf. Chapter 24, pp. 201–2).

APHASIA TESTS IN MONOLINGUALS

One of the most important targets in the assessment of aphasic patients is the objective description of their language deficits. As in the case of motor disorders, a detailed description of the linguistic functions that patients have lost following a cerebral lesion, and of their residual abilities is conducive to an appropriate diagnosis and the planning of corresponding rehabilitation. A detailed and objective analysis allows the assessment of the patients' recovery patterns with regard to their linguistic functions over time. The simple clinical description of an aphasic disorder—as in the past—is no longer considered sufficient, because it relies heavily on the personal abilities of the examiner.

To avoid describing aphasic disorders in an imprecise and subjective manner, psychometric tests have been developed since the 1940s—especially in English-speaking countries—aimed at the description and measurement of the residual linguistic abilities of aphasic patients. These tests ought to be easily applicable and accurately standardized so that an assessment carried out in London could be understood and repeated in, for example, New York or Canberra. During the 1970s a standardized test aimed at assessing linguistic abilities in Italian aphasic patients was also developed at the neurological department of the University of Milan. Subsequently, this test has been widely applied.

More recently, the Italian adapted version of the *Aachener Aphasie Test* (AAT)—an aphasia assessment test—developed at the neurological clinics of the University of Aachen was devised by Luzzatti, Wilmes, and De Bleser (1992). The AAT has been adapted into many European languages and is becoming one of the most frequently used clinical tests for the assessment of language disorders in adult aphasic patients. It is divided into six parts for the evaluation of six different aspects of linguistic function:

1. spontaneous speech;
2. comprehension without contextual clues (Token Test);
3. repetition;
4. written language;
5. naming;
6. comprehension.

During the assessment of *spontaneous speech* the examiner questions the patient for about 10 minutes on the history of the illness, previous job, family, hobbies, and spare time. The conversation is recorded and later transcribed. Essential aspects of the patient's spontaneous speech are scored: communicative behavior, articulation, prosody, automatic speech, semantic cohesion, and phonemic and syntactic integrity (0 is the lowest score, 5 the highest). The patient is administered the *Token Test*, consisting of 50 commands of increasing complexity involving the manipulation of geometric figures of various forms and color (the so-called tokens). For instance, when the examiner says: "Touch the green square", the patient is to point to the green square token among squares and circles of various colors, or "Touch the large red circle", "Touch the yellow square and the green circle", "Touch the small red circle and the large black square", "Take the black circle or the yellow square", "Before you touch the green circle take the white square", etc. The number of wrong trials is counted to assess comprehension of words, syntactic comprehension, and short-term memory. In the following section of the AAT, *repetition tasks* are administered to assess the patient's ability to repeat isolated sounds (vocal sounds /a/, /i/, /o/, and consonants /t/, /p/, /g/, etc.), bisyllabic words with different articulatory complexity, loan-words (pepperoni, salami, etc.), words with increasing bound morphemes (shortsightedness, unconventionality) and sentences of various complexity (0 is the lowest score, 3 the highest). In the *written language* tasks the patient is asked to read out loud words and short sentences. Afterwards a written dictation task is administered and the patient has to make up words and phrases using letter and word tiles. The *naming* section consists of 4 tasks of 10 stimuli each. In the first task the patient is asked to name simple objects when shown their picture; the second task is to name colors; the third task is to name compound words (washing-machine, dustbin, etc.); and the fourth task is to construct a sentence to describe a picture. The sixth part of the AAT is a *comprehension* task: auditory comprehension of isolated words, auditory comprehension of sentences, and lastly comprehension of written words and sentences (cf. Huber, Poek, Weniger, & Willmes, 1983).

This brief description of the AAT highlights its objective and systematic nature and its clear and relatively easy application. Once the raw scores of the various tasks have been obtained, they are stored in a computerized system that on the basis of a particular statistical program automatically shows the level of the patient's linguistic deficit (very low, low, mild, severe) with regard to each of the five sections of the test, and reveals whether the patient suffers from aphasia and—if so—which form of aphasia (global aphasia, Broca's aphasia, Wernicke's aphasia, anomic aphasia). If the linguistic deficits do not relate to any of these aphasic syndromes, then the patient suffers from a nonclassifiable aphasia, namely motor or sensory transcortical aphasia, or conduction aphasia.

APHASIA TESTS IN BILINGUALS

In the study and assessment of language disorders in bilingual aphasics at least one of the examiners ought to have a good knowledge of the languages spoken by the patient both with regard to the administration of the tests and test interpretation. In bilinguals who have become aphasic the need to assess linguistic deficits by means of objective criteria is even more important. If the degree of impairment of one language as against the other is to be assessed, both languages have to be assessed in a systematic, precise, and thus comparable manner. To this effect, some clinicians have suggested the use of the adapted versions of the AAT in the different languages to be examined. However, as the AAT has not been devised as a test for assessing bilingual aphasia, its various versions cannot effectively carry out a detailed and comparative analysis of the various languages known by the patient. For this kind of patient there is the need for accurate and systematic linguistic methods aimed at assessing various aspects of language so as to detect possible differential impairment of the two languages. Furthermore, the AAT shows its German origin (i.e. the compound noun task; compounds are an important aspect of German morphology but in Italian they are less important).

In an attempt to provide a solution for this type of disorder, 20 years ago Michel Paradis of McGill University, Canada, started an international project aiming at devising a proper test for the assessment of bilingual aphasia. This issue was live in Canada, a country where people officially speak two languages, English and French. Moreover, a great number of immigrants from all over the world live in Canada. A test aimed at assessing bilingual aphasia was needed to support research by experts in the field on clinical issues (i.e. which language has been affected most?, which language is to be rehabilitated, and why?) as well as on cognitive and scientific issues.

The end of the 1970s saw renewed interest in the study of bilingual and polyglot aphasia and, at the same time, a raising of awareness that bilingual aphasia could no longer be assessed as naïvely and approximately as had been done from the end of the 19th century up to 1950. Before the introduction of systematic assessment protocols for language disorders utilizing tests and objective neurolinguistic analyses, the study of bilingual aphasics was improvised and anecdotal. The collected data are hardly comparable, because they depend strongly on diverging observation abilities of the different researchers involved.

Michel Paradis developed a systematic and effective test for a detailed analysis of the various components of language (Paradis, 1987a). The original version of the test was aimed at assessing aphasia in English-French bilinguals, but from the very beginning the various tests had been devised so as to be applicable to all languages. The *Bilingual Aphasia Test* (BAT) is divided into three parts: *Part A* is common to both languages and assesses the linguistic history of patients and their family (when, how, and from whom patients have learnt the languages they know); *Part B* assesses the linguistic performance of patients in the various linguistic components of one language only; subsequently patients will undergo Part B in all the languages they know. *Part C* assesses the patient's translation abilities from language to language as well as grammaticality judgments containing grammatical elements of the other language. If patients are bilingual, they will undergo Part C only once, just to assess their translation abilities in both directions (L1→L2) and conversely (L2→L1). If patients speak three languages, they will undergo Part C three times (L1→L2; L2→L1; L1→L3; L3→L1; L2→L3; L3→L2). At present, the BAT is available in more than 50 languages, including Italian, Japanese, Chinese, Russian, Arabic, Spanish, and Hebrew. These versions include Part C of many pairs of languages (English-Farsi, Japanese-Chinese, German-French, German-Turkish, etc.). The adapted versions of the test not only requires translation at a formal level, but an accurate restructuring of the stimuli to be administered so that they reflect and investigate the most typical and distinctive features of the language to be assessed as well as respect its cultural characteristics.

Part B of the BAT investigates the following aspects of a language:

1. spontaneous speech;
2. pointing;
3. comprehension of simple orders;
4. comprehension of complex orders;
5. verbal auditory discrimination;
6. comprehension of syntactic structures of increasing complexity;
7. semantic categories;
8. synonyms;

9. antonyms;
10. grammaticality judgment;
11. semantic judgment;
12. repetition of real words and nonwords, and related lexical decision;
13. sentence repetition;
14. series;
15. verbal fluency;
16. naming;
17. sentence construction;
18. semantic opposites;
19. derivational morphology;
20. morphological opposites;
21. description of a story through pictures;
22. mental arithmetic;
23. text listening comprehension;
24. reading words or sentences aloud;
25. text reading comprehension;
26. copying of words and sentences;
27. word reading comprehension;
28. sentence reading comprehension;
29. spontaneous writing.

Part C consists of the following tasks:

1. Word recognition; words are given in L1 or L2 by the examiner and the patient points to them in a list containing the same words written in L2 or L1.
2. Translation of concrete or abstract words from L1 to L2, and conversely.
3. Translation of sentences from L1 to L2, and conversely from L2 to L1. The sentences to be translated vary in syntactic complexity, containing one to three contrastive grammatical differences between the two languages. For instance, a contrastive difference between Italian and English is the use of the preposition "in". In English one says: "*I live in New York*". In Italian, the preposition "in" is not to be used in this context, because the right preposition here is "a": "*Io vivo a New York*". The construction of the six sentences to be translated from L1 to L2 and the six sentences to be translated from L2 to L1 requires the isolation of 12 contrastive differences between the two languages;
4. In the last task of Part C the patient makes grammaticality judgments with regard to sentences presented in L1 and L2, respectively. In this case, eight contrastive differences between the two languages are also to be identified. Errors in the sentences are not coincidental, they

reflect the grammatical structure of the other language. For example, the English-Italian patient is asked to judge whether a sentence such as "Io vivo *in* Milano" is grammatically correct.

The BAT should be administered on successive days. If patients cooperate and their expressive abilities are not severely damaged, it can be administered in two hours in one language by a person without a background in speech-language pathology, for instance a relative of the patient or anyone knowing the language to be examined. This possibility has been taken into consideration because sometimes one or more languages known by patients are spoken by none of the hospital staff, only by a relative. In this case the relative introduces the tests to the patient and writes down the answers, stating whether they correspond to the choices offered as possible responses to the test. The assessment of the results takes place afterwards. There are two assessment patterns for the BAT: (i) an immediate evaluation pattern, where answers are stored in a computerized program that automatically analyzes results and provides an immediate visualization of the patients' residual linguistic abilities in the languages they know and in the translation processes; (ii) a more complex evaluation pattern, which implies a neurolinguistic assessment of all tests so as to obtain quantitative data on the patients' linguistic performance in the languages they know and on the type and quantity of errors they made.

Those who are concerned with the neurolinguistics of bilingualism will acknowledge that the application of the BAT in the assessment of language disorders is satisfactory and constructive, because it provides a systematic view of the linguistic deficits of aphasic patients and reveals interlinguistic differences (Fabbro, 1997a).

The Bilingual Aphasia Test (BAT) is available in 57 languages and 106 bilingual pairs. [For orders write to: Lawrence Erlbaum Associates, Inc., 10 Industrial Avenue, New Jersey 07430-2262, USA, Fax (201) 236-0072.]

The BAT is now available in the following single languages (Parts A and B): Amharic, Arabic (Jordanian), Arabic (Maghrebian), Armenian (Eastern), Armenian (Western), Azari, Basque, Berber, Bulgarian, Catalan, Chinese (Cantonese), Chinese (Mandarin), Croatian, Czech, Danish, Dutch, English, Farsi, Finnish, French, Friulian, Galician, German, Greek, Hebrew, Hindi, Hungarian, Icelandic, Inuktitut, Italian, Japanese, Kannada, Korean, Kurdish, Latvian, Lithuanian, Luganda, Malagasy, Norwegian, Oryia, Polish, Portuguese (Brazilian), Portuguese (European), Rumanian, Russian, Somali, Spanish (American), Spanish (European), Swahili, Swedish, Tagalog, Tamil, Turkish, Ukrainian, Urdu, Vietnamese, Yiddish.

Bilingual pairs (Part C) of the BAT are now available in: Amharic/ English, Amharic/French, Arabic/Armenian, Arabic/English, Arabic/ French, Arabic/Somali, Arabic/Swahili, Armenian/English, Armenian/ Farsi, Armenian/French, Armenian/Russian, Basque/English, Basque/ French, Basque/Spanish, Berber/English, Berber/French, Bulgarian/English, Bulgarian/French, Bulgarian/German, Bulgarian/Russian, Catalan/ Spanish, Chinese (Cantonese)/English, Chinese (Mandarin)/English, Chinese/French, Croatian/English, Croatian/French, Croatian/Italian, Czech/ English, Czech/German, Czech/Russian, Czech/Swedish, Danish/English, Danish/German, Dutch/English, Dutch/French, Dutch/German, Dutch/ Hebrew, English/Farsi, English/Finnish, English/French, English/Friulian, English/German, English/Greek, English/Hebrew, English/Hindi, English/ Hungarian, English/Icelandic, English/Italian, English/Japanese, English/ Korean, English/Latvian, English/Lithuanian, English/Luganda, English/ Norwegian, English/Polish, English/Portuguese, English/Rumanian, English/Russian, English/Serbian, English/Somali, English/Spanish, English/Swahili, English/Swedish, English/Tagalog, English/Turkish, English/ Urdu, English/Vietnamese, Farsi/French, Farsi/Hebrew, Finnish/French, Finnish/Swedish, French/Friulian, French/German, French/Greek, French/ Hebrew, French/Hungarian, French/Italian, French/Japanese, French/ Malagasy, French/Polish, French/Rumanian, French/Russian, French/Serbian, French/Somali, French/Spanish, French/Swahili, French/Urdu, French/Vietnamese, Friulian/German, Friulian/Italian, Galician/Spanish, German/Greek, German/Hebrew, German/Hungarian, German/Italian, German/Polish, German/Russian, German/Spanish, German/Swedish, Greek/Spanish, Greek/Turkish, Italian/Rumanian, Italian/Spanish, Portuguese/Spanish, Russian/Swedish, Somali/Swahili.

CHAPTER SEVEN

Methods for studying the organization of language in the brain

Besides the study of residual linguistic abilities in patients with cerebral lesions, a number of techniques aimed at investigating the cerebral organization of language have been devised, some of which [dichotic listening, finger-tapping, tachistoscopic viewing, electroencephalographic techniques (EEG), mapping EEG, event-related potential (ERP), positron emission tomography (PET), and functional magnetic resonance (fMRI)] present no danger to the subjects' health. Therefore, they can be used not only in the study of aphasics but also of normal adult subjects. Other techniques are available to study the cerebral representation of cognitive functions (intracarotid sodium amytal test, electric stimulation of the brain), but their use is restricted to subjects affected by diseases of the nervous system for their clinical examination or during neurosurgical operations.

Over the past 40 years many techniques aimed at studying the cerebral organization of language have been devised. For clarity's sake these techniques are grouped into two major categories: studies on normal subjects and studies with people suffering from neurological diseases (cf. Bryden, 1982; Botez, 1996; Kolb & Whishaw, 1990; Poeck, 1982; Stemmer & Whitaker, 1998; Trevarthen, 1984).

STUDIES ON NORMAL SUBJECTS

Broca's studies showed that in most of the subjects the same cerebral hemisphere controls the right hand and language. Therefore, cerebral organization of language—or with neurologists, cerebral lateralization of linguistic functions—may be easily established by assessing the subject's manual preference. Between 85 and 90% of individuals are right-handed, with the remaining 10–15% ambidextrous or left-handed. Over 95% of individuals generally exhibit aphasia following a left hemisphere lesion. This statistical data shows that language is lateralized in the left hemisphere in most left-handed individuals, too. The control exerted by the left hemisphere over language and the motility of the dominant hand has drawn the attention of scholars to the possible relationship between fine motor tasks performed by the right hand and man's linguistic functions. Some scholars have claimed that the ability to make complex stone tools, such as hatchets, arrow-heads, scrapers, etc., might depend on the particular ability to perform fine movements in a given sequence—common both to right-hand control and language. Other scholars have made an attempt at proving that human language probably derives from a previous gesture language. They claim that the basis for right-hand gesture communication precedes verbal language, which, in turn, developed by means of the same structures of the left hemisphere responsible for the control of the right-hand gesture communicative functions.

However, the assessment of manual preference is at most only a rough method of establishing the cerebral asymmetry of language. Hence, techniques have been devised (i.e. dichotic listening, finger-tapping, and tachistoscopic viewing) that permit a deeper understanding of hemispheric specialization of language. These techniques are not invasive and can thus be applied in the study of both adults and children.

Dichotic listening

Two different messages are sent concurrently to the right ear and the left ear through earphones. Stimuli can be verbal (digits, words, syllables), musical (chords, melodies), or other sounds (the flow of a river, the wind rustling the leaves, etc.). Immediately after having listened to a series of stimuli, subjects repeat or write down the stimuli they remember. Under these circumstances stimuli sent to the right ear are recognized and processed by the left hemisphere, whereas stimuli sent to the left ear are processed by the right hemisphere (cf. Fig. 7.1). Many studies on right-handed adults have proved a left hemispheric (right ear) superiority in recognizing verbal stimuli, whereas the right hemisphere (left ear) is better at recognizing environmental noise or musical stimuli (cf. Fig. 7.1).

The verbal-manual interference paradigm (finger-tapping)

This technique allows one to study cerebral lateralization for cognitive function, e.g. verbal expression. The subject, while remaining silent, is required to tap a key as rapidly as possible with the right index finger (the

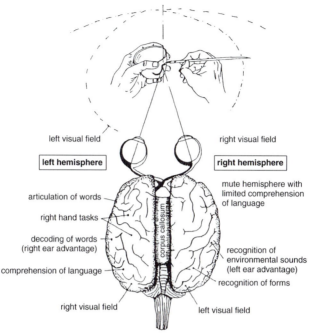

left visual field   right visual field

left hemisphere   right hemisphere

                                 mute hemisphere with
articulation of words   limited comprehension
                                 of language
right hand tasks

decoding of words
(right ear advantage)
                                 recognition of
comprehension of language   environmental sounds
                                 (left ear advantage)

                                 recognition of forms
right visual field   left visual field

corpus callosum

FIG. 7.1.   Hemispheric specialization for different cognitive tasks (adapted from Trevarthen, 1984).

right hand being controlled by the left hemisphere) and then with the left index finger (controlled by the right hemisphere). The key is connected to a digital counter. This task is performed several times, in sessions lasting 15 seconds each, alternately with the right and the left hand. The number of finger-taps produced by both hands in the control condition is thus established. The control condition is matched by an experimental condition where the subject, while tapping, concurrently performs a verbal task (saying prayers, days, counting, etc.). If the verbal activity is mainly controlled by the left hemisphere, the subject will reduce the number of taps by the right finger while speaking, thus showing that the finger's movement interferes with speaking. The right-hand interference is caused by the involvement of the left hemisphere in two concurrent tasks, namely controlling the right index finger and verbal expression. On the other hand, the degree of left-hand interference will be lower, because in this condition the right hemisphere is involved in the motor activity, whereas the left hemisphere controls verbal production. Finger-tapping has raised considerable interest on the part of neuropsychologists, because it allows the study of the organization of different cognitive functions such as verbal expression in the languages known by a bilingual, or cerebral organization of arithmetic and musical abilities.

Tachistoscopic viewing

Hemispheric specialization for the processing of rapidly presented visual stimuli can be studied through the tachistoscope (the word tachistoscope derives from Greek and means rapid vision). Given the particular configuration of human visual pathways, if subjects watch an image, focusing their glance on a central fixation point without deviating to the right or the left, the information in their right visual field is sent directly to their left cerebral hemisphere. Conversely, the information in their left visual field is sent directly to their right hemisphere. Numerous studies have proved that in right-handed adults verbal stimuli (words, letters) are better and faster recognized when they are presented to their right visual field (left hemisphere) as opposed to their left visual field (right hemisphere). On the other hand, the reverse applies if stimuli are of a spatial nature, namely faces of unknown people or arrows with different directions, etc. In this case, the right cerebral hemisphere (left visual field) recognizes them better and faster (cf. Fig. 7.1).

Unfortunately, the results obtained through the techniques mentioned in the preceding paragraphs also hold only if groups of subjects are studied, and not single subjects. Results obtained in this way can sometimes be difficult to interpret. For example, subjects can modify the superiority of their right ear and/or their right visual field with regard to certain verbal stimuli by voluntarily focusing their attention on their left ear and/or their left field. In addition, the study of a single right-handed subject with these techniques often produces contradictory results. For example, the same right-handed subject can present a left hemisphere specialization on two of the techniques (finger-tapping and tachistoscopic viewing), whereas results of the dichotic listening task can point to a right hemisphere specialization of language. For these reasons, these methods are used at most in experimental research studies and not as clinical examinations. At least for the time being, the results produced by these techniques are certainly lower—in terms of knowledge of cognitive functions—than the neuropsychological study of brain-damaged patients. Therefore, they are to be considered reliable only if their results coincide with the results of clinical studies on brain-damaged patients.

Recording the electrical activity of the brain

The most widespread techniques used to record the electrical activity of the brain are the electroencephalogram (EEG), EEG mapping, and event-related potentials (ERPs). The recording of cerebral electrical activity during cognitive tasks is probably one of the most promising techniques used to study the cerebral organization of cognitive functions. Some of these techniques reach a resolution in time at the level of milliseconds, which, for the study of language processing, is much more interesting than present functional brain imaging techniques. In addition, they can be used to study real verbal production. For example, it is possible to make EEG studies on subjects while they are talking out loud, because nowadays there are computerized programs that subtract from EEG records the muscular artifacts produced during articulation. Yet, results so far obtained have not borne out theoretical expectations (cf. Segalowitz & Chevalier, 1998).

Functional brain imaging

Lately, two further techniques for the study of neural structures selectively activating (or "deactivating") during specific cognitive tasks have been developed and used: positron emission tomography (PET) and functional magnetic resonance imaging (fMRI). PET involves the injection of slightly radioactive substances (radioactive glucose or oxygen) into the bloodstream. These substances are used by the brain as sources of energy during the execution of sensory-motor or cognitive tasks. The prime structures activated during the execution of a cognitive task take up the injected radioactive substances more than others. A computer processes this data by reconstructing and showing the cerebral structures that are most active during a task. Particular detectors identify the distribution of radioactive emissions released by the neural tissue; an appropriate computerized system can thus reconstruct a map of activated cerebral structures. Several functional anatomy studies in both monolinguals and bilinguals have been carried out by means of this technique (see Chapter 25). However, its major limits are the temporal resolution, which is greater than 10 seconds (whereas many language processes only last tenths of seconds, see Chapter 2), and the fact that normal subjects are being administered radioactive isotopes, a necessary practice that, although legal, is not completely harmless. Finally, another important aspect is the very high cost of the equipment necessary for PET studies, which so far has drastically limited the number of experimental investigations carried out worldwide.

Functional magnetic resonance imaging (fMRI) is a type of tomographic functional imaging that does not use radioactive compounds and has a better spatial and time resolution than PET (about 2 millimeters of spatial resolution and 4–8 seconds of time resolution). It consists in the recoding local hemodynamic changes and in particular blood oxygenation during cognitive tasks. Thus, fMRI also measures the activation of cerebral structures during cognitive tasks in general and during language in particular. It has been recently used to study language representation in bilingual subjects (see Chapters 10 and 25) and is gradually substituting for PET in studies of neurofunctional anatomy. Results obtained with these two techniques, both with the subtraction method and the correlational approach, were very appealing to most neuroscientists and fascinating for the public interested in scientific breakthrough. It is hoped that the methodological limits presently characterizing these techniques, at least as far as the study of language representation in the brain is concerned, will be eliminated for the sake of further knowledge (Démonet, 1998).

INVESTIGATION TECHNIQUES FOR NEUROLOGICAL PATIENTS

Some highly effective techniques for the study of the cerebral organization of cognitive functions have been developed, but they can only be used in the study of subjects affected by diseases of the nervous system during clinical examinations or neurosurgical operations. These studies provide interesting results, but vary in level of invasiveness for the subject.

Carotid sodium amytal injection (Wada test)

A neurosurgeon who has to remove a tumor or an epileptic focus needs to establish clearly in which cerebral hemisphere language is organized. If the tumor is in the left hemisphere and language is organized in the left hemisphere as well, the neurosurgeon will remove the cerebral cortex sections that might cause aphasia with great caution. The need to clearly establish in which hemisphere language is organized cannot be met by using dichotic listening, finger-tapping, or tachistoscopic viewing. Not even the concurrent application of all three techniques on a single subject can clearly establish which hemisphere is dominant for language. The injection of the barbiturate sodium amytal or of benzodiazepine (valium) into the right or left carotid artery causes temporary anesthesia (1 to 2 minutes) in the cerebral hemisphere of the same side (ipsilateral hemisphere) as the injection. Anesthesia also implies a total, yet transient paralysis of the muscles of the side of the body that is contralateral to the anaesthetized hemisphere as well as a loss of the ability to speak, if language is lateralized in the anaesthetized hemisphere. In 96% of right-handed subjects studied through this technique language was lateralized in the left hemisphere, whereas in only 15% of left-handed subjects was language lateralized in the right hemisphere. As in right-handed subjects, in most left-handed subjects (70%) language was lateralized in the left hemisphere, and in only the remaining 15% was language lateralized in both cerebral hemispheres.

Electrical stimulation of the brain

During neurosurgical operations the need might arise to delimit specific language areas so as not to damage them. To this effect, cortico-electrical stimulation can be carried out in conscious patients under local anesthesia because the brain is insensitive to pain. This procedure was devised by neurologist Wilder Penfield during the 1950s at the Neurological Institute of McGill University, Montreal. North-American neurosurgeon George Ojemann, who is at present the most active in this field, is used to stimulating the cerebral cortex with bipolar electrodes situated at a distance of 5mm from each other (Calvin & Ojemann, 1980, 1994). The weak electrical charge applied (1msec; 3-8mA; 60Hz) provokes a transient inhibition of the functional activity of the neural tissue under the stimulated area. As a consequence, the patient is temporarily no longer able to perform a given cognitive task (e.g. naming). Through this technique the cerebral organization of numerous language components has been investigated (e.g. phoneme recognition, sentence completion, reading, verbal memory, and naming). To assess the cortical representation of the process of naming a patient is presented with slides showing a sentence: "This is a ...", followed by a picture describing the different objects to be named (e.g. a star). The patient has to read the sentence and name the object (Fig. 7.2). An electrical charge in a given cortical area is applied concurrent with the presentation of the slides. If the area is involved in naming the patient can no longer name objects (anomia), because the electrical stimulation provokes a transient inhibition of the process. A series of cortico-electrical stimulations enables one to draw a map of the cortical organization of language components.

Ojemann's studies seem to point to a concentric organization of language (cf. Fig. 7.2). The central portion subserves oro-facial movements. Stimulation of these structures interferes both with oro-facial movements and with motor sequences necessary to produce language. Stimulation of the temporal or frontal areas adjacent to the area subserving oro-facial movements inhibits phonemic perception, whereas stimulation of even more peripheral areas elicits interference of other language components. In addition, stimulation of the inferior temporal lobe inhibits naming, stimulation of the inferior frontal lobe elicits syntactic errors, and stimulation of the inferior temporal and parietal lobes interferes with the performance of semantic tasks. Finally, stimulation of the posterior temporal lobe and of the inferior central frontal lobe inhibits reading, whereas stimulation of the margins of the perisylvian areas interferes with short-term verbal memory processes. In particular, the frontal lobe seems to be involved in the retrieval of stored information, whereas the parietal lobe is apparently involved in both the retrieval and storing of verbal information. Cortico-electrical stimulation of the right hemisphere provokes alterations to language components, such as prosody and some semantic aspects, as well as short-term memory. Through this technique the role of some left hemisphere deep structures (thalamic nuclei and basal ganglia) with regard to perception, production, and control of language (cf. Chapters 9 and 19) has been investigated.

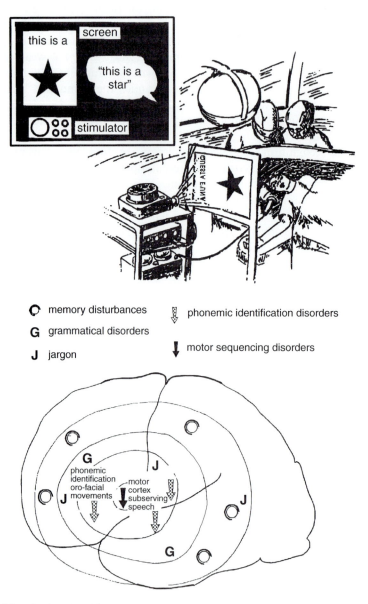

FIG. 7.2. Cortical electrical stimulation during linguistic tasks (Calvin & Ojemann, 1980).

Carotid sodium-amytal injection and the electrical stimulation of the brain present relevant limits, as far as both their use and their potential to contribute to knowledge are concerned. For example, Wada test can only be used with patients waiting to undergo a neurosurgical operation. These subjects obviously suffer from a nervous system disease that might have somehow interfered with the organization of the functions to be studied. In addition, the test only lasts a few minutes, and in this short span of time both research activities and clinical examination have to be carried out. Furthermore, in the case of cortico-electrical stimulation, the methodological objection holds that it can be applied only to subjects with severe illnesses affecting the brain—often present for many years, such as epilepsy—that can have greatly modified the cerebral organization of linguistic functions. One of the harshest methodological criticisms leveled at electrical stimulation studies is that they are not very accurate, because the area of cerebral tissue inhibited by the electrical charge is not constantly the same and thus the same stimulation cannot be repeated twice for two reasons: (1) it is difficult to mark the cortical areas to which electrodes are to be applied, and (2) the area of cortical tissue inhibited can vary slightly in width during different stimulations of the same area.

Computerized axial tomography

Computerized axial tomography (CT scan) enables visualization of the main cerebral anatomic structures. This technique was devised at the end of the 1970s and is based on a different absorption of X-rays by intact cerebral tissue as opposed to that affected by a lesion (cerebral infarction, tumor, edema, etc.). The CT scan reveals the site and the extent of a cerebral lesion. Together with magnetic resonance imaging, it has been a watershed in neuropsychological and neurolinguistic studies, because it allows one to link acquired cognitive disorders to specific cerebral areas without a post-mortem (Damasio & Damasio, 1989).

Magnetic resonance imaging

Magnetic resonance imaging (MRI) was devised at the end of the 1980s. It can show brain morphology through the creation of a magnetic field around the head that modifies some characteristics of the hydrogen atoms present in cerebral structures. The presence of a lesion is revealed by the different reaction of the hydrogen atoms to the pathological tissue as opposed to intact neural tissue. MRI defines the cerebral structures better than CT scan and, in addition, it is not as dangerous as exposure to X-rays because magnetic fields do not represent a risk for human health.

CHAPTER EIGHT

The representation of language in the brain

Neurons are the basic elements of the brain. One of their essential features is that they are organized in circuits, within which information (of both excitatory and inhibitory type) is continuously exchanged. J.H. Jackson, an English neurologist of the last century, proposed and described a hierarchical organization of cerebral functions. Jackson reached the conclusion that basic functions (respiration, swallowing, sleep, etc.) are controlled by the lower structures of the brain, whereas voluntary functions, including language aspects, are organized in the higher structures of the brain, namely in the cerebral cortex. In the second half of the 20th century A.R. Luria's contribution was crucial for the emergence and the development of neuropsychology and neurolinguistics. He proposed the application of the historico-cultural method to the study of neurology. This approach is based on the hypothesis that psychic processes do not have a natural origin, but they are based on social structures within which an individual is raised from infancy. With regard to language in particular, Luria claimed that it is organized into different subcomponents (articulation, naming, phonemic analysis, etc.) localized in separate areas of the brain. The activation of a cognitive function depends on the coordinated activity of numerous cortical centers. More recently, these hypotheses have been further developed into a neurofunctional model of language organization at three levels: (1) the hierarchically higher level comprising underlying systems, known as the extended system of language; (2) the intermediate level, made up of various subsystems (verbal production, word comprehension, reading, writing, etc.); and (3) the lower system, consisting of numerous neurofunctional modules (modules for phonation, articulation, co-articulation, etc.), which can be equated—from an anatomo-functional point of view—with the "neuron assemblies" described by D. Hebb.

FUNDAMENTALS OF NEUROPHYSIOLOGY

The human brain is made up of neurofunctional units, neural cells or neurons, and by the supporting cells of the glia. Each neuron processes information, as it receives information from, and transmits information to, thousands of other neurons. Neurons coordinate the activity of the body organs and determine the behavior of the living organism. Some neuronal groups are organized into systems that are responsible for a specific function in order to reach particular objectives. Some of these functional systems and some specific functions are innate, or genetically preprogrammed, and thus need not be learnt (e.g. a baby's crying), whereas other functions, such as language, are acquired. The simplest functions organized by the nervous system include *reflex arcs*. A stimulus (e.g. a prick on the foot) activates sensory neurons that, in turn, activate intermediate neurons (interneurons) of the spinal cord. Finally, the latter activate motoneurons inducing muscle contraction so that the foot is moved away from the source of pain. Stress is to be laid on the fact that between the prick and the movement of the foot only a few milliseconds pass and this type of reflex occurs without the subject being aware of it. Awareness of the pain caused by the prick occurs only when the foot has already moved away from the source of pain. The structures responsible for both tactile sensitivity and sensitivity to pain send information to the higher cerebral centers, up to the sensory cortex, which—together with other cortical structures—informs the subject of the stimulus. Many other reflexes involved in posture, scratching, in some aspects of mastication and swallowing, etc. have been described and analyzed.

Probably the most important feature of neural cells is that they send information by means of electrical signals. Each neuron has structures connecting with other neural cells (dendrites and the cell body) and structures that send information (axons). Circuits are established between the various groups of neurons and can involve several areas of the nervous system. A case in point is the involvement of at least four structures with four neuronal groups in the production of vocalizations, namely the limbic system, the motor cortex, some structures of the midbrain and the pons, and motoneurons controlling the larynx (cf. Fig. 3.2). Importantly, neurons and the neural circuits they form in the brain reduce the activation threshold, so that the more frequent the activation of a circuit, the lower the amount of energy needed for its re-activation. This is due to the fact that contact points responsible for information transmission between neurons are structurally and functionally modified according to their frequency of activation: the energy needed to activate a neural circuit is greater in the early phases and tends to diminish when the same circuit is activated repeatedly.

Second, in neural circuits *inhibitory* neural cells are active. They are extremely important, because they inhibit the electrical activity of the neural cells with which they establish contact. For example, when walking or jogging muscles extending the leg are activated and concurrently inhibitory interneurons inhibit muscles flexing the leg. Otherwise the different stages of walking could not occur and in some cases the leg's bone might even break owing to a lack of synergy in muscle contraction. Neural circuits organizing a given function thus have activating and inhibitory mechanisms whose complexity depends on the type of function they subserve.

CORTICAL REPRESENTATION OF LANGUAGE

J.H. Jackson (1835–1911) was one of the 19th century's neurologists who contributed greatly to the study of cerebral organization of language (Taylor, 1958). He proposed a model of neural functions organized in layers, where the first layers accounting for basic capacities overlapped with more complex functions. Jackson divided nervous system functions schematically into three layers:

1. *Basic functions*: respiration, heart rate, regulation of endocrine functions, sleep, etc. These functions are fundamental for life and for the organization of behavior. They are also present in animals with simple brains and in new-born babies. Neural structures subserving these functions are localized in the developmentally lower structures of the brain (medulla, pons, midbrain; cf. Fig. 3.1).
2. *More complex functions* such as posture, walking, reaction to dangerous stimuli, and vocalizations are organized in the intermediate structures of the nervous system (midbrain, thalamus, cerebellum, basal ganglia, limbic system; cf. Fig. 3.1).
3. *Voluntary functions* such as voluntary movement, numerous aspects of language, thought, and other higher cognitive functions are organized in the developmentally higher structures of the nervous system, namely in the cortex of the two cerebral hemispheres. Jackson claimed that the more complex functions of the nervous system exerted control over, and inhibition of, the underlying structures and the basic functions of behavior. For example, he suggested that in children basic functions controlling sphincters increasingly depended on will, which led to the acquisition of voluntary cultural behavior, thus easing social life. A lesion in the higher areas of the brain could produce *negative symptoms* owing to the loss of the highest and most voluntary aspects organized in the neural structure affected by the lesion and, concurrently, *positive symptoms* manifesting themselves in automatic and stereotyped behavior patterns caused by the loss of inhibition that is generally exerted by the cortical centers of the lower neural centers.

Jackson explained through this model why patients suffering from global aphasia could sometimes speak, however, producing stereotyped sentences, such as curses. Such automatic expressions are organized in structures of the nervous system that are developmentally lower than cortical areas. Genuine verbal expression occurs only when new and creative utterances are produced. This type of conscious (nonautomatic) expression presupposes that the dominant hemisphere is intact. For example, a patient with a diffuse left hemisphere lesion lost the ability to speak. When asked his daughter's name, whom he had not seen for a long time, he could not pronounce her name (which was Mary), even though he had understood the question. During the same session, however, his daughter suddenly entered the room and the patient—greatly surprised because he did not expect his daughter to be there—exclaimed: "Oh, Mary!". Another patient, a very pious priest, who was affected by aphasia, had lost the ability to speak. The only verbal expressions he could utter were vulgar words and curses. These spontaneous speech expressions with a strong emotional impact in aphasic patients led Jackson to propose a hierarchical organization of language.

More recently, American neuropsychologist Jason Brown proposed a new hierarchical model of language organization (Brown, 1977, 1990). In Brown's opinion, aphasic symptoms emerge following an interruption of the microgenetic process of language at a given point. The study of aphasia should thus lead to an understanding of the various phases, from the intention to communicate to verbal expression. Furthermore, the correlation between language disorders and the areas affected by the lesion would allow insight into the brain structures involved in the various stages of verbal production.

MODELS OF LANGUAGE PROCESSING

The studies on the correlation between brain and language carried out by Russian neuropsychologist Aleksandr R. Luria between 1935 and 1975 were a watershed in this field of neuroscience. Together with psychologist Lev S. Vygotsky, Luria proposed the *historico-cultural approach* to neurology, which is based on the hypothesis that higher psychic processes not only have a natural origin, but are also founded on the social structures within which subjects have been educated since infancy (Luria, 1973, 1976a, b, 1980; Vygotsky, 1986). An explanation of the origin of language thus requires one to abandon the purely organic field and look for its source in human relationships and in the evolution of their social history. Obviously, only brains with the same degree of development as the human brain could develop the same degree of social complexity developed by human cultures.

A second extremely important methodological aspect is Luria's attention to the analysis and description of symptoms caused by a cerebral lesion. If a lesion brings about a cognitive disorder, analysis is not to be limited to a rough and anecdotal description of the deficit. One has to use all available instruments to provide a description and a psychological analysis of the patient's general behavior. The application of this approach to the study of brain-damaged patients led to the emergence of a new scientific discipline, namely *neuropsychology*. Apart from Luria, the "founding fathers" of neuropsychology were French neurologist Henri Hécaen (Hécaen, 1972) and American neurologist Arthur L. Benton (Benton, 1969). With regard to the study of language disorders, the accurate analysis of the symptoms could not be just in psychological terms, but also in linguistic terms. Together with linguist Roman Jakobson, Luria laid the foundations of a systematic linguistic analysis of aphasia, thus developing a new branch of science, namely *neurolinguistics* (Jakobson, 1971; Hécaen & Dubois, 1971; Paradis, 1986; Stemmer & Whitaker, 1998).

Luria developed a modular model of language organization. Each linguistic function, e.g. verbal expression, naming, repetition, auditory comprehension, etc., depended on the involvement of several subcomponents. The following are the main subcomponents Luria identified (cf. Fig. 8.1):

1. The subcomponent accounting for text comprehension and production (f), localized in the frontal lobes, causes communicative behavior disorders if it is affected by a lesion. Patients affected by such lesions exhibit poor communicative attitude and attention because they find it impossible to inhibit the tendency to concentrate on irrelevant stimuli.
2. The subcomponent for the construction of the linear scheme of verbal expression (g), localized in the left frontal-temporal cortex (Broca's area). Patients with a lesion in this subcomponent are not able to construct a sequence out of verbal elements. The temporal sequence of verbal expression and comprehension is thus disrupted.
3. The subcomponent for switching from lexical element to lexical element (c), localized in the inferior premotor cortex of the left hemisphere. Patients with disorders affecting this subcomponent cannot switch from the name of an object to the name of the next object and are likely to exhibit perseveration.
4. The subcomponent for phonemic analysis (e), localized in the left temporal region (Wernicke's area). A lesion affecting this subcomponent causes an alteration in word processing at the phonological level, thus causing errors in the comprehension and production of phonemic sequences (i.e. production of phonemic paraphasias).
5. The articulatory subcomponent (d) localized in the postcentral region of the left hemisphere. This structure is responsible for the sensory control of lips, face, and tongue. A lesion in this component prevents patients from establishing the correct spatial position of their articulatory organs, which is a prerequisite for verbal expression.
6. The subcomponent for naming (b) is localized in the left parieto-occipital region. It allows the correct selection of the words to be uttered through inhibition of irrelevant alternative words. Lesions in

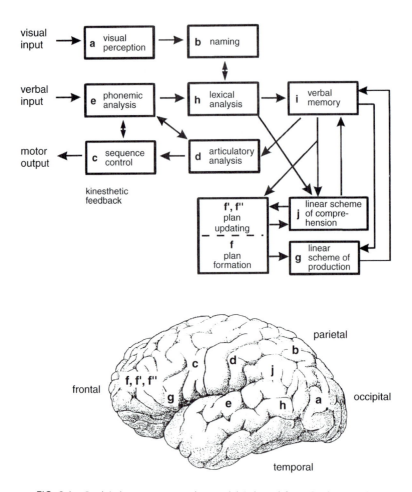

FIG. 8.1.   Luria's language-processing model (adapted from Caplan, 1990).

this area determine the production of phonemic, semantic, and verbal paraphasias that may be similar to the word selected.

7. The subcomponent for lexical analysis (h) is localized in the left temporo-occipital region. Patients with a lesion in this area exhibit severe disturbances in accessing lexical meaning, because in this structure lexical items establish object and thought representation relationships through different modalities (visual, tactile, and proprioceptive modalities).

8. The subcomponent for comprehension of logico-grammatical relations within sentences (j) is localized in the temporo-parieto-occipital joint of the left hemisphere. Patients with a lesion in this area cannot understand sentences requiring a synthesis in a logical scheme.

A case in point is the following question: "Is an uncle the brother's father or is he the father's brother?".

9. The subcomponent for verbal memory (i) is localized in the left temporal lobe.

Luria claimed that the subcomponents accounting for neurolinguistic processes are localized in separate areas of the brain. The activation of a neuropsychological function thus depends on the coordinated activity of many cerebral centers. For example, naming activates the subcomponent for vision and perception of the object to be named (i.e. a ball), the subcomponent for naming (b), the subcomponent for phonemic analysis (e), the subcomponent for switching from a previous verbal action to the name to be produced (c), and finally, the articulatory subcomponent (d). Acoustic comprehension activates the subcomponent for phonemic analysis (e), the subcomponent for lexical analysis (h), and the subcomponent for semantic analysis. They, in turn, consist of modular elements accounting for verbal memory (i), the analysis of the logical scheme of sentences (j), and the analysis of the most significant features of verbal communication (f). In Luria's opinion, human behavior in general, and verbal behavior in particular, depend on a complex interaction between numerous cerebral structures. Therefore, disorders—mainly caused by a cortical lesion—involving one subcomponent only can affect more than one function.

A NEUROFUNCTIONAL MODEL OF LANGUAGE PROCESSING

Numerous recent neuropsychological and, in particular, neurophysiological studies have revealed that mental activation of the various aspects of language occurs through the cooperation of many separate systems. Different aspects of language such as naming, syntax, reading, etc. are distinct systems that can be separately compromised, inhibited, or preserved following a brain lesion or after transient inhibition (due to electrical stimulation, paroxystic charge, or pharmacological inhibition of a cerebral hemisphere; cf. Ojemann, 1991).

Recently a model of the *neurofunctional organization* of language has been proposed by several authors (Fodor, 1983; Paradis, 1987b; Shallice, 1988). This approach presupposes that each function (e.g. language, music, or mathematics) is organized at three levels: a more general level known as an extended neurofunctional system, an intermediate level comprising many subcomponents, and a basic system formed by neurofunctional modules.

1. The *extended system* is generally called a neurofunctional linguistic system with regard to verbal functions, and comprises all three levels

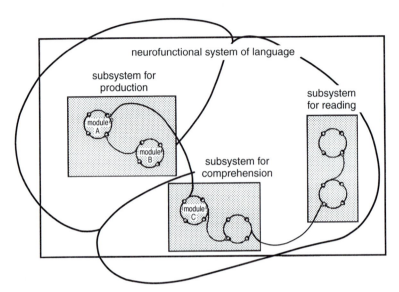

FIG. 8.2. Modular organization of the neurofunctional system of language.

(cf. Fig. 8.2). The whole set of extended systems (language, mathematics, music, etc.) forms a subject's cognitive capacities.

2. An extended system such as language is formed by a number of *subsystems* controlling particular aspects of language such as verbal
   production, repetition, comprehension of words, sentences and texts,
   reading, writing, etc. Not all subcomponents of language have as yet
   been accurately identified. They can be detected through the description of patients who, following cerebral lesions, exhibit a *dissociation
   pattern* between two components of verbal expression (i.e. the patient
   is able to understand but not speak) or a *double dissociation pattern* (a
   patient exhibits a loss of reading but not of writing, whereas another
   patient cannot write but can read). The detection of double dissociations is one of the most reliable methods for proving the existence of
   two separate subsystems.

3. The lowest level is represented by *neurofunctional modules*. The functional assembly of a given number of modules forms a subsystem and,
   hence, a higher level. Therefore, modules of phonation, articulation,
   co-articulation, memory for motor sequences of words, etc. form the
   subsystem subserving the production of words. Not all modules
   forming the language subsystems have yet been identified, because this
   research is still at an early stage and relies on the description of
   patients exhibiting particular double dissociation patterns. For

instance, the study of a patient who, following a cerebral lesion, lost the capacity to read vowels, but not consonants, and of a second patient who lost the capacity to read consonants, but not vowels, led to the hypothesis being advanced of the existence of two separate neurofunctional modules accounting for the reading of consonants and of vowels, respectively.

At this juncture, an anatomical-physiological description of neurofunctional modules is in order. I believe the best theoretical hypothesis—supported by the results of numerous experimental studies—was put forward by Canadian psychophysiologist Donald Hebb of McGill University, Montreal (Hebb, 1949, 1980). Hebb proposed that during the execution of a given function (e.g. word recognition), cortical neurons tend to become connected reciprocally, forming a closed multicircuit system. Hebb called this system *neuron assemblies*. The prolonged activation of a given number of neurons during the execution of a functional task enhances transmission of information between neurons (due to a modification of synapses, i.e. the contact points between neurons). The more frequent the activation of the circuit, the less the amount of energy needed for its activation. However, neuron assemblies do not contain activating neural cells, otherwise, once activated, the circuit would discharge electric impulses indefinitely. However, inhibitory cells are also active and mediate the activity of the circuit. Hebb's studies suggest that probably the best way to describe the anatomical and physiological level of a neurofunctional module is the "unit" of neuron assemblies in its various levels (first and second order).

The neurofunctional model of language organization is still a rough and temporary scheme, mainly useful for future research on brain and language. However, it provides answers to a series of objections raised by many previous studies.

1. This model is not strictly linked to anatomy, even though the distinction between neuron assemblies involving only cortical neurons and the assemblies involving cortical and subcortical neurons (of thalamus, basal ganglia, and cerebellum), or even circuits formed by subcortical neurons only, is to be stressed. Several neurotransmitters may be involved in the various types of neuron assemblies. With learning, it is probable that the capacity to undergo modifications also varies. This capacity reaches its highest point in the cortical and subcortical modifications.
2. Neurofunctional modules and their neuron assemblies of first and second order are influenced by learning.
3. The elements of the neurofunctional modules (neural cells and their components) and the mechanisms regulating neural activity are the

same for all modules, even though the latter belong to different cognitive systems.

4. Neurofunctional modules may share some subsystems (i.e. the module accounting for phonemic articulation may be involved in both the subsystem of verbal production and the subsystems of working memory), whereas some subsystems (i.e. those accounting for syntax and working memory) may concurrently subserve different cognitive systems (language and mathematics).

CHAPTER NINE

The role of subcortical structures in language

Recently many studies investigating the involvement of subcortical structures in language have been carried out. It has been noted that probably only certain structures of the basal ganglia (caudate nucleus) and of the thalamus (ventral anterior nucleus) of the left hemisphere account for the first stages of verbal expression, whereas left cortical areas regulate the upcoming stages of the language production process. The basal ganglia and the left thalamus are also involved in the semantic, grammatical, and phonemic control of units to be uttered. Furthermore, other brain structures, such as the cerebellum, which were once considered to be involved exclusively in motor control, are also involved in the regulation of cognitive functions. For example, the right cerebellar hemisphere (which is directly connected to the left cerebral hemisphere) seems to play an important role in word-selection tasks. Neural structures underlying the cerebral cortex are thus crucial for the regulation of language, but further research is needed to establish their functions clearly.

Numerous studies have described the functions of some left cortical areas with regard to language organization. On the other hand, the role played by the main subcortical structures is still difficult to define. Over the past 30 years considerable data on this issue has been gathered and present knowledge is encouraging and stimulating. Subcortical structures have raised researchers' interest because, even though the cerebral cortex is responsible for the organization of the finest and most detailed components of motor and cognitive behavior, cortical nuclei seem to control initiation of, and support for, the motor behavior and cognitive functions.

Furthermore, they are also involved in the regulation of emotional systems and memory. Suffice it to say that many drugs, above all those used to treat the most severe mental illnesses, act mainly at subcortical level.

Subcortical structures lie in the middle of the brain; more precisely, at the base of the two cerebral hemispheres. They are localized under the cerebral cortex, hence their name. They have many connections with the cerebral cortex and the neural structures of the brainstem. Schematically they can be divided into two groups: the basal ganglia and the thalamus (cf. Fig. 9.1). The basal ganglia are formed by three main nuclei: the *caudate nucleus*, the *putamen*, and the *globus pallidus*. The thalamus is formed by a set of nuclei, the most important of which are involved in some language functions, i.e. the *ventral anterior* nucleus (VA), the *ventral lateral* nucleus (VL), the *dorsomedial* nucleus (DM), and the *pulvinar* (P). Studies of clinical neurology and experimental neurophysiology have

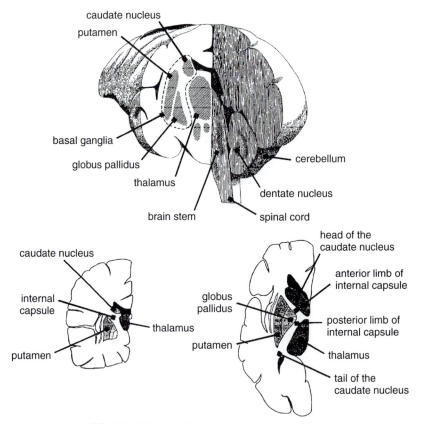

FIG. 9.1.   Subcortical structures subserving language.

shown that the basal ganglia and the thalamus form a series of neural circuits activating and controlling functions that until recently were ascribed to the cerebral cortex only.

A brief explanation of the process is in order. The cerebral cortex of the frontal, parietal, and temporal lobes sends excitatory information to two nuclei of the basal ganglia, namely the caudate nucleus and the putamen (cf. Fig. 9.2). Further, these two nuclei receive information from a very important area of the brainstem, that is, the *substantia nigra*, whose role was discovered by studying patients affected by Parkinson's disease. These patients exhibit degenerative lesions in this structure. The most important symptoms of the disease are muscle rigidity, resting tremor, and a general difficulty in starting thought and movement. The caudate nucleus and the putamen inhibit the globus pallidus, which, in turn, inhibits the activity of some thalamic nuclei, namely the ventral anterior nucleus, the ventral lateral nucleus, and the dorsomedial nucleus. When they are activated (from inhibition of the globus pallidus) these nuclei excite the frontal lobe cortex that is involved in the organization and planning of motor and cognitive behavior patterns.

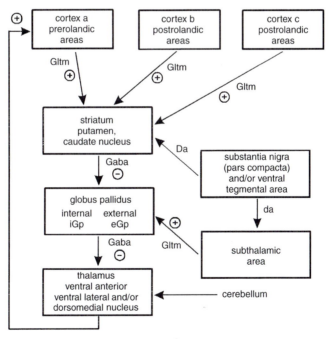

FIG. 9.2.   Basic structures of the cortico-striato-pallido-thalamo-cortical loop (adapted from Crosson, 1992).

Recent research by Alexander (1994) and Bhatia and Marsden (1994) has led to the identification of the two main circuits of the basal ganglia that are involved in the regulation of movement and language:

1. The "cortico-striato-thalamo-cortical loop", also known as the direct pathway (inner putamen-pallidus pathway), collects and processes information from all cortical lobes and exerts an activating influence on the frontal lobe (positive feedback).
2. The "cortico-striato-subthalamo-thalamo-cortical loop", also known as the indirect pathway (outer putamen-pallidus pathway), inhibits the frontal lobe (negative feedback), suppressing those motor or psychic schemes that are in competition with the movement or the cognitive action to be performed.

A NEUROPSYCHOLOGICAL MODEL OF SUBCORTICAL STRUCTURES IN LANGUAGE

Over the past 30 years the results of many studies have shown that the basal ganglia and the thalamus of the left hemisphere are involved in language organization (Alexander, 1989; Fabbro, 1997b; Nadeau & Crosson, 1997; Vallar, Cappa, & Wallesch, 1992; Wallesch & Papagno, 1988). In particular, studies on patients with vascular or surgical lesions in the basal ganglia and the thalamus have revealed the presence of aphasia. The most frequent language disorders caused by a lesion in the *basal ganglia* of the left hemisphere include:

1. non-fluent aphasia, characterized by a general reduction in spontaneous speech;
2. voice disorders (hypophony, foreign accent syndrome);
3. presence of semantic and verbal paraphasias (language disorders which generally accompany fluent aphasias);
4. presence of echolalias and perseveration;
5. generally preserved repetition and comprehension;
6. writing disorders.

On the other hand, the most frequent language disorders caused by lesions to the left *thalamus* include:

1. alteration in verbal expression, which is fluent with many anomias, whereas comprehension is generally less compromised;
2. presence of anomias, verbal, semantic, and neologistic paraphasias;
3. mild comprehension deficits, spared repetition;
4. disorders in reading, writing, arithmetic, and long-term verbal memory.

Subcortico-electrical stimulation during neurosurgical operations may induce patients to utter words or whole sentences involuntarily. This is a crucial result, because applying cortico-electrical stimulation only does not produce this effect, which implies that only specific structures of the basal ganglia and of the thalamus subserve verbal expression, whereas the cortex, once expression has been activated, regulates the final stages of the language production process. The structures accounting for word or sentence production by electrical stimulation are the caudate head and the most anterior nuclei of the thalamus. Stimulation of the dominant caudate head induces conscious patients under local anesthesia to produce sentences irrelevant to the clinical and experimental occurrence following electrical stimulation. On the other hand, during electrical stimulation of the most anterior left thalamic nuclei subjects exhibit a strong compulsion to speak, accompanied by the production of words, sentences, or speech irrelevant to the contextual situation.

Equally interestingly, the left thalamus has a high concentration of noradrenaline. This neurotransmitter is rather similar to two notorious substances, caffeine and cocaine, which, among other things, enhance the impulse to speak and render their user's conversation fluent and lucid. As early as the end of the last century Sigmund Freud described the effects of cocaine on conversation. The two aforementioned substances probably activate the left thalamus, thus enhancing verbal fluency.

Recently, on the basis of numerous studies on this issue, North-American neuropsychologist Bruce Crosson (1992) proposed a model of subcortical functions of language, which will be presented in a rather modified version because data from other studies have been added to simplify Crosson's original model based on five fundamental systems (cf. Fig. 9.3).

1. The first *activating* system is a circuit providing "energy" and "motivation" for the subject's verbal expression. A similar system had already been proposed over 20 years ago by Russian neuropsychologist A.R. Luria. The activation of the cerebral cortex leading to verbal expression occurs through participation of neural structures of the reticular substance of the brainstem, of the intralaminar nuclei of the thalamus, and of the cingulate cortex.
2. Once the frontal cortex is activated, specific areas of the frontal lobe control the "construction of chunks", whose selection depends on a system accounting for the assessment of their *semantic acceptability*. The system accounting for the selection of words at semantic level is formed by a neural circuit involving the frontal cortical areas, the pulvinar, and the left posterior cortical areas.
3. Once a chunk has been assessed at semantic level, a *"green light" system* disconnects it from the assessment stage, while connecting it to the systems accounting for expression. Once the chunk has been

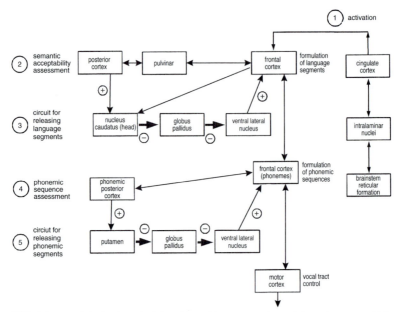

FIG. 9.3.   Model of subcortical functions of language (adapted from Crosson, 1992).

checked off, areas of the anterior and posterior cortex are activated, which, in turn, activate the caudate nucleus inhibiting the globus pallidus. The latter inhibition activates the thalamic ventral anterior nucleus and, consequently, the areas (anterior to Broca's area) responsible for the production of the phonemic sequence forming the sentence to be uttered.

4. The motor program for the production of the phonemic sequence, too, is subsequently activated in order to carry out the *phonemic acceptability* assessment. This system uses a circuit involving Broca's area in the frontal lobe, Wernicke's area in the temporal lobe, and the arcuate fasciculus, ensuring communication between the two areas.

5. After phonemic check-off, the phonemes to be produced are sent to a circuit activating actual *phonemic production*. In this case, the phonemic temporal cortex (Wernicke's area) and the phonemic frontal cortex (Broca's area) synergically activate the putamen, which inhibits the globus pallidus; the inhibition of the globus pallidus activates the ventral lateral nucleus of the thalamus, which, in turn, activates the cortex responsible for the correct execution of the vocal tract movements producing language sounds.

Like all schematic representations, this model may be useful for clinical and cognitive studies, but must be updated further. Indeed, as geographical maps have to be modified after the redrawing of frontiers or relevant geographical changes caused either by nature or man, new findings in the field of neuroscience may determine the abandonment or the radical revision of models.

THE ROLE OF THE CEREBELLUM

During World War I English neurologist Gordon Holmes studied many cases of soldiers with cerebellar lesions caused by gunshot wounds (Holmes, 1917). He was able to describe typical alterations in word production due to cerebellar disorders, namely ataxic dysarthria. A diffuse cerebellar lesion may cause severe coordination difficulties. In fact, patients with a cerebellar lesion walk as if they were drunk (ataxia), and with their legs slightly open in order to balance themselves. When they perform a voluntary movement, their motor systems, without the normal coordination exerted by the cerebellum, are unstable and thus provoke a diffuse tremor to all parts of the body involved in movement. These disorders also affect motor production of speech. For this reason, speech is slow and characterized by many errors in phonation and articulation. The voice sounds irregular owing to the tremor of the articulatory organs.

Although neurologists in the past have claimed that the cerebellum was also involved in the organization of cognitive functions, until 10 years ago almost all experts in this field believed that it was involved in the regulation of movement only. Data gathered over the past 10 years have shown that they were incorrect. Indeed, some structures of the cerebellum (neocerebellum) participate in the regulation of nonmotor cognitive functions (Leiner, Leiner, & Down, 1991). The neocerebellum is formed by the right and left cerebellar hemispheres and by the dentate nuclei (cf. Fig. 9.1); it receives information from many cortical areas, processes it, and sends it back to the motor and premotor cortical areas. With regard to the role played by the cerebellum in language organization, recent PET studies on the activation of neural structures during the execution of cognitive tasks have shown that the right cerebellar hemisphere, which is directly connected to the left cerebral hemisphere (specialized in language), activates during purely linguistic tasks, for example, production of verbs from nouns (e.g. fire → to burn; water → to drink, etc.).

These findings have stimulated interest in the study of language in patients with cerebellar lesions. A recent case is that of patient R.C., aged 49, working as a lawyer, who suffered a diffuse lesion of the right cerebellar hemisphere following a cerebral infarction (Fiez, Petersen, Cheney, & Raichle, 1992). After the insult he became aware that he made errors in verbal expression that his wife and he dismissed as slips, yet they were semantic paraphasias. Moreover, he could not match the name of his clients to the details of the case. A routine neuropsychological examination showed a high intelligence level without memory or language disorders. However, a more detailed analysis revealed that R.C. had above-average difficulties in word production tasks. This deficit also emerged in other production tasks: e.g. categories (Columbus → explorer), attributes (bike → pedals), synonyms (swine → pig). Furthermore, the patient did not show any improvement after many repetitions on similar tasks, showing that the cerebellar lesion had impaired his capacity to learn linguistic tasks. The patient was almost unaware of all the errors he made.

MOTOR ASPECTS OF LANGUAGE FUNCTIONS

Numerous cerebral structures subserving movement control are involved in language production (Aronson, 1980; Buckingham & Hollien, 1978; Darley, Aronson, & Brown, 1975; Gracco & Abbs, 1987). For example, during phonemic production the larynx and the supralaryngeal vocal tract perform coordinated movements producing appropriate air vibrations that are perceived by the brain as language "sounds". In order to perform these movements correctly the brain must constantly be informed of the position of the articulatory organs. The execution of a movement requires knowledge of the position of the organ to be moved, so that it can take the *target* position according to the sound or sounds to be produced. Sensory information on the position of the articulatory organs is sent to the brain through some cranial nerves, namely the trigeminal (V), the glossopharyngeal (IX), the vagal (X), and the hypoglossal nerves (XII). Before reaching the cortex sensory information is reorganized in two areas: in the sensory nucleus (SN in Fig. 9.4) of the cranial nerve and in the thalamus (ventral posterior medial nucleus, VPM, in Fig. 9.4). The information from the thalamus reaches the sensory cortical areas (3b), the pre-motor areas (6) and, lastly, the motor areas of the tongue, the pharynx, and the larynx. A pathway starts from the sensory, pre-motor, and motor areas, namely the pyramidal tract controlling the motor nuclei (MN in Fig. 9.4) of the cranial nerves involved in language production: the trigeminal (V), the facial (VII), the glossopharyngeal (IX), the vagal (X), and the hypoglossal nerves (XII). The cortical control on the motoneurons of the cranial nerves seems to be one of the neural bases allowing humans to learn with relative ease the whole sequence of movements contributing to language production. This direct neural pathway, which leads from the cortex to the cranial nerves, is much less developed in primates (chimpanzees, orangutans, gorillas). Partly for this reason, these primates cannot speak. In many passeriform species (chaffinches, canaries, etc.) there is a direct neuronal bundle connecting the telencephalic hemispheres to the cranial nerves controlling the tongue and other structures involved in song. This fascicle permits songbird species to modulate a considerable variety of sounds accurately (cf. Chapter 3).

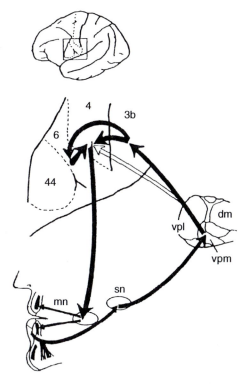

FIG. 9.4. Sensory-motor structures involved in verbal articulation (adapted from Gracco & Abbs, 1987).

Some neurophysiological studies have measured the time needed for a sensory stimulus (e.g. the tip of the tongue being bitten) to provoke a movement (the tongue being moved away from the teeth)—in other words, the time needed for the circuit to activate (cf. Fig. 9.4). It generally takes less than 50msec (1/20 second), less than the duration of a vowel or a consonant. These results led some researchers to claim that language production might make use of a constant sensory control, on the basis of which the nervous system—before producing a phoneme—needs to await sensory information (acoustic, tactile, and proprioceptive information) related to the previous phoneme (peripheral feedback model). However, many empirical studies contradict this hypothesis. For example, subjects may continue to speak well even though they become completely deaf in old age (acoustic feedback exclusion). Furthermore, a subject may speak with little difficulty even after bilateral anesthesia of the oropharyngeal tract (tactile and proprioceptive feedback exclusion), which implies that in adults language production is preprogrammed in the brain and may be expressed even in the absence of sensory information.

Sensory information is, however, crucial for foreign language learning. As a matter of fact, children who are born deaf do not learn to speak and become "mute". The learning of a second language implies listening stages and stages of repetition-production in order to obtain, for example, a correct pronunciation. In addition, the correction of systematic articulatory errors implies the learning of the correct sequence of movements for the selected sound to be uttered. These sensory-motor learning stages are similar both in aphasics, who have lost the capacity to produce language appropriately, and in students who are trained in the correct phonemic repertoire of the foreign language they are studying.

In adults speaking their mother tongue and in fluent bilinguals the sequential movements of the supralaryngeal vocal tract are produced and coordinated as a set of motor programs that may function independently of sensory information. The whole set of programs underlying the execution of movements subserving language production may include the activation of complex neural structures such as the basal ganglia, the thalamus, the cerebellum, etc. (central feedback model). Finally, models of language motor production based on preprogramming have been proposed. Once a motor program for word production has been activated all minor movements are performed in the selected sequence by means of a hierarchical structure that is called "syntax" by linguists.

At present, these models can contribute to the formulation of experimental hypotheses. However, further research is needed before a sufficiently clear framework on the motor programming of language in monolinguals and bilinguals is available.

CHAPTER TEN

Memory in language acquisition and learning

One of the most useful strategies for survival is forecasting the future. For this reason, during their evolution creatures have developed memory. For a creature it is of fundamental importance to remember both dangerous and pleasant situations so as to avoid the former and repeat the latter. It is the brain that subserves the capacity to store information. The neural structures responsible for the process of storing (temporal lobes, diencephalon) have been identified, as have been the structures where information is stored (cortical areas). Studies of patients with lesions in specific brain areas have substantiated the existence of two general models of memory, namely short-term memory and long-term memory. The short-term memory system, recently revised and redefined as working memory, receives and processes information by means of a series of subcomponents (the central executive, the phonological loop, etc.). Long-term memory includes explicit memory and implicit memory. Explicit memory refers to learnt knowledge of which subjects are aware and, in turn, consists of semantic memory (encyclopedic knowledge of the world) and episodic or autobiographical memory. Implicit memory concerns learnt knowledge of which subjects are not aware, even though they use it (e.g. the use of mother tongue syntax). Implicit memory is divided into three subtypes: procedural memory, priming, and conditioning. In bilinguals the mother tongue and the second language may be stored in separate systems. The mother tongue is mainly stored by implicit strategies, whereas the second language is stored to a wider extent with the involvement of explicit strategies.

One of the most interesting issues of neuroscience is the study of memory and its organization. One aspect of memory is that it plays an important role in the preservation and selection of individuals and species. Animals remember dangerous and pleasant experiences and are thus able to avoid the former and repeat the latter. Swedish neuropsychologist D.H. Ingvar claimed that one of the most useful strategies for the survival of an individual or of a species is the capacity to forecast the future, so as to avoid those situations that can be potentially dangerous or fatal on the basis of past experiences (Ingvar, 1985). Of course, forecasting the future is very complex, but the nervous system has devised an effective strategy to tackle this problem. Because what has happened is likely to occur again, recall allows animals with very complex brains to make hypotheses about the future. Specific situations lead to the selection of the most appropriate hypotheses. For this reason, Ingvar speaks of "memory of the future". The idea that memory and future-forecasting are connected is also present in Middle Eastern cultures, for example in the Jewish culture, where recall of the past, and hence history, are keys to understanding the future.

Animals remember because they have a nervous system. The more complex the nervous system, the greater the extent and the complexity of recall. North-American neurobiologist Paul MacLean and French neuropharmacologist Henri Laborit have investigated the limits and the performances of memory in the various classes of animal species (Laborit, 1976, 1983; MacLean, 1973). They claim that reptiles have a limited memory span, which is mainly related to the learning of motor tasks, whereas memory is richer and more differentiated in mammals. Unlike reptiles, mammals look after their offspring for a certain period of time after birth, because mammal offsprings are very immature and cannot look after themselves; moreover, mammal offspring have highly developed affective systems. The immature nature of the brain at birth and a marked development of emotional functions are two aspects that are strictly connected to memory organization in mammals. During its development, an immature brain can learn more than a strongly genetically preprogrammed brain (typical of reptiles). Furthermore, the usefulness of remembering situations involving the emotional system, both negative and pleasant, is explained by the need to avoid what is dangerous and repeat what is pleasant. For this reason, the emotional structures of the nervous system in mammals are considerably involved in the storing of memory traces.

Many studies have attempted to understand what happens in the brain of an animal after it has learnt a task. The most reasonable hypothesis claims that following learning, functional and structural modifications occur in specific cerebral structures. Even though these studies are still at an early stage, experimental results have documented these kinds of modifications. Repeated electric stimulation of a neural circuit reduces the energy needed to activate it, which means that the circuit has undergone a functional modification, thus reducing its activation threshold. This effect, which may be lasting, has been termed *long-term potentiation* and is believed to be functionally correlated to long-term memory. In addition, significant structural modifications of synapses at anatomical and biochemical levels have been observed as a consequence of learning. For example, an increase in the number of receptors for a given neurotransmitter has been observed, as has an increase in the size of dendritic spines (Ito, 1994; Kandel et al., 1991).

Finally, with regard to the neural structures subserving explicit memory (semantic and episodic memory), a distinction between structures essential for the storing of information in memory and structures involved in the storing of stimuli is necessary, as underlined by Russian neuropsychologist Alexander Luria and his American colleague Larry Squire (Luria, 1976a; Squire, 1987). The most important neural structures accounting for the storing process lie in the temporal lobes (medial-basal portions of the temporal lobes, amygdala, and hippocampus), in the diencephalon (thalamic dorsomedial nucleus), and in the basal portions of the anterior brain above the optic chiasma (septal nuclei, Meynert's nucleus, pre-frontal cortical structures, see Fig. 10.1). The structures "containing" memories correspond to the cortical areas subserving cognitive processes. In this regard Hrayr Terzian, one of my professors of neurology, used to say: "The brain is capable of learning!", thereby implying that the brain learns pathological behavior patterns, too. The treatment of neurological diseases, such as epilepsy, should also be aimed at making the patient "forget" pathological behavior that is dangerous to the patient's life.

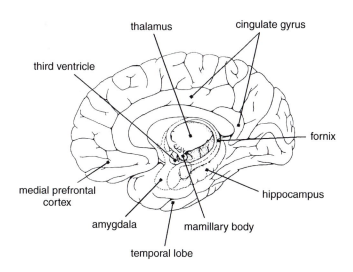

FIG. 10.1.   Brain structures involved in memory.

TWO GENERAL MEMORY SYSTEMS:
SHORT-TERM AND LONG-TERM MEMORY

Scientific studies on memory date back to the end of the last century. One of the most important approaches is the assessment of some aspects of memory by means of objective criteria, such as the memory capacity, also known as *span*. Memory *span* for digits or words corresponds to the number of elements of a sequence that a subject can repeat correctly for at least 50% of the trials. It has been observed that adults generally repeat sequences of digits containing up to seven elements. A second crucial aspect that has been underlined in the first scientific studies on memory concerns the attempt to distinguish eventual subcomponents of memory. For example, William James claimed the existence of a *primary memory*, lasting a short period of time, and a *secondary memory*, lasting longer (James, 1890).

More recent neuropsychological studies proved the existence of at least two general types of memory: short-term memory and long-term memory. The patient who has contributed most to the substantiation of this hypothesis is well known and usually described as H.M. This patient has been observed for more than 30 years by Canadian neuropsychologist Brenda Milner (Cohen & Eichenbaum, 1994; Milner, Corkin, & Teuber, 1968). In an attempt to treat a severe form of epilepsy H.M. underwent a bilateral surgical ablation of the temporal lobes (cf. Fig. 10.1). After the operation H.M.'s intelligence and normal linguistic competence were pre-served. His short-term verbal memory span was also unaffected. However, his capacity to store information in long-term memory was severely damaged. H.M. could not recognize his psychologist's face and name, he did not know whether he had already read a magazine or not, and he did not remember his new address, even though he had moved years before. It was thus clear that he could no longer store new information, whereas he could remember what he had learnt in the remote past, or experiences he had had before the operation, such as his school, his childhood friends, etc. H.M. could learn motor behavior patterns of relative complexity, such as drawing a picture while looking at his own hand reflected in the mirror, or com-pleting very difficult puzzles. In motor or perceptive learning tasks he behaved like a normal subject, even though he could not remember that he had already performed these tests. This series of disorders is known as *pure amnesic syndrome*. A few years later, in 1969, English neuropsychologists Elizabeth Warrington and Tim Shallice had the opportunity to observe a patient affected by the reverse syndrome (Warrington & Shallice, 1969). Patient K.F. had suffered a left hemisphere lesion in an area adjacent to the Sylvian scissure (cf. Fig. 5.1). He did not exhibit relevant aphasic symptoms, but had a very limited short-term verbal memory span of only two or three digits (normal subjects usually have a memory span of seven digits).

Nevertheless, the patient exhibited normal learning capacity and long-term memory. The presence of two opposite deficit syndromes (in H.M. loss of storage in long-term memory capacity and preservation of short-term memory; in K.F. preservation of long-term memory and marked reduction in short-term memory span) is an example of *double dissociation*, which reliably substantiates the existence of two general memory systems, namely a short-term memory system and a long-term memory system.

On the basis of this data and other experimental studies, models of memory based on the processing of information have been proposed. According to one of the most renowned models, by R.C. Atkinson and R.M. Shiffrin, the environmental stimuli are first stored in short-term memory and only then is part of the information stored in long-term memory (Atkinson & Shiffrin, 1968). In this model short-term memory has a limited capacity and thus cannot sustain highly extensive global learning such as human learning. However, the description of patients like K.F., with severe short-term memory disorders, does not meet the expectations raised by this model, whereby patient K.F. would have had severe cognitive disorders; these were absent. These clinical cases and the results of experimental studies led to a more exhaustive and consistent hypothesis replacing Atkinson and Shiffrin's model.

In the same period a group of researchers underlined the need for a multilevel analysis of information to improve understanding of the mechanisms subserving memory. Given the acoustic processing of a verbal message, traces are kept in short-term memory for a relatively short period of time. Phonological processing produces a more lasting trace, whereas deep semantic processing of information establishes a more stable recall. These remarks on the relationship between memory and the levels of processing of information have been substantiated experimentally many times, but in this case the model became the only reference point, thus creating confusion between the model and the issue to be studied.

WORKING MEMORY

The theoretical and experimental attempts to solve some of the issues related to the concept of short-term memory led English researcher Alan Baddeley to postulate the existence of a more consistent element, namely *working memory* (Baddeley, 1990). It is a system containing and processing information only temporarily and participating in other essential tasks such as reasoning, comprehension, learning, and consciousness. The working memory model consists of many components including the central executive and a series of slave systems, the most studied of which—with regard to verbal functions—are the phonological loop and the visuo-spatial sketchpad (cf. Fig. 10.2).

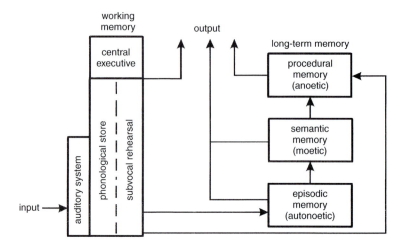

FIG. 10.2.   Human memory mode (adapted from Darò and Fabbro, 1994).

The *central executive* is a system regulating attention focalization, and controlling—and eventually modifying—behavior. Many neuropsychological studies indicate that this component is represented in the frontal lobes.

The *phonological loop*, in turn, consists of two components: the phonological store and the articulatory rehearsal process.

In the *phonological store*, verbal information is kept for a short period of time (about 1.5–2 seconds), after which mnestic traces decay. This temporal limit is a constant for verbal traces in all known languages.

The process of *subvocal rehearsal*, based on inner speech, refreshes the mnestic traces of the phonological store by means of an inner articulatory repetition mechanism. Verbal stimuli are thus maintained for about 10 seconds. A simple experimental study has contributed to assessing the effectiveness of subvocal rehearsal in digit span. If subjects—while performing a digit span task—are also required to pronounce irrelevant syllables, such as "bla, bla, bla", etc., loudly or mentally, their span invariably diminishes because the production of irrelevant sounds causes an articulatory suppression of the subvocal rehearsal process, thus partially inhibiting memory span.

A series of studies proved the effects of working memory on a variety of cognitive functions. For example, working memory can influence memory span for digits and, hence, mental calculation capacities, because the latter requires storage of the items to be calculated. In languages where words defining digits contain a greater number of syllables (e.g. 4 in Italian consists of two syllables, 4 in English consists of one syllable), the memory span for digits is shorter. This is due to the fact that the articulatory repetition component seems to take more time for digits whose articulation in one language (4 in Italian) takes longer than it does for shorter digits in another language (4 in English). For this reason, in bilingual children with Welsh as the mother tongue and with English as the second language, memory span for digits is greater in English than in Welsh. Numbers in Welsh take longer to be memorized, because most Welsh words defining numbers are much longer than English ones. This point raises another interesting issue. Welsh children observed during experiments obtained significantly lower scores than English children in some WISC tests with digits. Subsequently, it was noted that Welsh children did not have lower intellectual capacities than English children, but rather the difference lay in the higher speed with which numbers in English can be repeated mentally as against digits in Welsh (Ellis, 1992). At present, the record word articulation speed defining numbers is to be ascribed to Chinese. For this reason, mental calculation tasks are easier to perform in Chinese than in other languages. In 1988 Baddeley and Italian neuropsychologists Costanza Papagno and Giuseppe Vallar described an Italian patient, P.V., who following a left hemisphere lesion only exhibited a selective disorder affecting the phonological store of working memory, whereas long-term memory, verbal intelligence, and language were unaffected (Baddeley, Papagno, & Vallar, 1988). Because the patient had no difficulty in learning lists of words in Italian, her learning capacity in a language she did not know, Russian, was also tested. Whereas a control group of subjects performed the task without difficulty, the patient was not able to learn words in Russian. On the basis of this data, it was proposed that one of the working memory functions accounts for the learning of new phonological material. In particular, the phonological loop seems to play a fundamental role in the acquisition of both the mother tongue and foreign languages (Papagno & Vallar, 1995).

Working memory seems to be correlated to learning disorders, too. About 10% of children of school age with normal intelligence and without physical, emotional, or socio-economic disorders have difficulties in varying degrees with regard to language learning (developmental language disorder), reading (developmental dyslexia), calculation (developmental dyscalculia), and movement (developmental motor disorders). It has often been noted that children with dyslexia exhibit problems related to some components of working memory (Gathercole & Baddeley, 1993; Masutto, Bravar, & Fabbro, 1993). For example, these children have a memory span for digits that is shorter than the span of a control group of children of the same age. They present with difficulties in reading and in nonword repetition (e.g. "git", "seaw", or foreign names). They have a reduced vocabulary and have enormous difficulty in learning foreign languages (Ganschow, Sparks, Javrosky, Pohlman, & Bishop-Marbury, 1991). Even though it is not known which aspects of memory are compromised in children with reading disorders, it is assumed that working memory has a considerable influence on this type of learning difficulty. Future studies will better explain the emergence of this disorder, thus allowing more effective help for children with learning disabilities and for their families. Since these are clever and sensitive children, they suffer especially because the educational establishment is not tolerant or prepared to deal with this issue.

TYPES OF LONG-TERM MEMORY

The study of patients with amnesic syndromes has contributed to understanding that long-term memory is not a unitary system, but is organized in many separate systems or processes. As early as 1896 the French philosopher Henri Bergson, in a book on memory, distinguished between a memory of the body, comprising learnt sequences of gestures, which could be involuntarily recalled also by patients with amnesia, and a memory of the soul, comprising past experiences, which was severely damaged in amnesic patients (Bergson, 1911). At the beginning of this century, the Swiss neuropsychiatrist Edouard Claparède noticed that amnesic patients with poor learning capacities were, however, able to learn some things (Claparède, 1911). Claparède used to shake hands with his patients when he met them. One day he hid a pin in one of his hands and pricked the hand of an amnesic patient. The following day the patient refused to shake hands with him. She did not remember why, nor could she explain her behavior.

More recent studies on amnesic patients showed that they are able to learn new motor tasks (e.g. drawing the contour of a star by looking into a mirror to monitor their own hand movements) or cognitive tasks (e.g. recognition of a picture made of only a few salient features). The analysis of, and the scientific discussion on, these findings led to the idea that long-term memory is organized in separate systems. According to the current classification, long-term memory consists of explicit memory, which in turn is divided into semantic memory and episodic memory, and of implicit memory, divided into procedural memory, priming, and conditioning (Tulvig, 1987; Schacter, 1996; cf. Figs 10.2 and 10.3).

Explicit memory

This refers to learnt knowledge of which individuals are aware and which they can imagine or verbally express on request or at will. Examples of explicit knowledge are the elements of history, geography, or chemistry learnt at school, the rules of grammatical pedagogics (i.e. Latin, classical Greek, etc.), one's own past experiences, the face of a person seen only once for a moment, but who has caught the individual's attention, etc. The following are the typical features of explicit memory:

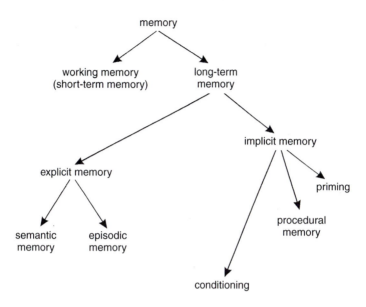

FIG. 10.3.   Hierarchical classification of memory components.

1. it comprises consciously learnt knowledge;
2. it accounts for the focalization of attention and the enhancement of the individual's performance;
3. its contents can consciously be retrieved and verbalized;
4. in some cases one exposure can be enough for an individual to preserve an indelible explicit memory.

Explicit memory, also known as declarative memory, consists of two subtypes, namely semantic memory and episodic memory. *Semantic memory* is the system storing the subject's encyclopedic knowledge of the world, for example, knowledge of the meaning of the words, and geographical, historical, and social knowledge. *Episodic or autobiographical memory* refers to the individual's past experiences that can be recalled consciously.

Amnesic syndromes, too, are characterized by the incapability to learn new semantic or episodic information (anterograde amnesia) and by the preservation of explicit memory prior to insult. Amnesic patients are, however, still able to learn implicitly, and furthermore, their working memory functions are preserved. On the other hand, patients with Alzheimer's disease, a severe presenile dementia, exhibit both an amnesic syndrome and a working memory deficit, caused by an alteration of the central executive system coordinating attentive functions. This is probably due to a reduced functionality of the frontal lobes.

Recent research by McEwen and Sapolsky (1995) has underlined that in the long-term stress situations—by increasing catecholamines and gluco-corticoids—determine a selective destruction of the medial temporal lobe (medial-basal portions of the temporal lobes, amygdala, and hippocampus), with consequent reduction in the storing capacity of the subject's episodic and semantic memory. This subtle form of amnesia can be defined as "stress amnesia" (LeDoux, 1996).

Implicit memory

Implicit memory refers to a type of learning or knowledge that depends on the repeated execution of a task, even though the subject is not aware of the nature of implicit knowledge, has forgotten, or cannot remember when he has learnt the task. Implicit memory subserves, for example, the ability to play musical instruments by ear, the learning of sensory-motor sequences for the production of phonemes, the learning of morphosyntax, the use of grammar in the comprehension and production of an individual's mother tongue, etc.

Implicit learning is characterized by the following distinctive features:

1. the acquisition of information is casual, with no direct focalization of attention, nor voluntary concentration;
2. information is memorized by means of implicit strategies, which do not make it available for conscious introspection;
3. information is automatically used independently of conscious control, letting the subject establish the objectives to be reached, but not consciously carry out the program (execution is automatic); the subject's attention can thus be focalized on the result, ignoring the process;
4. this type of learning occurs slowly and improves with practice (this holds true for procedural memory only, and not for priming; see below). Studies have suggested that in their first year of life children have implicit memory only. Explicit memory develops later. In addition, 3-year-old children still have an implicit memory which is considerably more developed than explicit memory. (Parkin, 1997).

Implicit memory comprises the following subtypes:

1. *procedural memory,* concerning the learning of motor and cognitive procedures and seemingly involving highly developed cerebral structures, also present in the brain of reptiles (i.e. basal ganglia and cerebellum).
2. *priming*, consisting of the learning of acoustic or visual fill-in-the-blank tasks, lexical decision, etc.

3. *conditioning*, which was studied by Russian physiologist Ivan P. Pavlov. For example, if each time a dog is fed a bell rings, after a certain number of trials the dog will immediately salivate when hearing the bell ring, even though there is no food. The acoustic stimulus, which is not normally associated with salivation, conditions the dog's behavior on the basis of an association produced by implicit learning.

As already stated, patients suffering from a pure amnesic syndrome are still capable of procedural learning, because they are still able to learn a foreign language (Hirst, Phelps, Johnson, & Volpe, 1988). Cases of patients suffering from Parkinson's disease (a degenerative disease mainly affecting basal ganglia) have been described, in which explicit memory or working memory was intact, whereas their capacity to learn procedures had been damaged. Patients suffering from an amnesic syndrome and patients suffering from Parkinson's disease are yet another example of double dissociation, because in the former explicit learning is affected, whereas in the latter procedural learning is damaged. Moreover, the fact that these two groups of patients exhibit lesions in different cerebral structures suggests that the two different types of memory are subserved by separate cerebral structures (Saint-Cyr, Taylor, & Lang, 1988). A third category of patients, those suffering from Huntington's chorea—a severe hereditary disease of the nervous system—exhibit disintegration of both systems in the acute pathological phase, but they show normal priming on a word completion test.

THE ANATOMY OF MEMORY

Studies on brain-damaged amnesic patients, experimental research on learning abilities of animals with lesions localized in areas subserving memory, and, more recently, the visualization of the cerebral areas activated during memory tasks by means of PET, have enabled us to draw a provisional map of the neuronal structures involved in the different types of memory (Meunier, Bachevalier, & Mishkin, 1994; Perani et al., 1993).

During tasks involving the activation of working memory, prefrontal areas of both cerebral hemispheres activate, as do the left superior temporal areas and the right parietal areas. During *episodic memory tasks* cingulate areas activate bilaterally, as do both sides of the hippocampus and the thalamic structures of both hemispheres. During *semantic memory tasks* only the left hemisphere structures activate, namely the cingulate cortex, the prefrontal cortex, and the superior temporal area (Squire & Zola-Morgan, 1991). During *procedural memory tasks*, prefrontal areas of both cerebral hemispheres, the basal ganglia and the cerebellar hemispheres activate (Salmon & Butters, 1995).

TYPES OF MEMORY INVOLVED IN LANGUAGE ACQUISITION AND LEARNING

Recently, Michel Paradis proposed that a bilingual's mother tongue and second language are stored in separate memory systems (Paradis, 1994a). For example, if a subject's mother tongue is a language acquired only in the oral form, as is the case with Swiss-German, Québécois (French spoken in Québéc), or Friulian (spoken in the north-eastern part of Italy), it is mainly stored by means of implicit strategies, whereas the learning of a second language by means of grammatical rules and the activation of the mental translation processes presupposes a minor involvement of implicit memory. In Paradis' opinion, in this type of bilinguals aphasia would compromise to a major extent the language memorized by implicit strategies, namely the subject's mother tongue. These patients would thus have less difficulty when expressing themselves in their second language or in a dead language, such as Latin or ancient Greek, because verbal expression in these languages depends mainly on aspects of semantic memory (explicit memory), which in certain types of aphasia is relatively better preserved than implicit memory.

A series of studies carried out by Helen Neville and co-workers by means of electrophysiological techniques have substantiated the hypothesis that syntactic processing and semantic processing are organized in separate areas of the brain (Neville, Mills, & Lawson, 1992; Neville et al., 1997; Weber-Fox & Neville, 1996). Furthermore, these studies have revealed differences in the brain organization of language depending on the age of acquisition and learning strategies. They have thus corroborated the results of previous clinical data indicating an involvement of left hemisphere structures (anterior to the Rolandic scissure; cf. Fig. 5.1) in the production and comprehension of syntax, and of areas (posterior to the Rolandic scissure) of both cerebral hemispheres in semantic comprehension. Event-related brain potentials (ERPs) showed that English monolingual subjects exhibited typical activation frames of the left frontal lobe structures during linguistic tasks concerning the processing of closed class words (articles, conjunction, prepositions, etc.), whereas during the processing of open class words (nouns, verbs, adjectives) they exhibited a greater activation of the left posterior structures. Subsequently, Helen Neville became particularly concerned with the study of the cerebral organization of languages learnt at different ages. It is well known that syntax acquisition of the second language is more difficult and rarely reaches very good levels when the language is learnt after a critical age, which more or less coincides with 6–8 years. For example, in the United States, subjects who are born deaf learn the American Sign Language (ASL) first, and American English as a second language later, during special courses. They usually have a huge vocabulary in English but they do not master grammar perfectly. When performing linguistic tasks requiring the analysis of closed class words in English, deaf subjects with ASL as mother tongue and English as second language do not exhibit any activation of the left frontal lobe structures, as is the case in subjects without hearing difficulties. The frontal lobe areas usually organize closed class words of the mother tongue, regardless of presentation and/or execution modalities (reading, writing, oral production), which means that the frontal lobe structures organize the syntactic components of a language only if it is learnt before the critical age. Afterwards, other brain structures account for the organization of the grammatical aspects of the second language, probably through explicit learning.

Recent studies using neuroimaging techniques (see Chapter 7) have shown a different representation of L1 versus L2 in Broca's area in fluent bilinguals who have learnt L2 after the age of 10, whereas no such difference has been found in Wernicke's area. However, in fluent bilinguals who have acquired L2 in early childhood, the cortical representation of the two languages was similar both in Broca's and in Wernicke's area (Kim, Relkin, Lee, & Hirsch, 1997). Learning a language in a school setting, however, is apparently likely to determine a less extended cortical representation of L2 as opposed to L1. If L2 has been acquired only formally (e.g. at school), cortical areas involved in the comprehension of stories in L2 are activated to a lesser extent than when the same stories are being listened to in L1. In addition, only the task requiring listening to stories in L1 was correlated to an activation of the right cerebellum (cf. Chapter 9, pp. 85–6), a brain structure that intervenes in the organization of procedural memory of language (Perani et al., 1996).

Paradis claims that subjects have to be aware of these two distinct strategies of language learning. Even though the difference is not so clear-cut, the mother tongue is generally based on implicit processes to a larger extent than is the second language. However, in the mother tongue both implicit and explicit strategies are constantly involved. For example, comprehension presupposes the concurrent activation of semantic (explicit) memory, which is responsible for lexical recognition, and of implicit memory, which is responsible for grammatical comprehension. To date, in the teaching of a foreign language grammar at school explicit strategies have usually been preferred, whereas the grammar-translation method has been applied for teaching expression. On the basis of present knowledge, it is important to underline that the recourse to conscious strategies for the acquisition of a second language has considerable limits (Sharwood Smith, 1981).

1. The use of explicit strategies for foreign language learning presupposes that subjects are older than 15, which means that the application of this method in primary and secondary schools is misguided and ineffective.

2. Furthermore, it has been noted that many adults do not use conscious strategies for foreign language learning; therefore, the use of strategies based on implicit memory is the most valuable.
3. Often students who obtain excellent marks in foreign languages by means of the explicit learning method are incapable of following a natural conversation in the foreign language.

Such contributions, together with other studies in the field (linguistic, pedagogical, psychological, etc.)—carried out with the aim of finding a solution to this problem and others—ought to be to the forefront in foreign language research and teaching. They are particularly desirable at the most critical ages, namely kindergarten, primary school, and secondary school (cf. Jacobs & Schumann, 1992; Penfield, 1959; Pulvermüller & Schumann, 1994).

CHAPTER ELEVEN

What does it mean to be bilingual?

Over 50% of the world's population is bilingual. However, ideological and political prejudices have established a deformed vision of reality, on the basis of which bilingual individuals are considered to be only a very restricted number. Because concepts like language and dialect cannot be scientifically defined, at a neurolinguistic level bilinguals are considered to be individuals who master, understand, and speak: (a) two languages, (b) two dialects, or (c) a language and a dialect. If they wish to do so, during verbal production bilinguals can make a clear-cut distinction between the two linguistic codes. Many neurolinguistic and psychological studies have distinguished between various types of bilingualism: compact, coordinated, or subordinated bilingualism; early or late bilingualism, or adult learning of a second language; balanced bilingualism or dominant bilingualism. At present, however, a distinction is made between language acquisition (naturally, in an informal environment, with the prevailing involvement of implicit memory) and language learning (by means of formal methodologies, with learnt and intentionally applied rules, mostly in an institutional environment). With regard to the education of a bilingual, it is known that the earlier the exposure to the two languages, the easier and more complete the acquisition. However, an individual can become bilingual at any age: at a more advanced age more effort will be necessary to obtain results that are often lower than those reached by children, especially with regard to pronunciation and syntax.

François Grosjean, a psychologist currently working in Switzerland, claims that the question "Who is bilingual?" has a simple answer, namely over 50% of the world population (Grosjean, 1982). Yet, paradoxically, until some decades ago bilinguals seemed to be few in number. Even in the study of language disorders caused by neurological lesions there seemed to be very few bilingual aphasic patients. However, since this issue has been approached on an empirical basis, the situation has changed radically. At present, in North-American universities, it is very difficult to find the number of monolingual students necessary to carry out psycholinguistic experiments. The same holds true in Italy.

The responsibility of a distorted view of reality, where bilinguals are considered a rarity, lies with politics, which in turn has influenced culture. Indeed, many people, e.g. in Italy, Great Britain, or China, master the official language of their country and at least one dialect. Obviously, these people are ideologically considered to be monolinguals. However, a certain notion of State has resulted in a rather distorted view of the language issue, a view that has been theorized by literati and linguists, generally more concerned with their academic or political career than with an unprejudiced study of speech and languages. Several expressions have thus emerged, such as "language and idiom" or "language and dialect" belonging—as under-lined by linguist Louis J. Calvet—to a colonialist, ideological dichotomic view that has contributed to the creation of opposing word pairs such as civilized-wild, language-dialect, people-tribe, etc. Calvet claims that what is known as a dialect is a defeated language, whereas what is called language is the dialect that has prevailed politically (Calvet, 1974).

As early as the end of the last century some linguists had noted that notions such as language and dialect could not be defined scientifically. More recently, North-American linguist Noam Chomsky has reiterated that the concept of language is an opaque term and that a linguist completely unfamiliar with borders or political institutions would not distinguish between languages and dialects, as is normally the case. On another occa-sion Chomsky stated that behind a language there are always a flag and an army (Chomsky, 1977). French linguist Claud Hagège, who studied the relationship between language and power in detail, writes in one of his books on language and human sciences that language is a political asset. Any politics of language endorses established power because language unity is important to power. Any changes will disturb it (Hagège, 1985).

As already stated, the neurolinguistic study of bilingualism is a multi-disciplinary approach to the issue of cerebral representation and functioning of more than one language. Because this branch of neurology also deals with ill people and, therefore, with diagnosis and treatment, the issue cannot be limited to plays on words, double meanings, and self-interests. For this reason, after many debates with experts in the field and esteemed neurolo-gists, neurophysiologists, and neurolinguists (Salvatore Aglioti, Giovanni Berlucchi, Yvan Lebrun, and Michel Paradis, to name but a few) I have reached the pragmatic conclusion that a subject is bilingual if he masters, understands, and speaks: (a) two languages, (b) two dialects, or (c) a language and a dialect (cf. Grosjean, 1994). Moreover, if required to, during verbal production a bilingual can make a clear-cut distinction between the two linguistic systems. For example, Sardinian-Italian bilinguals can appropriately speak Italian on certain occasions, or converse in their dialect, without mixing the two languages. If, on the other hand, subjects can speak only Venetian, or a variation of it, they are monolingual, even if para-doxically, according to the Italian State, they do not speak any language in theory! Similar opinions on the issue of language and dialect were expressed by German neurologist Arnold Pick (1913/1983). The study of brain-damaged subjects is a serious problem that can help shed some light on a subject that has often been dealt with in a misleading way. This has hap-pened in other fields of research as well, e.g. in the study of memory, reading, and writing.

It is thus clear why in the United States it is difficult to find truly monolingual university students for psycholinguistic experiments. In 1982 Grosjean estimated the number of people who are not of English mother tongue in the United States. At least 13 million people were of Spanish mother tongue, 3 million of German, 2 million of French, 2 million of Polish, 3 million of Italian, and 8 million people spoke languages other than English. At least with regard to Italo-Americans, Grosjean made a mistake that will be clarified by the following anecdote. Some years ago, an Italo-American was admitted to a hospital in New York City. She had suffered a stroke with consequent aphasia. She could no longer speak English, even though she had been living in the United States for the last 40 years. Documents showed that she was of Italian origin. Fortunately, a doctor who could speak Italian was available. (Many skilled and keen young Italian doctors leave for the United States to study or work there immediately after taking their degree.) The doctor started to speak Italian to the patient, only to find out that she spoke a language unintelligible to him, which later turned out to be Friulian. This episode draws attention to the fact that the aforementioned number of Italo-Americans do not speak standard Italian, but the dialect of their own region. For example, I noticed that in the Friulian community of Toronto, amounting to about 50,000 people, most people speak Friulian and English, and only a minor-ity speaks Italian as well. The same holds true for Argentina and Aus-tralia, both with regard to Friulian and other Italian dialects. An Australian or North-American neurolinguist concerned with the assess-ment of a bilingual aphasic patient need not assess competence in standard Italian if the patient comes from Calabria or Sicily because he or she will rarely speak standard Italian. Therefore, what has to be assessed is com-petence in Calabrian and English, or Sicilian and English, etc. For these reasons, some Australian researchers are currently devising standardized test batteries in Calabrian and Sicilian. The same holds true for people living in the former Soviet Republics or in China, where—together with the official language of the country—hundreds of different languages are spoken.

As early as 1919 neurologist Z. Bichowsky was fully aware of the issues outlined in this chapter, and indeed he wrote: "It seems to be quite improbable that the many aphasics whose extensive case histories have been published should have spoken and understood only the one language of the researcher" (Bychowsky, 1919/1983, p.131). Some linguists claim that monolinguals do not exist because everyone becomes bilingual as soon as—apart from the dialect spoken within their family or in that area—they are able to understand and/or speak the language of the élite or a register or jargon different from that spoken in their family (Paradis, 1994b).

IS BILINGUALISM USEFUL?

Bilingual subjects generally think they are absolutely normal. If they have learnt the two languages during childhood, they are likely to believe that being able to express themselves in more than one language is absolutely normal. Over the past few decades many experimental studies have been carried out—many of them by Wallace Lambert in Canada—to establish whether bilingual subjects, and children particularly, are as intelligent as monolinguals (Lambert, 1992; Lambert, Genesee, Holobow, & Chartrand, 1993). It is a question both legitimate and strange. It is legitimate because raising questions can be useful, and strange because mistrust towards bilinguals was so widespread in the past, particularly in some German academic circles, as to lead people to think that bilingualism was responsible for a lower degree of intelligence. Mistrust has extremely old roots: Parmenides and his disciple Zeno, too, were looked at with mistrust and suspicion by monolingual Greeks, because they were bilingual. However, the studies carried out on this issue proved that there are no significant differences in intelligence between bilinguals and monolinguals. Actually, bilingualism does not damage intelligence: rather, it enhances tolerance.

Many pragmatic, cultural, and economic reasons suggest that bilingualism and polyglossia—the capacity to understand and speak more than one language—bring important advantages to individuals. Those speaking two or more languages can visit other countries with ease, as they can communicate and become familiar with the cultural features typical of each language and country. Furthermore, knowledge of two languages increases employment opportunities as well as information sources (books, papers, etc.). With regard to personality psychology, too, bilinguals seemingly have more tools at their disposal than monolinguals do. For example, they can express some psychological traumas in their second language with relatively greater ease than in their mother tongue, the latter generally being more closely related to the centers of psychological pain (De Zulueta, 1984).

TYPES OF BILINGUALISM

Many linguists have thought it useful to distinguish between various types of bilingualism, i.e. compact and coordinated or subordinated bilingualism. The expression *compact bilingual* refers to an individual who has learnt the two languages concurrently before their sixth year, because they generally were each spoken by one of the parents. A *coordinated bilingual* has learnt the second language before puberty, within or outside the family, for example, because the child moved to a foreign country with the family. A *subordinate bilingual* has one language as the mother tongue and uses the second language as mediator of the first language. In this type of bilingualism subjects think of what they want to express in their first language first and then translate it into their second language. Many classifications and definitions have been proposed, including *early bilingualism* to refer to early acquisition (in infancy) of the two languages, *late bilingualism*, where the second language has been acquired much later than the mother tongue, and *adult learning of a second language*, if the individual has learnt a foreign language at an advanced age. Other definitions attempt at describing the degree of competence in the two languages: a *balanced bilingual* is a subject mastering the two languages to the same extent, whereas a *dominant bilingual* is a subject who is more fluent in one language than in the other. All these definitions have proved useful, especially to identify groups of bilinguals for psycholinguistic experiments (Hamers & Blanc, 1990; Vaid, 1986). However, for the purpose of neurolinguistics these definitions lose their usefulness. For example, if a bilingual French-English subject moves from France to the United States and stays there for 15 years, English is very likely to become the dominant language and French the second language. If afterwards the subject returns to France, after only 6 months French might become the dominant language again.

Some of these classifications of bilingual people (such as the "ideal", the "true", the "balanced", or the "perfect" bilingual) have also been fiercely challenged at the psycholinguistic level (Grosjean, 1989; 1992; 1994). Grosjean has repeatedly stated that "the bilingual is not one monolingual in one person", thus trying to weed out a belief that can be found among many researchers, educators, and bilinguals themselves as a result of the strong monolingual bias that has been prevalent in the language sciences. Actually, bilingual individuals have differential needs for their two languages or ascribe to them different social/emotional functions (what a language is used for, with whom, where, etc.), thus they do not necessarily have to develop a perfect knowledge, nor the same level of competence and/or performance in both languages.

At present, a neurolinguistic distinction between acquisition and learning of a language is essential. *Language acquisition* occurs by natural modalities in an informal environment, especially with the involvement of implicit memory. All children acquire their mother tongue in this way, and adults too can acquire a second language by informal strategies. *Language learning* occurs mainly by formal modalities, namely rules, often in an institutional environment. A case in point is that of the so-called dead languages. In Italian schools Latin and classical Greek are learnt, but not acquired. Unfortunately, very often in Italian state schools learning of modern foreign languages is preferred to acquisition. This distinction is important, because seemingly separate cerebral structures are involved, depending on acquisition processes (emotional systems, cortical and subcortical structures) or learning processes (mainly cerebral cortical areas).

BILINGUAL EDUCATION

One of the most topical issues concerns when and how children ought to start learning a second language. This question is very often raised by parents who want their children to become bilingual. Fortunately, their number is constantly rising. However, there are no definitive answers nor unequivocal scientific data to help them. To date, four general modalities of language acquisition have been described:

1. Children acquire the two languages within their own family. No previous deliberate planning of the use of either language is involved.
2. In other cases, each parent speaks his/her own mother tongue with the child (one person-one language).
3. A third method consists in using only one language until the child has reached a certain age, between 3 and 6 years, and gradually introducing the second language later.
4. Finally, a fourth strategy consists in using the parents' mother tongue at home, whereas children acquire the second language in the country where they live, i.e. at school or, more generally, outside their family. This fourth strategy of second language acquisition is widely applied at international schools. Many children of Italian mother tongue have attended elementary and secondary schools where the teaching is in English, German, or French. They become bilingual with a slight dominance of their second language in all school topics. This type of bilingualism is very frequent in Italy. Suffice it to say that a large majority of children speak a language or a dialect within their family, and only at school do they acquire standard Italian. These children,

unlike the children of immigrants, do not speak their second language at school, when playing, etc., but speak instead their mother tongue or their dialect.

In all acquisition modalities, stress has been laid on a general principle that must be respected, namely the child is to use both languages in daily life. Poor results are obtained if the child is taught the second language for only one hour a week, and they are further reduced if teaching methods are institutional and based on rules.

Finally, with regard to age limits there are no straightforward answers either. It is commonly known that the earlier the exposure to both languages, the easier and more complete their acquisition. Many studies indicate that the age limit (for a complete and correct acquisition of pronunciation and grammar rules) is about 6–8 years (cf. Flege & Fletcher, 1992; Johnson & Newport, 1989). Such an age limit is reasonable, but many other factors influence second language acquisition. One of these is the degree of linguistic vicinity of the two languages, which makes it easier for an individual of Italian mother tongue to learn Spanish than to learn Chinese (Epstein, Flynn, & Martohardjono, 1996). Individual abilities are very important, too. Some individuals acquire languages easily and even enjoy themselves while doing so, whereas others face greater difficulties. Generally, an individual can become bilingual at any age. However, at a later stage greater effort is needed to obtain results, which are generally poorer than those of children, especially with regard to pronunciation and syntax (Hagège, 1996; Lebrun, 1975; Locke, 1993; Paradis & Lebrun, 1984).

CHAPTER TWELVE

First-language recovery in aphasics

When a brain lesion affects language areas subjects can lose the ability to speak the languages they know, but can recover them in parallel (parallel recovery). In other cases, aphasia can affect only one of the languages known by the patient. In 1895 A. Pitres put forward the hypothesis that in the latter case patients recovered the language that had been the most familiar prior to insult. Pitres maintained that this was due to the fact that often the lesion did not cause the loss of the language but only inhibited it owing to an "inertia" of the cortical centers of language. On the basis of this hypothesis, if a patient becomes aphasic owing to a sort of inertia of the language areas, inhibitory pathological phenomena affect the language that shows weaker associations between the neural elements subserving it, namely the language least used prior to insult. The analysis of all published clinical cases of bilingual aphasia shows that 40% of patients exhibit a parallel recovery of languages, 32% a better recovery of the first language, and the remaining 28% show a better recovery of the second language.

The first systematic study of bilingual aphasia was published more than 100 years ago in 1895 by A. Pitres, a neurologist living in Bordeaux. In an attempt to explain the better recovery of one language than the others, he described the clinical case histories of seven multilingual aphasic patients (Lebrun, 1995; Pitres, 1895/1983).

Following a brain lesion affecting language areas linguistic deficits are not stable, but can change over time. In the case of cerebral infarctions or hemorrhages, which are the most frequent causes of aphasia, three phases have been identified in which linguistic disorders may change according to type and severity. The acute phase, generally lasting two or three weeks, may present typical neuropsychological disorders and language recovery patterns that can sometimes be very rapid. The intermediate phase, lasting from the third week to the fourth month of disease, is crucial because it clarifies the type and the degree of severity of the nontransient functional losses caused by the brain lesion. The late phase begins in the fourth month of the disease and lasts all life long. It is believed that the rapid recovery of speech in the *acute phase* depends on the resolution of two pathological phenomena present in the first weeks, namely edema and diaschisis. Immediately after the brain lesion, the destroyed cerebral tissue is encircled by a certain amount of liquid (edema), which impairs the functional activity of the intact neural cells that are adjacent to the lesion. Moreover, because neural centers coordinate their monitoring when organizing language functions, the sudden lack of cooperation between one or more of these centers determines a temporary inhibition of the whole system owing to an effect known as *diaschisis* (Cappa, 1998).

Pitres and other neurologists claimed that failure to recover a language during the *intermediate* and *late phases* was not due to the loss of that language, but rather to inhibitory effects caused by the lesion and acting on the language itself. Pitres had drawn this conclusion on the basis of one general assumption and of some empirical studies. The general assumption was supported by all neurologists of the time, including S. Freud, A. Pick, O. Pötzl, M. Minkowski, W. Penfield, and presupposed that all languages of a bilingual or a polyglot are localized in common language areas (cf. Paradis, 1989). This theory had developed in the wake of the scientific debate that was started by R. Scoresby-Jackson in 1867 and was developed during the second half of the 19th century. Scoresby-Jackson maintained that Broca's area was responsible for the representation of a subject's mother tongue, whereas the portions anterior to Broca's area were responsible for foreign language acquisition (Scoresby-Jackson, 1867). This hypothesis was rejected following a postmortem study of the brain of a polyglot, Sauerwein, who spoke 54 languages, both at poetry and prose level. In the brain of this exceptionally gifted individual Broca's area and the structures anterior to it were of a normal extension and showed a perfectly normal development (Veyrac, 1931/ 1983). It should be noted, however, that Scoresby-Jackson's contemporaries had not understood that their colleague referred to the capacity of the tissue adjacent to Broca's area to control further linguistic functions. This does not necessarily imply an increase in their anatomical extension (Kim et al., 1997; cf. Chapter 10, p. 101).

A second element derived from the empirical observation of bilingual aphasic patients led Pitres to claim that the language that was not available was not lost, but only inhibited. Pitres had repeatedly noticed that these patients could progressively recover a language in a shorter period of time than that needed to acquire a foreign language, which meant that the disorder provoked by the lesion did not cause the loss of the language, but only made it partially inaccessible. Pitres defined this disorder as "inertia" of the cortical language centers, which manifested itself by the temporary extinguishing of the motor and sensory images used to understand and utter words. He proposed to name this disorder *verbal amnesia*, because it is due to the incapability to retrieve words. In his opinion, the cerebral organization of language in polyglots was to be studied by a neurophysiological approach, rather than a neuroanatomical approach that was certainly more direct but less effective.

Polish neurologist Bychowsky observed rapid speech recovery in young aphasic polyglot patients who had suffered aphasia following brain lesions during World War I (Bychowsky, 1919/1983). Not only did these patients recover language even if suffering from Wernicke's aphasia, which is the most difficult aphasic syndrome to treat, but they also easily learnt to write with their left hand when the right side of their body was paralyzed. On the basis of this empirical data, Bychowsky advanced the so-called "vicariousness theory" and proposed that in young adults language recovery following a left hemisphere lesion might depend on a reorganization of language functions in the right hemisphere. Bychowsky put forward his theory on the basis of the ideas advanced by the German neurologist Liepmann and the Italian neurologist Mingazzini. In an article dated 1909, Liepmann had maintained that speech recovery in aphasic patients depended mainly on the right hemisphere, which was usually used to a lesser extent but, if necessary, could organize language. In a contribution dated 1913, Mingazzini had stated his conviction that the right hemisphere had linguistic functions; in particular, the right basal ganglia were also involved in articulation (Mingazzini, 1913). In infancy, in particular, the right hemisphere was involved in verbal expression tasks. In fact, language "engrams" were also present in the right hemisphere. As they were not completely inhibited, they could be made accessible again through practice.

RULES AND EXCEPTIONS IN RECOVERY PATTERNS

When bilinguals or polyglots suffer a brain insult affecting language areas, they may lose the ability to use all the languages they know and exhibit the same type of aphasia in all languages. Subsequent recovery may be parallel in all languages. In a study on the literature of bilingual aphasia published in 1977, Paradis stated that 40% of polyglot aphasics exhibited *parallel recovery* of languages. It should be noted, however, that these statistics are based on clinical case histories that have been published and, thus, are the most atypical. Paradis put forward the hypothesis that this type of recovery is even more frequent, because descriptions of single clinical cases of poly-glot aphasics with parallel language recovery are very rare, and neurologists tend to describe only "exceptional" cases, as they can be published more easily (Mimouni, Béland, Danault, & Idrissi, 1995; Paradis, 1977). This is one of the reasons why over 10 years ago Paradis started an international project on bi- and multilingual aphasia in Canada, which is still operative and sees the participation of numerous researchers from all over the world. This study also includes bilingual aphasic patients with any type of language disorders so as to have a large number of subjects and, thus, more reliable statistical data.

In some cases, aphasia affects only one of the languages known by the patient. In his study of 1895, Pitres was the first to draw attention to the fact that the dissociation of the languages affected by aphasia was not an exceptional phenomenon, but rather ordinary. Pitres described seven clinical cases of patients exhibiting differential recovery of the two languages they spoke. On the basis of the frequency of dissociation, Pitres put forward hypotheses on the causes that might determine a better recovery in one language, reaching the conclusion that patients tend to recover the language that was *most familiar* to them prior to insult. This hypothesis was subse-quently called *Pitres' law*. Curiously, Pitres—in proposing his theory—referred to a work by Ribot in which it was claimed that, in the case of memory diseases, the general rule held that the new deteriorates earlier than the old. Subsequently, numerous neurologists compared and contrasted the so-called "Pitres' law" (recovery of the most familiar language) with "Ribot's law" (recovery of the mother tongue), but it should be noted that neither of the two authors ever formulated a "law" on language recovery in bilingual aphasics.

In his work, Pitres proposed a reasonable explanation of language recovery in aphasics. He maintained that the recovery pattern could occur only if the lesion had not destroyed language centers, but rather had only temporarily inhibited them through pathological inertia. In the case of a temporary inhibition of language, aphasic bilinguals would present the following recovery stages:

1. The first stage was characterized by the total loss of the capacity to understand and speak all languages known by the patient.
2. In the second stage the aphasic patient progressively recovered the capacity to understand the language that was *most familiar* (most used) premorbidly. It generally coincided with the patient's mother tongue, but it might be a second language.
3. In the third stage the patient recovered the ability to speak the lan-guage that was most familiar.

4. In the fourth stage, the patient recovered the ability to understand the second or all other languages.
5. In the fifth stage, the patient recovered the ability to speak all other languages.

In Pitres' opinion, the patient generally recovered the most familiar language first because the neural elements subserving it were more firmly associated. If the patient had become aphasic owing to "functional inertia" of the language areas, these inhibitory pathological phenomena should have affected to a greater extent the languages that exhibited weaker associations between the neural elements subserving them. These hypotheses were both supported and opposed (Pick's concept of a more automatized language, or Chlenov's concept of basic language; cf. Chlenov, 1948/1983). To date, no unequivocal rule applicable to all clinical cases has been formulated.

THE RECOVERY OF THE FIRST LANGUAGE

With the exclusion of the cases of individuals bilingual since infancy, the mother tongue is often the most familiar and the most automatized language preferred for "thought" (basic language). By analyzing all clinical cases of bilingual and polyglot aphasics published so far, I have calculated that around 40% of patients present parallel recovery of all languages, 32% present a better recovery of the mother tongue, and the remaining 28% present a better recovery of the second language. Cases of parallel recovery substantiate the hypothesis that the two languages are organized in the same cortical areas. Given cases of aphasia with differential impairment and differential recovery of the two languages, the question of a separate cerebral organization of the two languages remains open. If in these patients the mother tongue is recovered earlier than the other languages, it is legitimate to presuppose—as Pitres suggested—that the initial inhibition has subsequently been overcome. Hence, the recovery of the mother tongue first and of the other languages at a later stage.

I felt it useful in this chapter and in the next chapters to present short clinical case histories of bilingual aphasic patients, so that the reader can become familiar with the specific difficulties and problems faced by these patients during their lives. I will briefly describe two cases of aphasia with a better recovery of the mother tongue. The first patient was observed by P. Denès, in 1914. She was a theater dancer of French mother tongue and with fluent Italian, as she had visited Italy very often. In 1905 she suffered a stroke affecting the left hemisphere with consequent right-sided paralysis and aphasia. When admitted to hospital, she could only say "oui" (yes). Subsequently, she slowly recovered language production. In 1913 she was visited by Denès, who assessed her residual capacities to understand and speak the two languages. She spoke French as if she were a foreigner, by producing grammatically incorrect short sentences with only the main lexical items and the verbs in the infinitive form. Language deficits in Italian were similar to deficits in her mother tongue, even though more severe (Denès, 1914/1983).

In 1940 Dimitrijevic described the clinical case history of a Jewish polyglot who had suffered a left vascular lesion with consequent aphasia and a mild right hemifacial weakness. At the time of insult, she was 60 years old. She had acquired Yiddish at the same time as Bulgarian, which had become her second language when she went to school. At the age of 34 she moved to Belgrade and began to speak Serbian. Afterwards she continued to speak Yiddish and Serbian and completely "forgot" Bulgarian. Immediately following the insult she could not speak and only made gestures. A month later she could repeat a few words. Spontaneous speech did not return until after the second month, when she could produce sentences in Yiddish or Bulgarian. She could still understand Serbian, but could not speak it. Her family was stunned. She herself wondered with amazement why it was that she could no longer speak Serbian, the language she had used every day over the past 25 years (Dimitrijevic, 1940/1983).

CHAPTER THIRTEEN

Second-language recovery in aphasics

Almost one third of bilingual aphasics exhibit a better recovery of their second language. In the first half of the 20th century, Swiss neurologist M. Minkowski investigated the reasons why many polyglot aphasics did not recover their mother tongue, or the language that was most familiar to them. Minkowski identified a series of factors determining a better recovery of the second language. (1) The visual factor, depending on the frequency with which the patient reads and writes in that language. (2) The affective factor, influencing the recovery on the basis of e.g. the number of positive experiences related to the use of that language. (3) The environmental factor, namely the language spoken in the hospital setting. (4) The use of a language in order to deal with specific topics, which makes it highly automatized for some topics only. (5) Conscious strategies applied during the acquisition process of a language. (6) Linguistic factors, such as the degree of linguistic proximity of the two languages, and organic factors, e.g. the age of the patient and the type and extent of the lesion.

In almost one third of the multilingual aphasics' cases reported in the literature there is no recovery of the mother tongue, but rather of the second language. Out of 75 cases of nonparallel recovery, 35 revealed a recovery of the second or third language. As the mother tongue is acquired first and, generally, is also the most familiar, the recovery of the second language in polyglot aphasics contradicts both "Ribot's law" (recovery of the old as against the new) and "Pitres' law" (recovery of the most familiar language).

In the first half of the 20th century, Swiss neurologist Mieczyslaw Minkowski described numerous cases of polyglot aphasics and attempted to find an explanation for the recovery of the second (or other) language rather than that of the mother tongue. The first clinical case he described in 1927 was that of a 22-year-old mechanic who had suffered a car accident (Minkowski, 1927/1983a). He suffered a severe cranial trauma, especially affecting the left cerebral hemisphere. His mother tongue was Swiss-German. As a child he had attended elementary school, where he had learnt to write and read in standard German ("Hochdeutsch"). Afterwards, he had continued to read a great deal: history, novels, and also the German classics (Goethe, Schiller, Keller). Before his accident, the patient had been boarding with a German family, where he conversed in standard German. For business reasons, he had also learnt French and Italian, which he could speak, read, and write.

For a few days after the accident, the patient was drowsy, disoriented, and incapable of understanding or speaking any language; furthermore, he had suffered a right-sided hemiparesis, which progressively disappeared. After a week, the patient began first to understand and then to speak standard German, although with frequent grammatical and pronunciation errors (phonemic paraphasias). Surprisingly, he could no longer speak Swiss-German. When conversing with his family, who addressed him in this language, he replied in standard German only. When asked, the patient answered that he visualized the written form when speaking and that he was helped in his verbalizations by, so to speak, "reading off" this written visualization. As he had learnt to read in standard German only, he could visualize words in that language only. In the course of the following months he only spoke standard German. The patient rapidly recovered the capacity to understand Swiss-German, but— strangely enough—a year after the accident he still could not speak it. If he was forced to speak it, e.g. during a language test, he had word-finding difficulties, he showed mixing phenomena between Swiss-German and standard German, and he had a tendency to switch back to standard German, then continuing to use the latter. With regard to French and Italian, immediately after the accident he could neither speak nor understand them. These disturbances regressed slowly, and the patient recovered the capacity to understand and translate common expressions in both directions for both languages.

In 1928 Minkowski described a second case of an aphasic polyglot showing a significantly better recovery of the second language (Minkowski, 1928/1983b). The patient was a Swiss-German from the canton of Glarus. At the age of 44, he suffered a stroke that left him with a right hemiplegia and aphasia. Minkowski maintained that the lesion had destroyed sections of the left internal capsule, partly affecting the basal ganglia (cf. Fig. 13.1). The patient's mother tongue was Swiss-German, which he had spoken almost exclusively until his adolescence. At primary

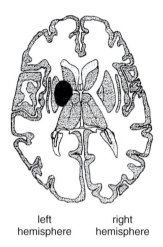

left   right
hemisphere   hemisphere

FIG. 13.1. Site of the lesion in the patient from the canton of Glarus.

school he had learnt to speak, write, and read standard German, even though he used it only at school. At the age of 19 he had moved to France, where he had lived for 6 years working as a cook. There he had learnt to understand and speak French fluently. At the age of 25, after marrying a young Swiss woman he had known since he was a child, he had returned to Switzerland. From that time on, he only spoke Swiss-German. He continued to read in French, because he had subscribed to the *Tribune de Genève*.

At the time of hospitalization, the patient had lost the capacity to speak and understand any language. The following day, he regained comprehension of all languages. Three days after his stroke, he started speaking French again. He started by stammering a few words and later produced short sentences. As his wife did not understand French, his children, who had learnt French at school, acted as interpreters for their parents. The patient spoke only French for three weeks. Afterwards, he began to speak some German. Six months after the insult, the patient spoke relatively fluent French, with a few residual disturbances of a mild Broca's aphasia. His standard German was slightly worse than his French. On the other hand, his mother tongue, Swiss-German, was almost nonexistent; the patient could only stammer fragments of discourse with great difficulty. After a month, during Christmas time, the patient—much to his surprise—started speaking Swiss-German fluently and, at the same time, he had difficulties in French (anomias and grammatical errors).

FACTORS ACCOUNTING FOR LANGUAGE RECOVERY

The aforementioned clinical cases led Minkowski to suggest a series of factors involved in language recovery of polyglot aphasics. He supported Pitres' theories on polyglot aphasia and thus maintained that the linguistic deficits and the recovery patterns of bilingual aphasics could be explained on the basis of physio-pathological modalities, rather than anatomical modalities. In the wake of Pitres, Minkowski held the general assumption that it was not necessary to assume the existence of separate centers responsible for each language known by a subject. With respect to this point, he stated: "But if we assume no spatially separate centers or areas in the cortex for the different languages, but instead assume that within the same area, the same elements are active, though in different combinations and interacting with a differential linguistic constellation, it is easy to explain the phenomena occurring in polyglot aphasia in terms of the interaction of such a large set of factors" (Minkowski, 1927/1983a, p. 229). Therefore, in Minkowski's opinion, the linguistic deficits and the language recovery patterns peculiar to polyglot aphasics were to be explained mainly by functional factors (physiological) which describe e.g. diaschisis, the imbalance between activation and inhibition of the two languages, the greater difficulty in switching from language to language, and the eventual pathological fixation on one language only (Paradis, 1996).

Therefore, a cerebral lesion alters the usual balance—which depends on functional relationships—between the languages known by the patient; the recovery of one language rather than another may depend on the presence of some critical factors influencing functional relationships between languages. Minkowski's main contribution to the study of cerebral organization in bilinguals was the proposal and description of a series of critical factors that may lead to differential recovery in polyglot aphasics (Minkowski, 1963).

THE DEGREE OF FAMILIARITY OF A LANGUAGE

Minkowski maintained that the most important factor influencing language recovery in bilingual aphasics was the frequency of use of the language recovered earlier. The more frequent the use of a language, the stronger the functional connections between the neural structures subserving it. Generally, the language that was most frequently used was the mother tongue; however, although this factor had been considered crucial for language recovery, Minkowski focused on polyglot aphasics who did not recover either the mother tongue or the most familiar language.

THE VISUAL FACTOR

Language is represented in the brain through motor, kinesthetic, acoustic, and visual components that are closely linked and reciprocally supportive. Minkowski claimed that the influence exerted by each single component depended on the individual's psychological organization or on the environment he/she had grown up or lived in. For example, there are subjects who organize their thoughts mainly by visual modalities, others by acoustic modalities, others still by kinesthetic modalities (Kosslyn, 1983; Paivio, 1986). Generally, the acoustic modality prevails in inner and verbal speech, but individuals possess all modalities. It has been noted that in individuals with a higher degree of education, inner visualization (mental imagining) of words or sentences is activated, especially with regard to classical languages such as Latin and Greek, which are acquired through writing. In Minkowski's opinion, this factor accounted for the recovery of foreign languages when they had frequently been used for reading. He presupposed that this factor had been crucial for the recovery of standard German in the case of the young mechanic, as prior to insult he had read a great deal in that language.

In 1941 Israeli neurologist L. Halpern stressed the role of the various orthographic systems in the recovery of a language in a polyglot aphasic. Halpern presupposed that cognitive systems responsible for reading in a European language were different from those responsible for reading in Hebrew or Arabic. Vowels are perceived acoustically in spoken Hebrew, but there are no letters corresponding to vowels in written Hebrew. This means that the process of reading in Hebrew is different from that of the European languages. For example, the word "RT" in Hebrew written without vowels could be read as rotir, rater, roter, etc. Therefore, reading in Hebrew depends on the comprehension of the context of discourse. For this reason, in Halpern's opinion, reading in Hebrew requires more concentration than reading in any European language; the European automatic, inattentive style of reading cannot be applied to Hebrew.

Halpern described the evolution of aphasia in a young Hebrew polyglot (M.J.), 24 years of age, who had suffered a gunshot wound to the left temporal lobe (cf. Fig. 13.2). The patient's mother tongue was German, as he had attended primary school in Germany. He also knew Yiddish, as it was spoken by his family. He had learnt literary Hebrew from the Bible during his adolescence because he had studied at a teachers' seminary for three years. At the age of 20, he had emigrated to Palestine where he had begun to use Hebrew with great frequency until his accident. When the patient awoke from the comatose state which had lasted five days, he uttered the following sentence: "*Lieber einziger Gott, danke dem Ewigen*"

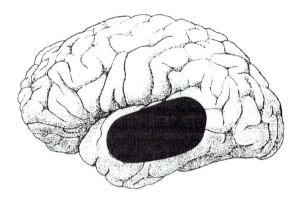

FIG. 13.2.   Site of the lesion in patient M.J.

(Dear One God, thank the Eternal Lord), which he continued to repeat for several days thereafter. After four weeks he began using both German and Hebrew; however, his expression in Hebrew was better than in German. After eight months, the differential recovery of the two languages was even more evident. In Halpern's opinion, the patient had recovered his second language better than his mother tongue because it was the most used in that environment, but also because reading systems in Hebrew were largely linked to conscious cognitive processes, which generally are less affected by aphasia than automatic cognitive processes (Halpern, 1941/1983).

Paradis, Hagiwara, and Hildebrandt (1985) systematically studied the effects of brain lesions on phonetic orthography (Kana) and ideographic orthography (Kanji) in Japanese aphasics. These patients showed interesting dissociations in their capacity to use the two orthographic systems. Following a brain lesion some patients could still read Kanji signs but not Kana signs and, conversely, other patients were no longer capable of reading ideographic signs, but could still read phonetic signs.

PSYCHOLOGICAL AND EMOTIONAL FACTORS

Minkowski stressed the importance of psychological and affective factors in language recovery of polyglot aphasics. He defined himself as a psycho-analytically oriented neurologist, and explained the clinical case of the patient from the canton of Glarus by affective factors (Minkowski, 1928/1983b). Minkowski had drawn this conclusion after he had asked the patient if he was fond of France and French. The patient, being emotionally involved, had told him that he had spent the happiest years of his life in France; he added he had had the first and most intense love affair of his life with a French woman he had left before returning to Switzerland. He had repeatedly tried to convince his wife to move to France. On the basis of this data, Minkowski proposed that the recovery of French was due to the fact that this language was mostly related to the instinctive and psychosexual sphere, unlike the other languages. It should be noted that the patient started to recover Swiss-German during Christmas time, when he spent some time with his family.

Another neurologist, E. Krapf, further analyzed the role played by affective factors in the recovery of one language. In Krapf's opinion, aphasic patients—like schizophrenic patients—after a psychotic crisis choose to use one language as a defense mechanism activated by a part of their psyche (Super-ego). The unconscious choice of one language only would thus correspond to a response to the fear unleashed by a brain lesion or an acute psychological crisis. Both types of patients would thus use the language that gives them a sense of security (Krapf, 1955, 1957/1983).

THE LANGUAGE SPOKEN TO THE PATIENT IN THE HOSPITAL

Bychowsky was the first to focus on the role of the language spoken in hospital settings in language recovery of aphasic polyglots. In 1919 he described the clinical case of a young soldier (K.K.) who had suffered a gunshot wound to the inferior portions of the left frontal and parietal lobe (cf. Fig. 13.3) with consequent aphasia (Bychowsky, 1919/1983). His mother tongue was Polish, his second language German, which he had acquired in Germany, where he had worked for some time. At the age of 24, he was conscripted into the Czarist army and learnt to read, write, and speak Russian. After the insult he was admitted to a hospital where Russian was spoken; he remained in a coma for three weeks. When he awoke he could

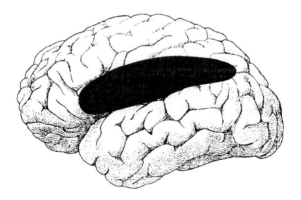

FIG. 13.3. Site of the lesion in patient K.K.

neither understand nor speak any language. A nurse taught him to speak and write Russian again. After more than two years K.K. spoke and wrote in Russian relatively well, but he could not speak Polish, even though his comprehension of the language was not impaired. When ordered to speak Polish, he could only utter a few words and switched to Russian, complaining that he could not speak Polish and that he had forgotten his native language. With respect to German he could no longer understand simple words such as *"Brot"* (bread); he could not speak it; he said he had forgotten everything.

LANGUAGES USED IN SPECIFIC CIRCUMSTANCES

In 1923 Austrian neurologist A. Bàlint described the clinical case of a polyglot patient (G.N.), 60 years of age, who had suffered a traumatic left hemisphere lesion with consequent aphasia (Bàlint, 1923/1983). The patient was born in Greece. During his adolescence he became first a servant and later the private secretary of a Russian ambassador. When the diplomat retired and went to Russia, the patient followed him and lived in Russia until the age of 20. In his position of private secretary, the patient learnt Russian and French, but above all he learnt about politics. When the diplomat died, the patient emigrated to Vienna, where he lived in extreme poverty. He exclusively concentrated on political propaganda activities. He wrote a few pamphlets in German in which he took a stance for Germany against French foreign policy. His pamphlets were written in a grammatically and stylistically correct German, but the contents were extremely naïve from a political point of view. During his stay in Vienna the patient paid visits to numerous Austrian politicians to whom he expounded his political ideas. Usually he was given a small sum of money on which he lived. He behaved like a gentleman and spent many hours a day giving speeches on international policy issues.

Immediately after the insult, G.N. began speaking his mother tongue, Greek, and German, relatively well. His spontaneous speech was fluent and presented typical errors of Wernicke's aphasia and mixing phenomena. He had completely lost the capacity to speak and understand Russian and French. To the doctor's amazement, his linguistic deficits largely disappeared when he was asked questions of international policy issues. He answered these questions in German, because he had never used Greek to discuss these matters. He showed a considerable improvement in his verbal expression marked by a reduction in phonemic and verbal paraphasias as against spontaneous speech. The improvement in German—only with regard to international policy issues—was explained by the presence of specific automatic expressions related to international policy. The patient was accustomed to repeating excerpts from his speeches by heart so as to be always ready to recite them before some important politician. The policy issues were a mission for him. He had invested a great deal in them in affective terms. For this reason also, his expression with respect to this issue was less impaired.

LANGUAGES LEARNT AT UNIVERSITY

Neurologist K. Kainz focused on the fact that the language better recovered is often a language whose use was not automatic, but rather depended on conscious efforts. In Kainz's opinion, aphasia mainly affects the most automatic language, namely the language that is used unconsciously (Kainz, 1960/1983; cf. Smirnov & Factorovich, 1949/1983). Often bilingual subjects acquire a second language in order to enroll at university, and mainly use it for scientific or business reasons. In this case, aphasics recover their second language better because it is less automatized than their mother tongue (cf. Gomez-Tortosa, Martin, Gaviria, Charbel, & Ausman, 1995; Paradis 1995b).

A few years ago I was asked for a consultation on the case of a colleague from Sofia (N.K.J.) who had a stroke at the age of 68. The stroke had caused an ischemic lesion to the left temporo-parietal region (cf. Fig. 13.4) with consequent right-sided paralysis and nonfluent aphasia. Until the age of 13 she spoke only Bulgarian, even though she understood Turkish, which was spoken by her parents. At high school she began to study German, Russian, and French. She moved to Vienna to study medicine at the university, and thus improved her German and her French. Prior to insult Bulgarian and German were the languages she spoke, read, and wrote best. A few days after the insult N.K.J. could still understand German and

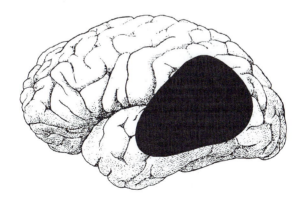

FIG. 13.4.   Site of the lesion in patient N.K.J.

Bulgarian, but—much to the patient's and her family's surprise—she could not speak Bulgarian, which was her native language, whereas she could still speak German. After more than three years, she has still not recovered Russian or French; her comprehension in Bulgarian is relatively good, but she only speaks and reads in German.

Recent studies on the various types of memory involved in the acquisition of the mother tongue as opposed to languages acquired through conscious strategies (cf. Chapter 14) have contributed to a better understanding of the type of dissociation exhibited by this Bulgarian patient and numerous other polyglot aphasics.

LINGUISTIC FACTORS

In his contributions to the study on polyglot aphasia, Minkowski stressed that there are peculiar antagonistic relationships between two languages that are structurally closely related, or between a dialect and the related standard language, and in this case these relationships are stronger than those between more distant pairs of languages. They imply mutual inhibition and are similar to those that inhibit L2 when L1 is used. Therefore, it seems that the brain paradoxically concentrates more resources in supporting, and keeping distinct, two structurally close languages (i.e. Venetian and Italian, Italian and Spanish) than two distant languages (i.e. Italian and English, French and Russian). Similarly, in a polyglot aphasic, only one language from the two structurally close languages is unaffected, whereas a very distinct language might be preserved. For example, if a polyglot knowing Spanish, French, and Chinese becomes aphasic, he might recover only one of the Romance languages (Spanish or French) and, paradoxically, Chinese. In this case there is a parallel recovery of the more distant languages at the expense of one of the two close languages.

ORGANIC FACTORS

Minkowski also investigated the effect caused by organic factors (i.e. the age of the patient, the type and extent of the lesion, etc.) on the recovery of one language in polyglot aphasics. He maintained that a diffuse lesion to the left hemisphere would diminish the possibility of supporting languages functionally. Therefore, the wider the extent of the lesion, the greater the amount of resources concentrating on one language to the disadvantage of others. In the case of a sudden emergence of a lesion (e.g. a stroke as opposed to a cerebral tumor) and/or the patient's advanced age, the linguistic deficit will be more severe.

CHAPTER FOURTEEN

Paradoxical recovery of a language

Medical literature describes many cases of bilingual aphasia with para- doxical recovery of a language that the patient had never used for commu- nicative reasons, such as Latin or classical Greek. Recently, Aglioti and Fabbro have studied the paradoxical recovery of the second language in a patient with a lesion to the basal ganglia of the left hemisphere. Surpris- ingly, prior to insult the patient had thought she could not speak the lan- guage as competently as she did after insult. Recent studies on memory contribute to the understanding of some aspects of paradoxical recovery of languages. For example, because the mother tongue is acquired uncon- sciously and at an informal level, it is mainly stored in implicit memory sys- tems, whereas the languages learnt through rules and used not automatically are mainly stored in explicit memory systems. Because aphasia mainly affects implicit memory systems, it is not uncommon to find patients who paradoxically tend to speak a language that they had never used before for communicative purposes more easily.

RECOVERY OF A DEAD LANGUAGE

A few cases of aphasic patients with "paradoxical" recovery of one of the languages they knew premorbidly have been described. Their peculiarity is that these patients had either never spoken or never used this language for communicative purposes before—the so-called "dead" languages such as classical Greek, Latin, and Hebrew. Indeed, before the constitution of the Israeli State, Hebrew was considered a dead language used only dur- ing religious ceremonies or in Hebrew schools to study the Bible (Carrez, 1983).

Recovery of languages used in liturgy

One of the first cases of paradoxical recovery of a dead language was described by Grasset in 1884. The patient, aged 60, knew only French; she was admitted to hospital because she could no longer speak and exhibited a right painful hemisyndrome as a consequence of a stroke that had affected her left cerebral hemisphere. Her verbal expression in French was non-existent, whereas comprehension was not impaired. Surprisingly, after a few days the patient started speaking Latin. She had never studied it, but she was a fervent Catholic and had always attended religious ceremonies conducted in Latin. After the insult the patient uttered only single words in Latin which recalled prayers, e.g. *fundamenta* or *Pater nisi Dominus*. She seemed unaware of the fact that she was not understood. In addition, she could still read prayers in Latin (Grasset, 1884/1983).

A second case of recovery of a language used during religious functions was described by Schwalbe in 1920. The patient was a pious Israeli who knew only German. When he was young, he had studied Hebrew which, however, he had used only during religious ceremonies. He had never used it for communicative purposes. At the age of 70, he suffered a stroke to the left hemisphere with consequent aphasia and right-sided paralysis. For many weeks after the insult the patient expressed himself mainly using Hebrew words that were often incoherent. Subsequently he slowly recovered his mother tongue (Schwalbe, 1920/1983).

A similar case was described by Durieu in 1969. At the age of 59, a Catholic priest of French mother tongue who knew Latin, classical Greek, and basic Biblical Hebrew suffered a stroke affecting the left hemisphere with consequent aphasia and right-sided paralysis. Three years after the insult the patient still exhibited severe agrammatism in French. His spontaneous speech was very limited and generally formed by incomplete sentences containing only the subject and the verb. However, each day the patient served Mass without difficulty. When one day Durieu attended it, he was very surprised to find that the patient's speech in Latin was quite fluent and free from errors (cf. Kraetschmer, 1982).

Recovery of a "classical" language

In 1902 Hinshelwood described the case of a polyglot patient who initially recovered the capacity to read dead languages and only later recovered his mother tongue. The patient was of English mother tongue and knew French, Latin, and classical Greek very well. At the age of 34 he suffered global aphasia following an infectious disease that had also affected the brain. He rapidly recovered verbal expression and comprehension of the languages he knew, but he still exhibited considerable reading difficulties.

He could read aloud only the alphabet letters and at most a few words in English, whereas paradoxically he could read classical Greek slowly, but without errors, and better than French and English. The patient continued to exhibit these symptoms for some months. Afterwards, he started reading in English and French fluently (Hinshelwood, 1902/1983).

A similar case was reported by Pötzl in 1925. The patient was a professor who knew many modern languages (German, French, Italian, and English) and had long studied Latin and classical Greek. Following a stroke he became aphasic. During the recovery phase he was able to express himself only in Latin and classical Greek, and he seemed to have lost the capacity to speak modern languages. Pötzl suggested that this phenomenon was due to the fact that only these two languages had been acquired through reading and they were thus organized in the patient's brain according to peculiar modalities (cf. Chapter 13, pp. 120–121). Apparently, aphasia had inhibited all modern languages acquired by the patient through acoustic-verbal strategies, but had spared the languages learnt by writing modalities (Pötzl, 1925).

In 1937, Gelb described the clinical case of an officer who became aphasic owing to a gunshot wound suffered during World War I. The lesion had affected the left frontal lobe and the patient had undergone a neurosurgical operation in order to treat the internal wound. Afterwards, the patient was no longer able to speak, but could still silently read and understand philosophy books. Before the war the officer had been a professor of classical languages, and after the operation he noticed that not only could he still read, but he could still express himself correctly in Latin. He decided he would rehabilitate himself by mentally constructing sentences he wanted to utter in Latin and then mentally translating them into German by the grammar-translation method. The patient recovered his mother tongue using a second dead language as a mediating system. On this basis, Gelb concluded that aphasic syndromes tend to affect the most automatized (i.e. unconsciously used) languages more severely, whereas the foreign languages or dead languages are best preserved because they require conscious efforts and reflection (Gelb, 1937/1983).

PARADOXICAL RECOVERY OF THE SECOND LANGUAGE

Recently, in collaboration with S. Aglioti of the University of Verona, I studied a peculiar case of recovery of the second language (Aglioti & Fabbro, 1993; Aglioti, Beltramello, Girardi, & Fabbro, 1996). The peculiarity of this clinical case is that the patient did not believe she could speak her second language as well as after the insult. The patient (E.M.), right-handed, aged 70, had the Veronese dialect—a variant of Venetan—as her mother tongue. Since infancy she had always spoken the Veronese dialect within her family, with her husband, children, and relatives. As a child she had attended elementary school for three years only, where she learnt to read and write Italian. All her life long, besides doing housework, she cultivated and sold vegetables. Even during this activity she used Veronese exclusively. Before the insult her husband made sure that she spoke Italian at least two or three times a year. On these occasions, the patient said only a few words in Italian and switched back to her dialect. In November 1990 E.M. suffered an ischemic infarction to the left hemisphere with consequent aphasia and a right sensory-motor hemisyndrome. She was admitted to hospital and she remained completely mute for two weeks. Magnetic resonance imaging revealed a lesion localized in some left subcortical structures only (mainly the caudate nucleus and the putamen) (cf. Fig. 14.1).

When she did start speaking, much to her own and her family's amazement, she expressed herself in Italian instead of the Veronese dialect, even though in the hospital ward the staff mainly spoke Venetan. When she was discharged from hospital a month after the insult, the patient's conditions had improved: she no longer exhibited clear signs of paralysis, and she understood both her dialect and Italian, but only expressed herself in Italian. When asked by the patient, doctors replied that this condition was temporary. E.M. had to use a new language to communicate with her family, which sounded rather artificial. E.M. expressed herself in Italian, whereas adults replied in Veronese dialect and her younger nephews in Italian. On these latter occasions, E.M. noticed that she understood Italian better than the Veronese dialect. She had communication difficulties with her acquaintances and friends who addressed her in the Veronese dialect, whereas she could only reply in Italian. These aphasic disorders were not understood by the patient's friends, who thought she was snobbish by speaking Italian instead of their dialect, as she had always done previously.

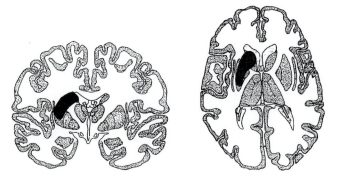

FIG. 14.1.   Extent of the subcortical lesion in patient E.M.

A year later, as the situation had not improved, E.M. decided to apply to the speech therapy service of the University of Verona to rehabilitate Veronese, a language that to her was socially more important than Italian. At this juncture, Aglioti and I were asked to analyze and study this para-doxical situation. Together with speech and language therapist Flavia Girardi we explained to the patient that rehabilitation required a thorough analysis of her linguistic capacities to understand the situation better and draw useful conclusions for the therapy. The patient and her family accepted this stage of the program, which lasted over six months and during which her collaboration was excellent.

Even following the lesion E.M.'s intelligence was normal. She underwent the Italian version of the Aachener Aphasie Test (cf. Chapter 6) as well as a Venetan version prepared by us. In both languages the patient exhibited Broca's aphasia. This test revealed that E.M.'s greatest difficulties were in her mother tongue (Veronese dialect) as opposed to her second language (Italian). The patient could name a significantly larger number of objects in Italian as against Veronese (L1, 12/24; L2, 29/30). With regard to oral description of events, results were also significantly better in Italian as against Veronese (L1, 3/30; L2, 28/30). Comprehension was well preserved in both languages. Another peculiar feature of the patient's language was her accent. Unlike most Venetans, when speaking Italian E.M. did not have a Venetan accent. On the contrary, her verbal output was characterized by a foreign accent. This phenomenon is known as the "foreign accent syn-drome" and is generally associated with a lesion to the basal ganglia.

The patient's spontaneous speech was also studied. During some sessions we explicitly asked E.M. to express herself in Veronese only, during other sessions we invited her to speak only Italian. We recorded some conversa-tions from which we obtained almost 20 minutes of spontaneous speech in L1 and 20 minutes in L2. These language samples were analyzed by counting the words and the sentences that were correctly pronounced in L1 and L2, as well as the sentences containing mixed elements (cf. spontaneous speech analysis in bilingual aphasics, Chapter 6). The results obtained confirmed that the patient's verbal production was better in Italian than in Veronese. During the sessions where only Italian was allowed, she produced 90% of words and 70% of sentences in this language; only 28% of sentences contained mixed elements (generally sentences in Italian with elements of Veronese dialect). During the sessions where only Veronese was allowed, she produced only 23% of sentences in that language, and 35% of sentences with mixed elements (sentences in Italian with a few words in Veronese dialect). Generally, in these sessions, she uttered 77% of the sentences in Italian. In addition, during the spontaneous speech sessions, when the patient expressed herself in Veronese, she constantly switched back to Italian, and she would have continued to speak Italian had she not been reminded to speak Veronese several times. During the sessions where Italian was allowed, the patient never spontaneously switched to Veronese. Stress is to be laid on the fact that in Venetan individuals with the same education as E.M. the reverse generally applies: when they are required to speak Venetan, their production is fluent. In contrast, when they are required to speak Italian, they exhibit difficulties and interferences with Venetan. In naming and spontaneous speech tasks the errors made by the patient were mainly phonemic and semantic paraphasias.

Her translation abilities from Italian into Veronese (L2→L1) and vice versa (L1→L2) were assessed by means of word and sentence translation tasks. Seventy-five words with different roots in Italian and Veronese [i.e. "sedia"-"*carega*" (chair)] and 20 sentences with lexical and syntactic differences in the two languages were presented to the patient who paradoxically could translate words (69.3%) and sentences (95%) better from Veronese into Italian (L1→L2) than vice versa (L2→L1; 41.3% words and 0.05% sentences). Generally, it is easier to translate into one's mother tongue rather than into a foreign language (L2 or L3). As a matter of fact, in the same word and sentence translation tasks E.M.'s husband, who acted as a control subject, showed better results when translating from Italian into Venetan.

THE ROLE OF MEMORY IN PARADOXICAL LANGUAGE RECOVERY

Paradoxical recovery of a language is an extreme case of aphasia. Generally, a language other than the mother tongue is recovered. This peculiar type of recovery was explained by referring to the role of writing suggested by Pötzl in 1925, and subsequently re-proposed by Minkowski, or to the conscious use of grammatical rules, as suggested by Gelb in 1937. However, recently an unequivocal interpretation based not only on hypotheses but also on a series of clinical and experimental data has been proposed.

Recent studies on long-term memory (Chapter 10, pp. 96–9) have provided an explanation for the reason why many patients exhibit a better recovery of the second language as opposed to the mother tongue, and hence for paradoxical recovery. The distinction between explicit and implicit memory is of crucial importance. The two memory systems are organized in distinct brain structures. Implicit memory involves subcortical structures, such as the basal ganglia and the cerebellum, and specific cortical areas; explicit memory is represented diffusely in the cerebral cortex. In a recent study, Paradis advanced the hypothesis that the mother tongue, being acquired unconsciously in informal contexts through constant repetition, is mainly stored in implicit memory systems (Paradis, 1994a). Therefore, the mother tongue seems to be mainly organized in the subcortical structures accounting for language and in limited areas of the cerebral cortex, whereas the second language and hence all other languages of a polyglot, being acquired through explicit strategies, seem to be more diffusely represented in the cerebral cortex. A case in point for languages being acquired and stored in explicit memory systems is that of "dead" languages. They are generally learnt at school, through reading, and their use requires a conscious knowledge of their grammar. However, many people use conscious learning strategies based on explicit rules to learn modern languages, too. As it has been claimed that aphasic syndromes mainly affect the implicit memory systems of language, it is not surprising that some bilingual or polyglot aphasics show a better recovery of the languages they spoke least well premorbidly, or that they recover those languages they had mainly learnt and used through explicit strategies. In the case of E.M. the lesion affected the basal ganglia of the left hemisphere, and the language least well known was recovered. Aglioti and I interpreted these results as a sign of a greater impairment of the implicit memory systems subserving the mother tongue and organized in deep cerebral structures. E.M. started speaking Italian (L2), because the cerebral lesion did not affect the cortex, and thus spared the second language that is organized in the explicit memory systems (mainly in cortical structures).

Beside this interpretation other hypotheses—not necessarily opposed to it—have been advanced. Numerous neurophysiological studies stress the importance of the basal ganglia for the selection of series of behavior patterns (Hikosaka, 1991). Language may be considered as a series of behavior patterns, too. Therefore, the basal ganglia of the left hemisphere may be mainly involved in the selection and activation of the mother tongue. The degree of involvement of these structures in the production of a less automatized language, such as the second language or a dead language, may be different from the degree of involvement in the production of the mother tongue. In fact, a group of Canadian researchers under the coordination of Denise Klein recently carried out a PET study on bilingual subjects exhibiting a greater involvement of the left putamen in tasks of verbal expression and translation into the second language (Klein, Milner, Zatorre, Evans, & Meyer, 1994; Klein, Zatorre, Milner, Meyer, & Evans, 1995).

CHAPTER FIFTEEN

Selective aphasia

Following aphasia bilinguals may exhibit language disorders selectively affecting one language. In the neurological literature Paradis has identified 37 cases of aphasic bilinguals presenting selective loss of one language only. This chapter gives a detailed description of one of the most recent cases of selective aphasia. This syndrome suggests that in the brain of bilinguals the two languages are isolated. There has been much debate on the type of isolation. Many authors have suggested an anatomical separation of the two languages. However, most authors (in the past as well as more recently) claim that the separation between the two languages is only functional, because the two languages are two distinct functional systems, even though they are organized in the same cerebral areas.

A CASE OF SELECTIVE CROSSED APHASIA

In 1989 Paradis and Goldblum described the clinical case of a polyglot patient (A.M.) who, following a neurosurgical operation, presented selective aphasia in one of the languages he knew for a certain period of time (Paradis & Goldblum, 1989). At the age of 24, A.M. started complaining of several episodes of jacksonian motor epilepsy of the left arm. Following a loss of consciousness a CT scan was performed, revealing a parasitic cyst the size of a walnut in the central prerolandic area of the right hemisphere (cf. Fig. 15.1). In April 1980, the cyst was neurosurgically removed.

The patient was right-handed and had no familial left-handedness. He was of Gujarati mother tongue, an Indo-European language spoken in a

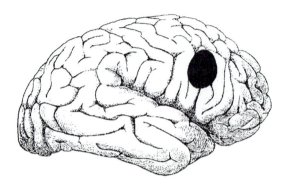

FIG. 15.1.   Site of the lesion in patient A.M.

central-western region of India, which he used mainly within his family. However, he was born and had lived in Madagascar and thus also spoke Malagasy, the country's official language. At the age of 6, he learnt French at school and continued to use it in his work as an accountant in an export firm.

Two weeks after the operation, in May 1980, the patient was administered a language test in French, which gave normal results. However, his family reported that since the operation the patient was having difficulties in Gujarati, so A.M. was administered the BAT (cf. Chapter 6) in this language, too. The test revealed deficits in spontaneous speech (very laborious, with articulatory disorders typical of Broca's aphasia), in naming (he named 2 objects out of 10), and in comprehension. He gave answers containing mixed expressions in French to questions in Gujarati, such as *enfin!*, *justement*, *par example*. The same language test in Malagasy did not reveal any deficit.

After a year and a half (November 1982), from a neuropsychological point of view the patient only exhibited a lack of dexterity in some fingers of his left hand. In the four months following the operation, he had gradually recovered Gujarati, but at the same time his family had noticed an increased difficulty in using Malagasy. Two years after the operation, he was again administered the BAT in both languages. No deficit was found with regard to Gujarati, whereas in Malagasy A.M. exhibited reduced verbal fluency and numerous errors in syntactic comprehension. Finally, four years after the operation (June 1984), the patient was tested for the last time. No disorder was detected with regard to either language, which meant he had completely recovered all linguistic functions.

POSSIBLE EXPLANATIONS OF SELECTIVE APHASIA

Paradis and Goldblum proposed a series of hypotheses for the clinical case they described and more generally on the neurological bases of selective aphasia. First of all, the selective aphasia case they reported contradicted the hypotheses put forward by neurologists in the past, including Sigmund Freud, who in 1891 claimed that a disorder in the mother tongue provoked by an organic lesion will also affect a language that has been acquired later (Freud, 1891). Penfield and Roberts suggested in their well-known book on the cerebral mechanisms of language that a lesion to the brain of a bilingual inevitably affected all languages (Penfield & Roberts, 1976). Penfield claimed that many bilingual patients he had visited had previously been considered aphasic in one language only. On the other hand, in all cases he had studied—after a thorough examination—he had detected deficits in both languages. The clinical case of A.M.—as well as others already mentioned—proved that selective aphasia is a real clinical situation, quite frequent, and that it needs a specific explanation.

A rather simple interpretation was first put forward by Scoresby-Jackson in 1867 (cf. Chapter 12) and implies that each language has a separate neuroanatomical localization. A lesion to a cortical area may thus provoke aphasia in one language but spare the other language, which is localized in a distinct cerebral area (cf. Gomez-Tortosa et al., 1995). Almost all neurologists in the past firmly opposed this rather simplistic hypothesis. Penfield and Roberts effectively put forward their own theory, and stated that there is no evidence in favor of Scoresby-Jackson's hypothesis. However, more recently, during experiments of cortico-electrical stimulation, Ojemann and Whitaker (1978) detected differences in the localization of the various languages known by a subject. The stimulation of some portions of the cerebral cortex sometimes inhibited only L1, whereas at other times the reverse applied (cf. Chapter 23). In addition, fMRI studies have shown a different cerebral representation of L1 and L2 in the Broca's area of fluent bilinguals who had learnt the second language after the age of 10 (Kim et al., 1997; see Chapter 10, p. 101).

Because the selective loss of one language is also observable in some psychiatric diseases, such as hysteria, the hypothesis that a psychiatric disease may cause selective aphasia is not to be ruled out. Stress is to be laid on the fact that hysteria generally affects subjects without lesions to the nervous system. In addition, in the clinical case of A.M., this hypothesis cannot effectively explain the partial loss of the mother tongue (Gujarati) with its subsequent recovery and concurrent regression of the second language (Malagasy).

Paradis and Goldblum claim that the most reliable interpretation of selective aphasia is not neuroanatomical, but neurofunctional (Paradis & Goldblum, 1989; Paradis, 1995b). The language impaired is not lost, but selectively inhibited by physiological phenomena caused by the lesion affecting the prerolandic area of the right hemisphere. The neurological lesion provoked a general increase in the activation threshold of the mother tongue. This inhibitory effect subsequently affected the patient's second language, Malagasy, and completely disappeared before the administration of the last language test in 1984 (Green, 1986; cf. Chapter 25). Paradis and Goldblum suggest that the languages known by a bilingual or a polyglot are separate mainly at functional level, not at anatomical level. Each language is thus a separate and independent neurofunctional system.

CHAPTER SIXTEEN

Differential aphasia

This chapter describes a few cases of bilingual patients exhibiting differential aphasia in their two languages (for example, Wernicke's aphasia affecting L1, and Broca's aphasia affecting L2). Some researchers claim that cases of differential aphasia suggest that the elements of the mother tongue and the elements of the second language are located separately in distinct cortical areas. This type of aphasia could corroborate once and for all the hypothesis that the two languages have separate neuroanatomical localizations. Other neurolinguists are reluctant to accept this conclusion, as they doubt that differential aphasia really exists and suggest that a lesion might imply different linguistic disorders according to the language affected.

The presence of two different types of aphasia in a bilingual patient, i.e. Wernicke's aphasia affecting L1 and Broca's aphasia affecting L2, is very convincing evidence of a partially separate cerebral representation of the two languages. This type of aphasia, known as differential aphasia, was first reported by Albert and Obler in 1975. They described the case of a young patient, of Hungarian mother tongue, who also knew French and English because she had lived for a long time in France, England, and the United States. At the age of 16 she had moved to Israel, where she had learnt Hebrew. At the age of 35 she underwent a neurosurgical operation to remove a tumor in the posterior section of her left temporal lobe. Ten days after the operation, the patient exhibited Broca's aphasia in Hebrew and Wernicke's aphasia in English, which means that she understood but hardly spoke Hebrew, whereas she did not understand English but spoke it fluently.

139

In her two other languages, Hungarian and French, deficits were mild. Albert and Obler interpreted this data as a result of a separate cerebral localization of English and Hebrew (Albert & Obler, 1978).

A few years later, in 1979, Israeli neuropsychologists R. Silverberg and H. Gordon gave a more detailed description of two other cases of differential aphasia (Silverberg & Gordon, 1979). The first patient (case 1) was a young nurse, aged 26, who was born and had lived in Chile until the age of 23, where she had acquired Spanish as her mother tongue; she had also learnt to read and write in English at school, but could not speak it. When she moved to Israel, she attended intensive classes in Hebrew for six months, five hours a day. At home she still spoke Spanish with her sister. However, since she had started working as a nurse, during working hours she spoke and listened to Hebrew only. One day, while at home, she exhibited a sudden deterioration of Spanish. When she arrived at work, her colleagues noticed she also had difficulties with Hebrew. She was soon admitted to hospital. During her stay there she still spoke Spanish with her sister, and Hebrew with the hospital staff. A neurological examination revealed a mild right-sided paresis, whereas the EEG revealed theta activity in the parieto-temporal region of the left hemisphere (cf. Fig. 16.1).

Three days after her hospitalization she was administered a language test in Hebrew. Her spontaneous speech was fluent, with numerous phonemic and semantic paraphasias; she was still good at describing pictures, whereas naming was very poor (2 objects out of 10). Repetition of 4- to 5-word sentences was correct. The following day she was administered a language test in Spanish. Her spontaneous speech was nonfluent, with telegraphic sentences coupled with word-finding difficulties. The patient succeeded in naming only 2 objects out of 20, and in describing only 5 salient elements of

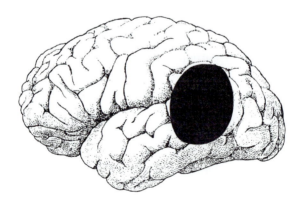

FIG. 16.1.   Site of the lesion revealed by the EEG in the patient of case 1.

a picture. In addition, she could not repeat a single word. She could understand complex orders in her two languages, such as "Put the watch on the other side of the pencil and turn over the paper", but she could not understand questions such as "Do you eat a banana before you peel it?". A month later she was retested with the same language tests in Hebrew and Spanish. Her linguistic abilities in both languages had improved considerably. Only in Spanish was her speech still characterized by stuttering and frequent pauses; no aphasic deficit was detected in Hebrew.

The second patient (case 2) described by Silverberg and Gordon was a right-handed physician who at the age of 54 suddenly exhibited language disorders. The patient was born and had lived in Russia until the age of 53. Subsequently, he had moved to Israel. Beside Russian, he had learnt German and English, which he could speak, read, and write. During his first three months in Israel he attended intensive classes in Hebrew (five hours a day, six days a week), and he learnt to express himself in very simple sentences only. At the hospital where he worked he had to ask for help to communicate with patients, and at home he still spoke Russian with his wife and friends. One day he suddenly exhibited word-finding difficulties in Russian (anomias). He was admitted to hospital where he was diagnosed an ischemic infarction in the posterior frontal area of the left hemisphere (cf. Fig. 16.2). The days after the insult he exhibited mild anomia in Russian, and global aphasia in Hebrew. He did not speak, nor did he understand Hebrew. After two months, he showed a partial recovery of both languages. In Hebrew he could understand simple sentences and speak with severe articulatory difficulties, paraphasias, and anomias. In Russian he no longer hesitated, nor resorted to circumlocutions. However, he still could not repeat sentences with more than 4–5 words. Three months after the onset of

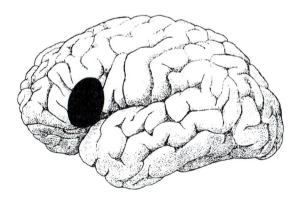

FIG. 16.2.   Site of the lesion in the patient of case 2.

the disease his Hebrew had improved considerably, but had not yet reached the level prior to insult.

Albert and Obler, like Silverberg and Gordon, claimed that the cases of differential aphasia they described suggest that elements of L1 and elements of L2 are localized in separate cortical areas. Differential aphasia would thus indicate that the languages known by a bi- or multilingual subject have separate neuroanatomical representations. However, some neurolinguists are reluctant to accept this conclusion, as they doubt the existence of this aphasic syndrome (Paradis, 1989, 1995a). They claim that a type of aphasia, i.e. Broca's aphasia, may imply different linguistic disorders depending on the languages in which it manifests itself. For example, an English-Italian bilingual patient with Broca's aphasia tends to omit free morphemes in English, a typical symptom of agrammatism, whereas in Italian the patient exhibits numerous errors in the flexion of obligatory morphemes—a typology of errors that until recently was considered to be typical of para-grammatism (Miceli, Silveri, Romani, & Caramazza, 1989; cf. Chapter 5). In this regard, in an article written in 1988, Paradis focused on the symptoms of agrammatism and paragrammatism and stated that it is important to understand how they manifest themselves in the various languages. In conclusion, a definitive interpretation of differential aphasia is not yet available. A detailed and standardized language test for the various languages of bilingual patients, such as the BAT developed by Paradis (1987a; cf. Chapter 6), will allow researchers to gather sufficient data and put forward a more reliable hypothesis on differential aphasia.

CHAPTER SEVENTEEN

Pathological switching and mixing

Two language disorders typical of bilingual aphasics are pathological switching and mixing between languages. Two different types of switching have been described: pathological fixation on one language owing to the inability to select the other language, and spontaneous switching, namely the frequent and uncontrolled switching to another language during the production of sentences. Pathological mixing in multilingual aphasics manifests itself in a variety of forms: word mixing, word root or suffix mixing, blending of syllables, use of the syntax of one language and concurrent use of the lexicon of the other language, etc. These disorders, peculiar to multilingual aphasics, drew neurolinguists' attention to the possible existence of specific neurofunctional systems (accounting for selection, activation, inhibition, and switching) in the brain of bilinguals.

Two pathological disturbances that are relatively frequent in cases of bilingual aphasia are *switching* and *mixing*. In 1929 Kauders defined them as *specific responses* of polyglot aphasics (Kauders, 1929/1983). Subjects may *switch* from language to language, alternating their verbal expression in both languages. On the other hand, subjects may *mix* linguistic elements from various languages within a single sentence. Generally, bilinguals use only one language while speaking and do not mix languages. This rule strictly applies when the interlocutor understands only one language; if bilingual subjects really intend to communicate, they will use the language that their interlocutor speaks. However, this rule no longer holds if all interlocutors speak two or more languages, in which case switching and mixing phenomena may occur.

The study of multilingual aphasics has led to the distinction between mixing and inappropriate switching phenomena. Some of these patients continue to present with inappropriate mixing, whereas others tend to produce mostly pathological switching. The latter phenomena seem to be more frequently associated with lesions to anterior structures of the frontal lobe (Fabbro, 1995b). Studying switching and pathological mixing in aphasics requires a very strict methodological approach, as recommended by Grosjean (1989, 1998). The assessment of each language should occur on two different days with two different examiners, each one knowing only one of the two languages, whereas a third bilingual examiner should assess the patient's translation abilities (see Chapter 6, p. 50).

SWITCHING DISORDERS

Pathological fixation on one language

Pathological fixation on one language, or the incapability to switch, refers to a polyglot aphasic's loss of the capacity to switch from language to language. Generally, patients' comprehension of the languages they know is preserved, but if they are addressed in the language that is nonavailable, they reply in the language whose expression is spared. This linguistic deficit was described for the first time by Czech neurologist O. Pötzl, who in 1925 reported two clinical cases of aphasic patients with this language disorder (Pötzl, 1925). The first patient was an Austrian businessman, aged 60. He had spoken only Czech until the age of 14, and later he had learnt German. He had moved to Vienna and since then used German only, both within and outside his family. During his last year of life, while paying a visit to his Czech parents, he suffered a stroke with consequent transitory aphasia. He could speak only Czech. After a few months, he suffered a second stroke, which affected the same areas of the brain. The neurological examination revealed that he had mild perception disorders accompanied by the loss of the visual capacity of the right field. Comprehension in Czech and German was spared, but he could speak only Czech. After a few months, the patient died. The autopsy revealed a destruction of cerebral tissue, mainly affecting the left supramarginal gyrus (cf. Fig. 17.1).

The second case described by Pötzl concerned a 52-year-old teacher of German mother tongue. One day, while going to work, he was hit by a car and suffered a severe cranial trauma. In the months preceding the accident he had concentrated on learning Czech, because he had become a member of a committee on school reforms where knowledge of both languages was required. At the time of hospitalization, doctors noticed that the patient mixed Czech words into the German conversation all the time. His behavior seemed involuntary, because he apologized to the doctors: "Es fehlen mir die *vyrazy*, es ist jà *nevìm*" [I am lacking the expressions, I don't know (the

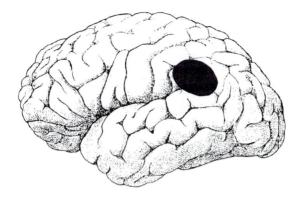

FIG. 17.1.   Site of the lesion in Pötzl's first case.

words in italics are Czech)]. On the following day the patient exhibited the typical symptoms of anomia, namely word-finding difficulties and the use of rare expressions in Czech. On the morning of the third day the patient died. The autopsy revealed a subpial hemorrhage that was localized on the surface exactly above the left supramarginal gyrus. The areas affected by the lesion in case 2 are the same as those in case 1 (cf. Fig. 17.1).

On the basis of this data, Pötzl suggested that the neural structures of the left supramarginal gyrus played a crucial role in the selection of a language in bilinguals and polyglots. In his opinion, when patients suffered a lesion to this area, their verbal behavior became "pathologically fixed" on one of the two languages known. Comprehension in the other languages remained almost unaffected, but expression was possible only in one language. However, Pötzl maintained that the reasons for a fixation on one language were not always clear, but rather accidental.

Pötzl had referred to the work of physiologist J. von Uexküll and drawn on the idea that in the brain there is a structure accounting for the selection and the switching of the "excitatory states" of the nervous system. Indeed, Uexküll had noticed that lesions in the nervous systems of animals induced the selection of a motor behavior—generally the behavior adopted immediately prior to insult—which was then constantly repeated as a sort of perseveration or fixation (Uexküll, 1956). Pötzl maintained that in humans the left parietal area was responsible for switching from language to language. This area coordinated all languages, allowing one language at a time to activate completely, whereas the nonselected languages were inhibited so as not to interfere with the activated system. In Pötzl's opinion, a lesion to this area provoked a pathological "fixation" on the language that had been spoken prior to insult. The neurological mechanism accounting for this disturbance was thus similar, though opposite, to the "reciprocal innerva-tion" phenomenon described by prominent English physiologist C. Sher-rington, who had proved that during the flexion of a limb agonistic muscles were activated to lift the limb, whereas antagonistic muscles were inhibited in order to avoid a painful stimulus. The pathological fixation on one lan-guage was a reverse mechanism to reciprocal innervation: it was as if ago-nistic muscles were inhibited, while antagonistic muscles were activated. Therefore, the subject did not move the limb away from the source of pain, but moved it closer.

In a study of 1930, Pötzl attempted to provide a neuropsychological explanation of the pathological fixation phenomenon, and considered it a symptom of the parietal syndrome, previously described by Italian neurol-ogist and Minister of Education Leonardo Bianchi. One of the symptoms of the parietal syndrome was the *démence aphasique*, namely loss of the ability to use all registers of a language, whereby in patients who—besides a lan-guage—used other registers (lawyers, professors, priests, etc. accustomed to using jargons), a lesion to the parietal area determined the incapability of using the most abstract linguistic registers (the rhetoric of lawyers, the style of lessons and sermons, etc.), whereas the ability of using the everyday language remained unaffected. On the basis of this syndrome, Pötzl con-sidered the pathological fixation phenomenon as a symptom of the *démence aphasique* (Pötzl, 1930).

Recently, I studied the case of a right-handed patient, A.G., aged 78, a housewife with Friulian as mother tongue (a Rhaeto-Romance language; cf. Haiman & Benincà, 1992) and Italian as second language (Fabbro, 1995b). During her life, the patient mainly used Friulian, and learnt Italian at pri-mary school. In 1992 she suffered a stroke affecting the left temporal lobe and causing fluent aphasia in both languages, with many errors in phoneme and word selection (phonemic and verbal paraphasia) and in the gramma-tical construction of sentences. Comprehension was relatively preserved in both languages. Besides these aphasic disorders, the patient exhibited a pathological fixation on Italian both during the language assessment test (Bilingual Aphasia Test) and during conversation with the hospital staff. She replied in Italian irrespective of the language spoken by her inter-locutors, even during the assessment of her spontaneous speech in Friulian. (E): "*Ce mistîr a e fàt te so vite, je siore?*" (What was your job in your life, madam?); (A.G.): "*Niente solo la la rasa, la lavorare, la mamma, sempre la mamma, ecco*" (Nothing, only the the *hone*, the work, the mother, that's it the mother); (E): "*A e lavorât pai cjamps?*" (Were you a farmer?); (A.G.): "*No, no, no, non abbiamo carpo, no!*" (No, no, no, we don't have *lant*, no!). Language tests revealed that the patient had more word-finding difficulties in Friulian than in Italian, which might explain her pathological fixation on the latter language.

Spontaneous switching

One of the first cases of pathological switching was described by German neurosurgeon O. Förster (1936). The patient underwent a neurosurgical operation in order to remove a tumor localized in the third ventricle, a small cavity delimited by the hypothalamus and the anterior portions of the thalamus (cf. Fig. 10.1). When the surgeon started manipulating the tumor, the patient who was conscious burst into furious speech and began to quote passages in Latin, classical Greek, and Hebrew. Furthermore, he produced typical phonemic associations with the word uttered by the surgeon. When the surgeon asked his assistant for a *Tupfer* (tampon) the patient started producing a series of words which had a phonemic assonance to that word: "*Tupfer ... Tupfer, Hupfer, Hüpfer, hüpfen Sie mal ...*" (tampon ... tampon, jumper, jumping). When he heard the word *Messer* (knife, scalpel) he immediately said: "*Messer, Messer, Metzer, Sie sind ein Metzel, das ist ja ein Gemetzel, metzeln Sie doch nicht so messen Sie doch Sie messen ja nicht Herr Professor, profiteor, professus sum, profiteri*". This sequence of words can roughly be translated as: "Knife, butcher, you are a butcher; this really is a massacre; you take the measures; why don't you take the measures? Professor, *profiteor, professus sum, profiteri*". It reveals a dual response to cerebral stimulation: on the one hand, the patient uncontrollably produced sequences of words that were linked by assonance and/or alliteration, yet without syntactic cohesion; on the other hand, he seemingly wanted to convey an important message to the surgeon, namely his fear of being butchered and his plea that the surgeon proceed with caution. The patient's pathological compulsion to speak probably depended on the stimulation of the ventral anterior nucleus of the thalamus (cf. Fig. 9.1), which seems to be involved both in verbal production and in language switching.

In a study of 1991, Belgian neurolinguist Yvan Lebrun described in detail the linguistic disorder known as spontaneous switching, namely the systematic and uncontrolled production of several sentences with constant switching between languages. For example, the first sentence is produced in L1, the second sentence in L2, the third sentence in L3, the fourth sentence in L2, etc. (Lebrun, 1991). De Vreese, Motta, and Toschi (1988) studied an Italian patient (N.T.) exhibiting this linguistic disorder. N.T. was a chemical engineer aged 65. He had begun to study French at the age of 13, and at the age of 28 he had started attending intensive classes in English and German. He had long worked as a consultant to the Italian Government at the European Community and had spent six months working in the United States. Prior to onset of the disease he had spoken Italian, French, and German fluently. At the age of 57, he started exhibiting memory disturbances whose severity increased to such a point that the patient was diagnosed with Alzheimer's disease. The CT scan revealed that the patient had a diffuse mild brain atrophy. Alzheimer's disease is often accompanied by language disorders similar to those observed in Wernicke's aphasia. On examination seven years after onset, N.T. presented with word-finding difficulties and poor spontaneous speech, with incomplete sentences and perseverations in all languages. When asked in Italian: "*Qual è il tuo mestiere?*" (What's your job?), he replied: "*Come mestiere?... sono... ho fatto... ho lavorato per una ditta per... per per... adesso sono... comunque... mi occupavo di acciaio... quello che c'era da fare per... questa... per questa, per quella faccenda...*". (Job?... I'm... I was... I worked for a firm as... as as... now I'm... anyway... I dealt with steel... what had to be done to... this... to tackle problems...). The patient answered the same question in French as follows: "*Dans l'acier... j'ai travaillé... ça marche mais*". His answer in English was: "I am... now... for steel... you know... all right that's it...". Comprehension in Italian was preserved, whereas comprehension in French and German was slightly lower. Naming in Italian was also better than in French and German.

Besides these deficits, N.T. switched between languages often and without reason. Generally, he uttered a sentence in one language and the following sentence in another language. When asked in French: "*Répétez-moi la phrase: L'équipe des ouvriers construirent le pont*" (Repeat the following sentence: the group of workers built the bridge), he answered: "*C'est très difficile, ma va tutto bene*" (It is very difficult /French/, but it's all right /Italian/). When asked: "*Quel est le contraire de rapide?*" (What's the opposite of rapid?), he answered: "*Le contraire de rapide est andare adagio*" (The opposite of the word rapid /French/ is slow /Italian/). Lebrun maintained that spontaneous switching is probably due to a deficit of the system accounting for the maintenance of verbal output in one language. In Lebrun's opinion, this system is localized in the right hemisphere, because the patient also exhibited other typical deficits due to an alteration in the functions of this hemisphere (Lebrun, 1991).

In a study of 1994 the English neurologist Martin Schwartz described the clinical case of a polyglot patient affected by right temporal epilepsy who exhibited switching disorders. During epileptic fits the patient spontaneously switched between languages. For example, while she was on the phone speaking Punjabi (an Indian language), she suddenly switched to English; or, while holding a lesson in English, she uttered a few words in Punjabi, a language that her students did not understand. These phenomena completely disappeared after the patient underwent an anti-epileptic therapy (Schwartz, 1994).

These two clinical cases suggest that the mechanisms accounting for the selection of and switching between languages are organized in the right hemisphere. However, I recently studied a 56-year-old right-handed patient

(S.I.) who, following a lesion to the left hemisphere, exhibited typical switching disorders. In August 1994, S.I.—a prominent land-surveyor of Friulian mother tongue and with Italian as second language—began to exhibit neurological disturbances caused by a space-occupying lesion of 6cm in diameter, affecting the left prefrontal lobe (cf. Fig. 17.2). While he was on holiday with a friend, he noticed that he often tilted to the right while walking or driving. Moreover, he had difficulties in speaking fluently and tended to concentrate his thoughts in a few short sentences. What struck him was the fact that he involuntarily alternated sentences in Italian and sentences in Friulian, even though his friend did not understand Friulian. In September 1994 he was admitted to the Neurosurgical Department of Trieste Hospital. Four months after his operation he underwent a language assessment test (BAT). During the examination in Italian, S.I. did not exhibit pathological switching phenomena, yet they were frequent in Friulian. Furthermore, during the assessment of his residual linguistic capacities, it was noticed that he frequently addressed the other patients and the hospital staff by alternating sentences in Italian and Friulian, even though he was aware that they did not understand Friulian, nor did they want to listen to it (Fabbro, 1995b).

Cases of spontaneous switching under hypnotic trance have been observed, too. For example, Sheehan (1993) described a hypnotic age regression experiment in which the subject spoke German (his native language) even though the examiner understood only English. During the interview after the hypnosis, the examiner learnt that the subject found it natural to express himself in German. This proves that in some cases of hypnosis the sociolinguistic rule of communication, whereby the language understood by all interlocutors is spoken, does not apply.

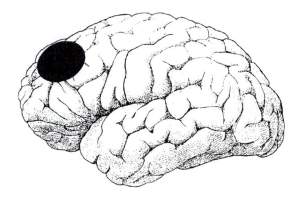

FIG. 17.2.   Site of the lesion in patient S.I.

Hypotheses on the neurological mechanisms of language switching

As has already been stated, producing a sentence in one language and the next sentence in another language is not a pathological behavior *per se*, as this occurs quite commonly, for instance, in bilingual communities, where both languages have the same social status (see Grosjean, 1998). The habits of bilingual individuals to alternate two languages within one coherent discourse may determine, at the psychological level, a low threshold of activation of switching phenomena and a reduction in the mutual inhibition of the languages (see Green, 1986, and Chapter 25, pp. 211–213). In such bilingual communities, it is quite normal for individuals to switch between languages while speaking informally. In other communities, however, such a behavior is intentionally avoided for sociolinguistic reasons. For example, in Brussels, where both French and Flemish are official languages, a public official or a bank employee would never switch between the two languages and would stick to the interlocutor's language, even though most natives understand and speak both languages. In Belgium each linguistic community has a strong identity, which is also fiercely defended through language use. The same is true for Friulian-Italian bilingual areas, where switching is generally avoided. Switching, however, has to be considered as a patholo- gical behavior when a bilingual aphasic produces sentences by mixing lan- guages, one of which one is not known by the interlocutor, as long as the aphasic did not do this premorbidly.

Many neurologists and neurolinguists have discussed the possible neurological organization of the switch mechanisms. Some of them, generally defined as *localizationists*, claim that there is a neuroanatomical center responsible for the activation of L1 and concurrent inhibition of L2 and L3. Both Pötzl and Leischner (1943/1983a) maintained that this center was localized in the left supramarginal gyrus; Stengel, Zelmanovicz (1933), and Zatorre (1989) claimed that it was localized in some anterior structures of the left hemisphere; and in Lebrun's opinion, this function is probably localized in the right hemisphere.

Other authors have criticized the idea of an anatomical center governing language switching. In a study of 1948, Goldstein maintained that any cerebral lesion impairs switching between mental processes, and that the faculty of switching is only an example of the more general faculty of abstraction (Goldstein, 1948/1983). M. Paradis (1993a) claims that switch- ing mechanisms are only one aspect of the more general systems involved in the decision-making processes. In Paradis' opinion, the switch function is part of a general system responsible for the selection of behaviors such as standing up or sitting down, speaking Italian or English, etc. In this regard, a neurofunctional system accounting for switching between behaviors is certainly to be postulated, yet its localization is still unclear even though it seems to involve some structures of the frontal system (e.g. part of the frontal lobe, the thalamus, and the basal ganglia, cf. the patient described by Förster and patient S.I.). This switching mechanism is peculiar not only to polyglot subjects, but also to monolinguals who use it in the selection of the different linguistic registers according to the communicative context. For example, individuals may ask their interlocutor to close the door by using a courtesy form ("Will you please close the door?") or a direct form ("Close the door"). In Paradis' opinion, the system accounting for the selection of one of the two registers is similar to the system accounting for the selection of one language rather than another.

At present, evidence in favor of any one theory has not yet been provided, even though Paradis' hypothesis of a neurofunctional system accounting for the selection and control of the switching mechanisms between languages is simple and exhaustive. There might be more than one neurofunctional system. Knowledge of their organization and of the neural structures subserving them is fundamental for future studies.

PATHOLOGICAL MIXING

Mixing occurs when sentences containing elements from different languages are produced. In language mixing phenomena, normal multilingual subjects usually respect the following rules:

1. In a sentence the subject (if it is a pronoun) and the predicate (verb) generally belong to the same language.
2. Hardly ever are prepositions alone expressed in a language other than the one used for the whole sentence.
3. In *mixing* there is a clear tendency to express function words or pro-verbs in the mother tongue.

Some authors claimed that in bilinguals, during verbal expression, the selected language exerts a functional inhibition on the nonselected language (reciprocal inhibition). On the other hand, during comprehension, both languages may be activated, because messages in different languages may be understood at the same time. The habit of frequently mixing languages, which is typical of some bilingual communities and of certain professions (e.g. simultaneous interpreting), seems to determine a lower level of reciprocal inhibition between languages. If a subject is accustomed to keeping the two languages functionally separate, when speaking in one language the inhibition systems of the other language will be effective (cf. Green, 1986). The language mixing phenomenon is not a pathological symptom. Therefore, during the examination of a multilingual aphasic it is important to know the frequency with which mixing phenomena occurred before insult (cf. Grosjean, 1989).

Several clinical cases of pathological mixing have been reported. One of the first cases was described by two neurologists of the University of Vienna, Stengel and Zelmanowich (1933), and concerned a patient, M.M., who had become aphasic at the age of 57, following a traumatic cerebral hemorrhage she had suffered years before (arachnoidean cyst in the proximity of Broca's area; cf. Fig. 17.3). At the age of 22 she had moved to Vienna, where she had worked as a cook. There she had acquired German so well as to be considered of German mother tongue. Between the ages of 51 and 54 she had returned to her homeplace; afterwards she had moved to Vienna again to work as a cook until the day she was admitted to the neurological clinic of the University owing to episodes of cephalea and word-finding difficulties. Her verbal expression was very poor, and marked by grammatical errors and numerous phonemic and verbal paraphasias. Moreover, the patient constantly mixed German and Czech. None of the two languages prevailed over the other. In particular, when she could not find a word in one language, she used the corresponding word in the other language without hesitation. Her comprehension of both languages was preserved—even in the case of complex instructions.

In 1943 German neurologist A. Leischner reported the case of a polyglot aphasic (J.S.) who was deaf-mute and had acquired sign language as his mother tongue (Leischner, 1943/1983a). Subsequently, he had acquired Czech as his second language and German as his third language. The latter he could read and write. Prior to insult the patient was used to accompanying his sign language with individual Czech words to emphasize relevant parts of his speech. J.S. sustained two strokes, one shortly after the

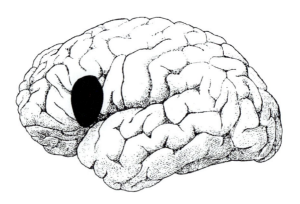

FIG. 17.3.   Site of the lesion in patient M.M.

other, with consequent right-sided paralysis and aphasia. After the second stroke, the patient made so many errors in his sign language that one could hardly understand it. In addition, he exhibited pathological mixing phenomena. Often he expressed a word in his sign language but uttered a different word, and wrote yet another word. When writing, he often mixed Czech syllables and German syllables within a word. The patient's ability to read Czech, but not German, had been preserved. The autopsy revealed a left hemisphere lesion affecting the superior temporal gyrus and the inferior parietal lobe (cf. Fig. 17.4).

From a neurolinguistic point of view the history of this patient is very interesting, not only because of the mixing phenomenon he exhibited, but also because it is one of the first cases of aphasia affecting sign language in a patient with a left hemisphere lesion. More recently North-American researcher Ursula Bellugi carried out research on aphasia in deaf-mute subjects and positively ascertained that sign language is a real language, not only at a linguistic level, but also at a neurological level (Hickok, Bellugi, & Klima, 1996). This currently widely accepted theory met with much opposition less than 30 years ago, especially with regard to the teaching of sign language to deaf-mute subjects, because this way of communication was not regarded as a language in the proper sense of the word but was equaled to inferior communication systems that are typical of animals.

In 1984 North-American neurolinguist Ellen Perecman described the clinical history of a patient (H.B.) who exhibited several mixing phenomena (Perecman, 1984). H.B. was an old man of German mother tongue who had acquired French as his second language as a child, and subsequently acquired English when he had moved to the United States at the age of 18. At the age of 75, H.B. suffered a cranial trauma and extensive bilateral

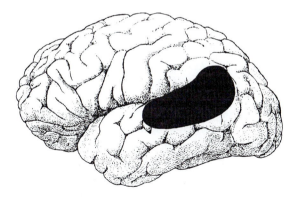

FIG. 17.4.   Site of the lesion of patient J.S.

temporal hematomas resulting from a car accident. Three months after the accident his verbal speech was fluent with numerous anomias, semantic and, sometimes, phonemic paraphasias; he also exhibited a marked tendency to mix his three languages and spontaneously translate many sentences he produced (cf. Chapter 24, pp. 199–200). Mixing phenomena affected different levels of his speech. H.B. exhibited mixing phenomena at a phonological level: "...standing that means *ständing ständing führen...*", at a semantic level: "*Ja ja c'est difficile*" (yes, yes, it is difficult), "The eggs were *verschwunden*" (The eggs had disappeared), and at clause level: Examiner (E): "*Haben Sie auf Deutsch die Bücher gelesen?*" (Have you read the books in German?); H. B.: "Yes I read I read some German books"; (E): "*Wie heißt das denn*" (How do you say it in German?); H. B.: "*Je ne sais pas*" (I don't know). Perecman's procedure and results have been strongly challenged by Grosjean (1989, 1998). It seems that H.B.'s language mixing was particularly pronounced when the investigator herself shifted from one language to another within the same conversation or task.

Bearing in mind and applying Grosjean's (1989) methodological suggestions, I recently studied an aphasic polyglot patient who exhibited an interesting, yet severe, mixing phenomenon (Fabbro, 1995b). E.G., right-handed, 55 years of age, was of Slovene mother tongue, with Italian as second language, Friulian as third language, and English as fourth language. After a stroke that provoked a lesion in the left temporal lobe (cf. Fig. 17.5) the patient exhibited Wernicke's aphasia in all the languages he knew. Aphasia was accompanied by a severe mixing phenomenon in Italian, Friulian, and English. These are a few examples of his spontaneous speech in his three languages: Examiner (E): "What was your job in Canada?"; (E.G.): "*In Canada? Co facevo la via?* I was working with *ce faccio coi... del... fare, i signori la che i faceva...*". (In Canada? What I did there? /Italian/ I was working with /English/ I do with... do... men there who did... /Italian/). (E): "What did you do?"; (E.G.): "*Allora le case, tante case, e dopo di notte lavoravo* for *i martesi,* for *i canadesi*" (Then houses, many houses, and during the night I worked /Italian/ for /English/ Martanians /Italian/, for /English/ Canadians /Italian/). Friulian: (E): "*Cemût ajal imparât l'inglês?*"; (E.G.): "*O Signor benedet!* Quando ero *cuan che jo o eri solduet jo o ai studiât inglês, o ai imparât par quindis dîs no, e o soi stât* English, mi mi ha fatto giusto un affare no, un sublan O. K.! English sì, oh ja, Svizzera sì, Svizzera sì *fat zingher zingher no*". [E: How did you learn English?; E.G.: O my God! /Friulian/ When I was /Italian/ when I was a soldier I learnt English, I learnt for fifteen days no, and I have been an /Friulian/ English /English/, it was a bargain no, a real /Italian/ sublan O.K. English yes, oh ja /English/, Switzerland yes, Switzerland yes /Italian/, done zingher zingher no /Friulian/]. English: (E): "Did you live in Germany?"; (E.G.): "Just think the wife, for *su e ju, su e ju* /Friulian/, because would the problem here in *Italia...* /Italian/ and he make everything for for my wife,

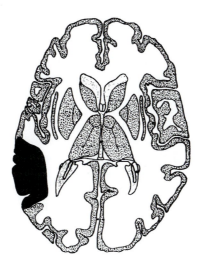

FIG. 17.5.   Site of the lesion in patient E.G.

that's was *sbagliât* /Friulian/ *tutto tutto* /Italian/ everything... that's right O. K., O. K.".

NEUROLINGUISTIC MODELS OF LANGUAGE MIXING

Perecman (1984, 1989) has analyzed and classified the various types of mixing phenomena in aphasic polyglot patients. A list of the most frequent types follows:

1. *Word mixing.* When they cannot find a word owing to anomia, bilingual aphasics are likely to substitute it with a corresponding word in another language. In this case, patients are usually aware of the mixing phenomenon. Sometimes they unconsciously mix words from different languages within a sentence, i.e. "... à la *I say* il est un peu", "... to think for my boys from England you know *und hab ich immer so gemacht und* one day I said to the boy" (... to think for my boys from England you know and I have always done this way and one day I said to the boy).

2. *Root and suffix mixing.* For example, E.G. uttered words with an English root and added the Italian suffix, "Per andare all'ospedale ho preso la *carra*" [To go to the hospital I took the *carra* (from the English "car" plus the Italian suffix "a"). Cases of patients adding the

English *-ing* form to the German verb *gelten* have been reported, as have cases of patients adding the German infinitive suffix *-en* to the English verb *to come*.

3. *Blending of syllables* from different languages within the same word.
4. *Intonation* of one language and concurrent use of the lexicon of another language.
5. Use of the *syntax* of one language and concurrent use of the lexicon of another language. For example, instead of reading the English sentence: "*I got home from work*", a patient said: "*I will home coming*", which is syntactically wrong, because it uses the German syntax where the verb takes the final position.
6. Utterance of a word in one language but *pronouncing the phonemes* in another language. For example, a patient pronounced the English word *door* like the French word *dur*.
7. Finally, the systematic tendency of a subject to answer in a language different from that spoken by the interlocutor is to be considered a *mixing phenomenon*.

As well as a linguistic description of the various types of language mixing, Perecman also proposed a neurolinguistic model to explain some aspects of this language disorder in polyglot aphasics. On the basis of her model, mixing phenomena, like other aphasic symptoms and slips, are errors in one stage of the process from the prelinguistic conceptual representation of language to the properly linguistic representation. Perecman based her hypothesis on a psycholinguistic model of sentence production that was developed during the 1980s by Garrett, who studied slips in normal subjects and identified four levels in the sentence production process (cf. Garrett, 1984):

1. Conceptual relations between the elements of the sentence are established at the *message level*, which is related to the linguistic and extra-linguistic systems.
2. Words relevant to the content of the sentence to be produced are selected at the *functional level*. They are assigned structural roles within the sentence (e.g. who does what, and who is done what to, etc.).
3. Closed class words are selected at the *positional level,* and a phonological form is assigned to words from both classes on the basis of the information coming from the previous levels.
4. The phonetic form of the words forming the sentence is specified at the *phonetic level*.

On the basis of this psycholinguistic model, Perecman suggested a classification of *mixing phenomena* in the following types: lexical-semantic, syntactic, morphological, and phonological. In addition, she proposed to correlate each single type of mixing to one of the stages of the sentence production process (functional level, positional level, and phonetic level, respectively).

CHAPTER EIGHTEEN

Alternating antagonism

This chapter describes the alternating antagonism phenomenon, which was first analyzed and discussed by Paradis, Goldblum, and Abidi in 1982. A bilingual aphasic patient affected by this disorders will always express himself/ herself in one language only (L1, but not L2) at a given time, and only in the other language (L2, but not L1) at another given time. The phenomenon tends to occur repeatedly and the capacity to speak one language selectively may last from a few hours to a day or a week. As patients cannot possibly recover language in this short period of time, it has been suggested that the language that is not available is not lost but only inhibited. Alternating antagonism has become an important paradigm for the study of aphasic linguistic disorders in general. It suggests that a cerebral lesion does not determine the loss of linguistic competence, but rather an inhibition of the execution systems, as had already been suggested by renowned French physician and physiologist Jean-Baptiste Bouillaud in 1825, over a century before linguists, including F. de Saussure and N. Chomsky, put forward their own theories.

A CASE OF DOUBLE DISSOCIATION IN LINGUISTIC BEHAVIOR

In 1895 the English physician Lewis C. Bruce described the clinical case of H.P., a Welsh tailor, aged 47, who had been admitted to hospital on October 25, 1892 because, having suffered from depression for 15 years, he had recently started showing symptoms of agitation, dementia, and destructive behavior (Bruce, 1895). Bruce noticed that the patient alternated between periods when he was noisy and destructive and expressed himself in English (L2) with periods when he was almost in a demential state and mainly spoke

Welsh (L1). Therefore, the physician defined the two states the "English phase" and the "Welsh phase", respectively, and for three months he carefully observed the patient's behavior. It might be of interest to dwell on some observations made by Bruce:

Nov. 30, 1892. The patient is sitting on a chair, pays no attention to his surroundings, does not seem to recognize tobacco and money. No understanding of English. Uses the left hand to pick up objects and cutlery. Speaks Welsh.

Jan. 2, 1893. He understands the word tobacco in English and uses the left or right hand as most convenient. Speaks Welsh with occasional English words.

Jan. 5, 1893. Uses mainly English, sometimes Welsh. Understands English and is ambidextrous.

Jan. 8, 1893. Back to the "Welsh phase", rather confused and uses the left hand exclusively.

Jan. 11, 1893. The patient is in an intermediate stage between the "English phase" and the "Welsh phase". Ambidextrous, i.e. holds the tea mug with the right hand as easily as with the left hand.

Jan. 20, 1893. Back to the "Welsh phase".

Jan. 24, 1893. Speaks both English and Welsh and is ambidextrous.

Jan. 27, 1893. Completely demented and left-handed. A Welsh patient acting as interpreter reports that he speaks an unintelligible jargon with a few words in Welsh only. After numerous questions, H.P. laconically states in Welsh: "I will no longer answer".

Jan. 29, 1893. 10 a.m.: Uses the left hand. Slightly restless, and mixes English words in his Welsh verbal production. *12 a.m.:* At lunch the patient is ambidextrous. Understands English, but answers mixing English and Welsh. When requested to write down his name with the right hand, he obeys the order, but with difficulty. He writes down his name with the right hand without difficulty, but in what is commonly known as mirror writing. *6 p.m.:* Completely right-handed and speaks only English. Writes down his name without difficulty with the right hand. Recognizes money and its value without difficulty, repeatedly asks for tobacco. Is able to understand Welsh, but does not speak it.

Jan. 30, 1893. "English phase". Uses the right hand, is very restless, destructive, constantly stealing small objects from the other patients.

Jan. 31, 1983. "Welsh phase". Uses the left hand only, understands and speaks only Welsh.

Feb. 2, 1893. "English phase" at 6 a.m. Welsh phase at 9 a.m., uses only the left hand. English phase at 6.30 p.m.

Feb. 3, 1893. "English phase", restless and destructive.

Feb. 4, 1893. Dirtier and more restless than usual. Speaks English and uses the right hand.

Feb. 5, 1893. "English phase" during the night. Less restless and more confused at 10 a.m.. "Welsh phase" at noon. Mixed expressions at 11 p.m.

Until March 1, 1893 Bruce continued to observe the patient who, during this period, continued to alternate between Welsh and English sentences. Bruce interpreted this phenomenon as the result of the alternating supremacy of one cerebral hemisphere over the other. In the "English phase" the patient presumably exhibited a left hemisphere superiority, proved by his being right-handed, and spoke English, even though he understood and sometimes spoke Welsh, too. He was restless, hyperactive, euphoric, and had a good intelligence; he was bold and fearless, recognized objects, physicians, and nurses; however, he did not remember what had happened in the latest phase. In the "Welsh phase" the patient showed a right hemisphere superiority, proven by his being left-handed; his verbal expression was often unintelligible. He seemed to understand Welsh, but he generally refused to answer questions. In this phase he did not understand English, not even the simplest sentences, he sat doubled up in a chair for hours without making a movement, he was shy and suspicious, did not recognize physicians and nurses, and seemed to constantly wait for unseen danger. He did not recognize money and tobacco, did not show any preference for sugar to salt, and did not react to strong and pungent odors. Besides these two phases H.P. exhibited an intermediate phase when switching from the "Welsh phase" to the "English phase" and vice versa. In this phase he was ambidextrous and he mixed and understood both languages.

In his conclusions Bruce put forward the hypothesis that each of the two cerebral hemispheres subserved an independent mental system. His intuition was substantiated during the early 1960s by the findings of Nobel Prize winner for Medicine Roger Sperry and by a colleague of his, Michael Gazzaniga (1985). They carried out research studies on patients who had undergone complete removal of the corpus callosum. In addition, Bruce claimed that both cerebral hemispheres were involved in the control of sensation, movement, and lower physiological reflexes, but only the left hemisphere could be instructed and was thus responsible for most abstract mental abilities.

RECENT CASES OF ALTERNATING ANTAGONISM

The first case of alternating antagonism was described in 1948 by the German neurologist A. Leischner, who considered it to be an aspect of the aphasic syndrome in polyglots, without analyzing its neurolinguistic significance in detail. The patient, aged 54, right-handed, had acquired Czech and German as a child. He suffered a left hemisphere insult with consequent right-handed paralysis and sensory aphasia. For a certain period of time he alternated days when he spoke only German and days when he spoke only Czech. His comprehension in both languages was preserved, but when he spoke German only, he also answered in German to those who addressed him in Czech. Leischner interpreted this phenomenon as a result of the loss of the capacity to switch from language to language owing to a lesion of the left parietal area, which accounted for the *switching* mechanisms described years earlier by Pötzl (Leischner, 1948/1983b).

The alternating antagonism phenomenon was first thoroughly described by Paradis, Goldblum, and Abidi in 1982. In a first case of alternating antagonism the patient, a nun (A.D.), right-handed, aged 48, born in Casablanca from a French-speaking family, had started learning classical Arabic at the age of 10 through a traditional grammar-translation method. She had worked as a pediatric nurse for 24 years in a hospital where she spoke Arabic with patients and their relatives, and French with physicians and nurses. On November 24, 1978, she suffered a left temporo-parietal lesion owing to a car accident (cf. Fig. 18.1). After a short episode of loss of consciousness the patient awoke with global aphasia. Four days later, the patient was able to utter only a few words in Arabic and nothing in French. On December 6, she was transferred to a hospital in Paris. The patient was lucid, knew where she was, and remembered all past events; her intelligence was preserved, no particular neuropsychological problem was detected, but she was aphasic. In the following month she was administered language tests in French and Arabic, as she exhibited an alternated use of the two languages. A brief account of her neurological examination follows.

Dec. 8, 1978. Only French is assessed. The patient has word-finding difficulties, exhibits occasional paraphasias, understands simple orders, but

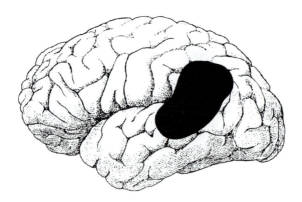

FIG. 18.1.   Site of the lesion in patient A.D.

has difficulty in understanding complex orders. Naming of objects is moderately good (80 trials out of 100 are correct), reading is good.

Dec. 11, 1978. The patient is fluent in French, except for pauses due to word-finding difficulties. Comprehension of simple and semicomplex orders is good, object naming is reduced (60 trials out of 100 are correct).

Dec. 12, 1978. The patient is disoriented, does not know whether she is in Paris or Rabat. In French she has difficulties in describing pictures; word repetition, object naming, and comprehension are very limited. In Arabic word and sentence repetition is good, with mild difficulties in naming and comprehension. Spontaneous writing is good.

Dec. 13, 1978. Arabic is worse than the previous day. Her expression is poor and impeded. She has word-finding difficulties and makes numerous grammatical errors in contrast with the previous day. On the other hand, her competence in French is very good. The patient expresses herself in French better than in Arabic. When she is requested to speak Arabic, she tends to switch to French or uses French intonation. Naming and comprehension are preserved.

Dec. 14, 1978. The patient speaks Arabic very well.

Dec. 21, 1978. The patient speaks French very well, her spontaneous speech is fluent and she rarely has word-finding difficulties. Naming in French is very good. She has difficulties in expressing herself in Arabic. She names only 1 object out of 10.

Jan. 3, 1979. Her spontaneous speech in French is fluent, with mild anomias. Object naming is good. Her spontaneous speech in Arabic is slow, but correct. Naming is discrete.

Jan. 4, 1979. Her spontaneous speech in French is moderately good. The patient has recovered Arabic almost completely, with a few word-finding difficulties, which she overcomes by using French words.

When she was discharged from hospital the patient was no longer able to say the Hail Mary in Latin, despite the fact that, according to Paradis et al.'s calculation, she had practiced the prayer at least half a million times during her life. In addition, the patient confessed she was no longer able to say the Lord's either, a prayer that she said she still "knew by heart".

The second patient described by Paradis, Goldblum, and Abidi (1982) was a right-handed young man, aged 23, who had become aphasic subsequent to the removal of an arterovenous malformation deep in the left parietal lobe. The patient was of French mother tongue and had acquired English as a child. In the six years prior to the operation, he had mainly used English for business reasons. Immediately after the operation he exhibited aphasic disorders for some weeks. During the first week he could not say a word in French, whereas he could express himself in English. As his wife did not understand English, his father acted as interpreter between them. Comprehension in both languages was preserved. During the second week the patient recovered French, but was no longer able to speak English, which was the language used by the hospital staff. Therefore, he could no longer communicate with them. During the third week he also recovered English.

In 1989, Iranian neurolinguists R. Nilipour and H. Ashayeri described a case of a polyglot aphasic (A.S.) who exhibited the alternating antagonism phenomenon (Nilipour & Ashayeri, 1989). The patient was an orthopedic surgeon, aged 49, right-handed. Until the age of 18 he had spoken only Farsi, Iran's national language. He had attended university in Germany and had worked there, thus acquiring German as well. He had also spent a year in England where he had learnt to speak, read, and write in English. In 1985, following an explosion, he was injured in the head and suffered a lesion to the left frontal-temporal lobe with consequent aphasia and right-sided paralysis. During the first few days after the accident the patient was completely mute. In the following five days he uttered a few words in Farsi. Thereafter, much to the hospital staff's and to his friends' amazement, he started speaking only German, even though he still understood Farsi. He remained in this condition for three weeks. Afterwards he again spoke only Farsi. During this first period he could neither speak nor understand English, and only after the recovery of the first two languages did he recover English as well.

The alternating antagonism phenomenon—exhibited by some bilingual and polyglot aphasics—corroborates the hypothesis that in many cases of aphasia the language that is unavailable is not lost, but only inhibited by the cerebral lesion (Green, 1986; Paradis, 1993a, b; cf. Chapter 25). The temporary incapability to use this language mainly affects production, whereas comprehension in both languages is spared.

CHAPTER NINETEEN

Subcortical aphasia in bilinguals

The development of computerized axial tomography (CT scan) and of magnetic resonance imagining (MRI) has led to the identification of patients with acquired language disorders due to focal lesions in the left subcortical structures. The study of subcortical aphasia has revealed that language functions are not only organized in the cerebral cortex but also in numerous subcortical structures. The study of two bilingual patients with lesions to the left thalamus suggests that this structure is involved in the control of the phonemic, morphological, lexical, and syntactic aspects of both languages. The study of three polyglot patients with lesions to the basal ganglia of the left hemisphere reveals that these subcortical structures are involved in the process of verbal production and comprehension, in semantic control, and in translation.

Neuroanatomical and neurophysiological studies have revealed that subcortical structures are crucial nodes of the neural circuits involved in the regulation of general functions such as movement, ideation, attention, memory, etc. (cf. Chapter 9). Four main circuits (cf. Fig. 19.1) accounting for the regulation of language have been identified:

1. A "*cortico-cortical*" loop mediating communication through the arcuate fascicle between Broca's area and Wernicke's area. It is involved in phonemic comprehension and production, and in verbal short-term memory.
2. A "*cortico-thalamo-cortical*" loop connecting the posterior areas and the anterior areas of language through some thalamic nuclei. It is

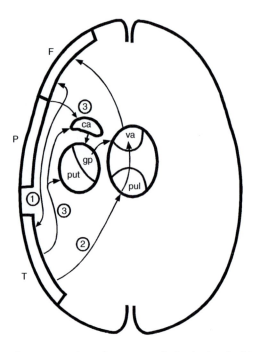

FIG. 19.1. Schematic representation of some neural circuits involved in the regulation of language.

    involved in the selection of words and in the organization of verbal long-term memory.

3. A *"cortico-striato-thalamo-cortical"* loop allowing the structures of the left parietal, temporal, and frontal lobes to control the language-planning functions developed by the left frontal lobe through the basal ganglia and the thalamus. The circuit regulates verbal communication by alternating listening and verbal production, and is also involved in the correct construction of sentences at grammatical and word-selecting level.

4. A *"cortico-cerebellar-thalamo-cortical"* loop seemingly involved in the control of grammar and production of language.

A lesion to the thalamus or the basal ganglia of the left hemisphere may provoke an interruption in one or more of these circuits, thus generating language disorders that so far have been studied in monolinguals only. In contrast, the study of bilingual aphasic patients with subcortical lesions may lead to the identification of the role played by these circuits in the comprehension and production of the mother tongue (L1) as opposed to the second language (L2), and in some verbal behavior patterns peculiar to bilinguals (i.e. switching, mixing, translation, etc.).

THALAMIC APHASIA IN MONOLINGUALS

Electrical stimulation or coagulation of some thalamic nuclei in the treatment of patients affected by Parkinson's disease has revealed three thalamic nuclei of the left hemisphere involved in the regulation of language: the ventral anterior nucleus (VA), the ventral lateral nucleus (VL) and the pulvinar (P). The VA and VL nuclei receive information mainly from the globus pallidus and the cerebellum and project fibers to the motor cortex (VL nucleus) and the premotor cortex (VA nucleus). The pulvinar is mainly linked to the parieto-temporo-occipital cortex (cf. Chapter 9).

Numerous studies on monolingual patients showed that lesions localized in the left thalamus may provoke aphasic syndromes characterized by: (a) fluent speech; (b) anomias, verbal and semantic paraphasias, and neologisms; (c) mild deficits of comprehension with unaffected repetition; (d) reading, writing, and calculation disorders, as well as impairments of verbal long-term memory. Language disorders accompanying "thalamic aphasia" have many aspects in common with sensory transcortical aphasia (cf. Chapter 5, p. 45), which is characterized by fluent speech and severe comprehension deficits as opposed to repetition.

THALAMIC APHASIA IN BILINGUALS

Reynolds, Turner, Harris, Ojeman, and Davis (1979) described a clinical case of thalamic aphasia in a bilingual. The patient, aged 40, of Navajo mother tongue and with English as second language, suffered a hemorrhage to the left thalamus. After the insult he could no longer speak his second language, whereas he was fluent in his mother tongue although with numerous paraphasias. The lack of accurate neurolinguistic studies on bilingual patients with thalamic aphasia leaves many questions still unanswered, especially those concerning the role played by some thalamic nuclei in the regulation of language in polyglots. For this reason, I recently carried out a detailed analysis of two cases of bilingual patients with lesions to the left thalamus (Fabbro, Peru, & Skrap, 1996, 1997).

The first patient, D.B., is a right-handed engineer of Italian mother tongue (L1). When he was 3 years old, his family moved to Australia where he attended primary and secondary schools using English (L2). When he returned to Italy, he continued to use English for business and study reasons. At the age of 41, he suddenly suffered a confusional state with memory disturbances. The CT scan and MRI revealed a bilateral ischemia of the thalamus that affected the left thalamic nuclei to a greater extent (cf. Fig. 19.2). The lesion was due to a venous malformation that was surgically repaired. The operation was successful and after seven months the patient was administered neuropsychological tests (intelligence and memory assessment) and neurolinguistic tests (BAT in Italian and English). The patient's intelligence was preserved, but he exhibited severe verbal short-term and long-term memory deficits as well as calculation disorders (Peru & Fabbro, 1997). His spontaneous speech in both languages was fluent with phonemic, semantic, and verbal paraphasias. In Italian D.B. exhibited only one type of agrammatism (omission of an obligatory morpheme), whereas in English he produced numerous agrammatisms and paragrammatisms. In both languages repetition was better than comprehension (repetition: L1 = 100% of correct trials, L2 = 94%; comprehension: L1 = 88.4%, L2 = 84.2%). D.B.'s morphology (L1 = 73.9%; L2 = 30.4%) and lexicon (L1 = 92.6%; L2 = 80.1%) in English were worse than the morphology and lexicon in Italian.

The second patient, L.M., is a right-handed housewife, aged 69, of Friulian mother tongue, who acquired Italian at primary school and mainly used it after her marriage as her husband did not speak Friulian. The patient was admitted to hospital owing to convulsions characterized by clonic spasms of her right hemiface, and a transitory fluent aphasia. MRI revealed a tumor affecting the left thalamus (cf. Fig. 19.2). The patient's intelligence was preserved, whereas her verbal long-term memory was impaired. Her speech was fluent, yet with many agrammatisms and paragrammatisms in both languages. In Italian (L2) repetition was better preserved than com-prehension (C = 81.7% of correct trials; R = 97%), whereas in Friulian

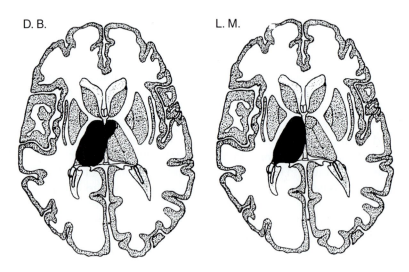

FIG. 19.2.   Extent of the thalamic lesions in patients D.B. and L.M.

(L1) results in both tasks were similar (C = 93.2%; R = 94%). Moreover, L.M.'s morphology (L1 = 86.9%, L2 = 56.5%) and syntax (L1 = 91.1%, L2 = 80%) of her second language were more severely impaired than those of her mother tongue.

The two cases have contributed to the identification of some characteristics that are typical of thalamic aphasia in bilinguals:

1. Generally, language disorders are moderately severe in both languages.
2. Speech is fluent, yet with phonemic, semantic, and verbal paraphasias and with grammatical disorders (both agrammatisms and paragrammatisms).
3. Repetition is better preserved than comprehension.
4. The major deficits concern morphological aspects, in particular of the second language. The aforementioned cases may lead to the conclusion that the left thalamus is involved in the control and regulation of phonemic, morphological, lexical, and syntactic aspects of both languages. The greater impairment of the second language morphology suggests that in bilinguals the left thalamic structures are involved in the regulation of the morphological aspects of L2 to a larger extent than of L1.

BASAL GANGLIA APHASIA IN MONOLINGUALS

The basal ganglia are a group of subcortical nuclei (caudate nucleus, putamen, globus pallidus; cf. Fig. 9.1) involved in the regulation of motor and cognitive behavior. Systematic studies of clinical neurology revealed that lesions to the *caudate nucleus* provoke motor disorders (dystonia, hemichorea) in 25% of the patients, whereas in 75% of the patients they provoke behavior and cognitive disorders (apathy, depression, disinhibition of behavior, memory disturbances, and language disorders). Lesions to the *putamen* provoke motor disorders (dystonia) in 95% of the cases, whereas in the remaining 5% they provoke behavior disturbances (dysprosody and obsessive-compulsive behavior). Lesions to the *globus pallidus* provoke motor disorders (rigidity, tremor) in 70% of the cases, and behavior and cognitive disorders (apathy, obsessive-compulsive disturbances, and language disorders) in 30% of the cases (cf. Marsden & Obeso, 1994).

Over the past few years cases of monolingual aphasics with lesions to the basal ganglia of the left hemisphere have been reported. The main characteristics of basal ganglia aphasia in monolinguals are:

1. nonfluent aphasia with reduction in the initiation of speech;
2. voice disorders (reduced voice volume, foreign accent syndrome);

3. semantic and verbal paraphasias (language disorders typical of fluent aphasia);
4. echolalias and perseverations;
5. generally preserved repetition and comprehension.

BASAL GANGLIA APHASIA IN BILINGUALS

Recently, Paradis and I studied the neurolinguistic features of basal ganglia aphasia in polyglot patients (Fabbro & Paradis, 1995a). This study was carried out in an attempt to find answers to important questions concerning the neurolinguistics of bilingualism, namely: (a) are basal ganglia involved in the organization of linguistic functions typical of bilinguals?, and (b) are language disorders following a lesion to the basal ganglia quantitatively and/or qualitatively similar in all languages known by a polyglot?

The first patient, C.B., a right-handed housewife, aged 71, of Friulian mother tongue (L1) attended primary school in Italian (L2), and moved to England at the age of 22, where she got married. The patient lived there until the age of 60, thus learning English (L3), too. Following a stroke, she exhibited a severe right-sided hemiplegia. MRI revealed an ischemic infarction affecting the head of the caudal nucleus, a small portion of the putamen, and the anterior portion of the internal capsule of the left hemi-sphere (cf. Fig. 19.3). In addition, the patient exhibited nonfluent aphasia in all the languages she knew, with semantic and verbal paraphasias. Her spontaneous speech was characterized by numerous echolalias and repeti-tions. She spontaneously translated echolalias into another language before uttering them (*echolalic spontaneous translation phenomenon*). For example, the examiner addressed her in Friulian: "*Ce mût stae?*" [How are you?] and she replied in Italian: "*Come sta?* (echolalia) *Bene!*" [How are you? I'm fine]. The BAT revealed severe comprehension deficits in all three languages (50% of correct trials), whereas repetition was relatively preserved (95%). C.B.

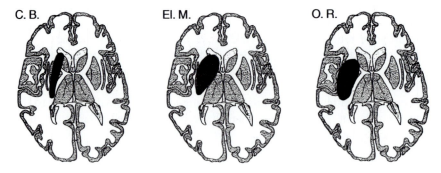

C. B.   El. M.   O. R.

FIG. 19.3. Extent of the subcortical lesions in patients C.B., El.M., and O.R.

translated words from Friulian into English (L1→L3) correctly, but could not translate the same words from English into Friulian (L3→L1), even though this direction is generally considered to be simpler.

The second patient, El.M., was a 56-year-old right-handed shopkeeper of Friulian mother tongue (L1), with Italian (L2) as second language, which he had acquired at primary school and used for business reasons. A cerebral hemorrhage had affected the caudal nucleus, the putamen, part of the globus pallidus, and the internal capsule of the left hemisphere (lesion evinced through MRI; cf. Fig. 19.3). Besides a right-sided paralysis, the patient exhibited a severe nonfluent aphasia with numerous echolalias and repetitions. Both languages were assessed through the BAT. Comprehension in both languages was more impaired than repetition (C = 64% of correct trials; R = 83%).

The third patient, O.R., was a 63-year-old right-handed bricklayer, of Friulian mother tongue (L1) with Italian as second language (L2), which he had acquired at primary school. Following a stroke he exhibited a right-sided hemiplegia and aphasia. MRI revealed that the lesion affected the caudate nucleus, the putamen, and portions of the insular cortex of the left hemisphere (cf. Fig. 19.3). The patient exhibited fluent aphasia in both languages, with numerous phonemic, semantic and verbal paraphasias, neologisms, repetitions, and echolalias; his syntactic errors were mainly omissions of bound grammatical morphemes (agrammatisms). The BAT revealed severe repetition and comprehension deficits in the mother tongue (R = 65% of correct trials; C = 60%). Comprehension in his second language was more impaired than repetition (C = 55%, R = 90%).

The neurolinguistic study of these polyglot aphasics corroborate the hypothesis that the basal ganglia of the left hemisphere are involved in the regulation of language functions in bilingual subjects, namely:

1. They are involved in the processes of speech initiation and maintenance through the limbic-striato-thalamo-cortical loop.
2. They participate in the construction of grammatically correct sentences.
3. They are involved in the semantic and phonemic control of the words to be uttered (cf. Huang & Peng, 1986).
4. They regulate switching from one element of language to the next.
5. They are involved in the most automatic aspects of the translation process.

The presence of certain characteristics of the "isolation of the speech area syndrome" (reduced spontaneous speech, impaired comprehension, and preserved repetition; cf. Chapter 5, pp. 40–41) in all three patients corroborates the hypothesis that the basal ganglia of the left hemisphere are almost certainly a fundamental node of the complex neuronal network accounting for organization and control of language functions in bilinguals.

Recently a group of North-American neurologists, under the coordination of Speedie, described a bilingual patient (L1 = French; L2 = Hebrew), aged 75, with a subcortical lesion to the right hemisphere (Speedie, Wertman, Ta'ir, & Heilman, 1993). The patient did not exhibit language disorders in the languages he knew. However, he was no longer able to say his prayers in Hebrew, an automatic language task he had been performing all his life. By studying this clinical case, Speedie et al. concluded that the subcortical structures of the right hemisphere are involved in the regulation of automatic verbal output of high emotional significance.

CHAPTER TWENTY

Aphasia in bilingual children

This chapter describes the only two reported cases of aphasia in bilingual children. In children aphasia presents typical features. Regardless of the site of the lesion, immediately after the onset of the acquired language disorder children tend to speak little, whereas their comprehension is generally preserved. Moreover, children show a rapid recovery of their linguistic skills. Recent research has proved that aphasic children will continue to exhibit language, writing, and calculation disorders for the rest of their lives. In bilingual aphasic children these permanent language disorders may affect one language more severely than another.

ACQUIRED APHASIA IN CHILDREN

Aphasia in childhood refers to acquired language disorders due to cerebral lesions (cranial trauma, tumor, hemorrhage, and cerebral infarction) that occur after language acquisition. Therefore, it is to be distinguished from developmental language disorders, namely neurological disturbances affecting language acquisition. The world's medical literature describes more than 1000 cases of acquired aphasia in subjects aged between 3 and 15 years.

Acquired childhood aphasia presents with typical features. Independent of the site of the cerebral lesion, mutism emerges immediately post-onset, or children speak little; in either case, acquired childhood aphasia is not fluent, unlike numerous cases of aphasia in adults. This symptom persists for weeks. Second, children recover most of their linguistic abilities rapidly. However, for the rest of their lives they will continue to have mild word-finding difficulties and will exhibit an impoverished lexicon compared to normal subjects of their age. They often have a simplified syntax and exhibit writing and calculation disorders. Mutism and articulatory disorders are generally associated with lesions to the left frontal lobe or the left Rolandic structures, whereas phonemic comprehension disorders are more frequently associated with lesions to the left temporal lobe (Hécaen, 1976, 1983).

What drew neurologists' attention toward acquired childhood aphasia is the extent and the rapidity with which aphasic children recover language. Numerous explanations have been proposed. North-American researcher Eric Lenneberg claims that if a lesion affects a child before the age of 10, language recovery is complete, because the linguistic functions damaged by the left hemisphere lesion are reorganized in the corresponding area of the right hemisphere (Lenneberg, 1967). In Lenneberg's opinion, a similar reorganization of linguistic functions is possible only before the 10th year of age, because children have not yet passed the critical stage at which it is impossible to transfer language from the left hemisphere to the right hemisphere. Other researchers have subsequently lowered the critical period from 10 to 5 years of age (Satz & Lewis, 1993).

Recently numerous hypotheses have been advanced in an attempt at explaining language recovery in aphasic children. Some neurologists have claimed that before a given age the two cerebral hemispheres organize language in almost the same manner. However, for genetic reasons, with growth language is preferentially represented in the left hemisphere, whereas the right hemisphere specializes in other cognitive functions. Therefore, if the left hemisphere is affected by a lesion during the first years of life, language will develop in the right hemisphere, but to the detriment of other functions that are generally organized in this hemisphere. According to another hypothesis, a child's brain, like the one of a newborn baby, contains excess neural circuits, some of which would normally be lost with growth owing to a selection process influenced by the natural and cultural environment. When a lesion affects a child's brain, some of the circuits that would have decayed because they were redundant are recycled and activated in order to reorganize the damaged function.

In the past neurologists were baffled by the quality and rapidity of language recovery in aphasic children as opposed to aphasic adults. Over the past 20 years, however, it has been observed that most aphasic children continue to exhibit more or less severe linguistic deficits. Few succeed in following a normal progression through school. Language recovery depends on the type of lesion: it is less likely to be complete following a vascular lesion (infarction or hemorrhage) than following a cranial trauma. However, the persistence of symptoms does not depend on the age of onset of the cerebral lesion (Murdoch, 1992).

ACQUIRED APHASIA IN BILINGUAL CHILDREN

The first case of acquired aphasia in a bilingual child was described by Bouquet, Paci, and Tuvo (1981). The patient was a right-handed child, R.B., with Italian as mother tongue and Croatian as second language. He spoke Croatian with his grandmother and cousins who did not understand Italian, whereas he spoke Italian with his parents and with his friends at kindergarten. At the age of 4 years and 4 months he suffered a severe cranial trauma that affected the temporo-parietal areas of the left hemisphere. When he awoke from a 13-day long coma, he remained mute for a month. However, during this period he understood words in Italian. After the first month, he started first to utter bisyllabic words in Italian and then three-syllable words, whereas in Croatian he could only utter two words: *nos* (nose) and *tresnje* (cherries).

In the third month, he started to recover Croatian, too, probably because his grandmother, who had been away, started to nurse him. When he was discharged from hospital at the end of the third month, the child seemed unaware of the right side of his body and preferred to use the left hand. He expressed himself in correct Italian, even though he had a poor lexicon and a tendency to speak very slowly. In Croatian his sentence construction was highly impeded, but correct. He was visited six months after the trauma and was diagnosed as having recovered Italian completely. The only residual sign of aphasia was a mild uncertainty in using his second language, in his mother's words: "He speaks well, but not naturally, as if he were translating from Italian into Croatian". In addition, his mother reported that the child spoke Croatian only with people who did not understand Italian, whereas he hardly ever did it with his parents, even though they were bilingual.

Three years after the trauma R.B.'s linguistic abilities were tested for the last time through the Wechsler Intelligence Scale for Children (WISC) and were found to be good both with regard to verbal aspects and non-verbal aspects. He was diagnosed as having recovered both languages completely.

NEUROLINGUISTIC ANALYSIS OF APHASIA IN A BILINGUAL CHILD

During my activity as a clinical neurologist I studied a bilingual child, K.B., who at the age of 7 years was affected by "idiopathic childhood hemiplegia" (Bickerstaff, 1972) accompanied by aphasia. Seven years after the emergence of the acquired language disorder, in April 1993, K.B. was administered the BAT both in her mother tongue and in her second language, so as to assess recovery of her linguistic functions or, conversely, her residual linguistic deficits (Fabbro & Paradis, 1995b).

Clinical history of K.B.

K.B. was born in 1978 and grew up in a small town in central Friuli. She had always spoken Friulian with her parents, grandparents, and sister. At the age of 3, she started to attend kindergarten, where mainly Italian was spoken. At the age of 6 years, she started primary school and learnt to read and write without difficulties. In March 1986, at the age of $7\frac{1}{2}$ years, while in her second year of primary school, she suddenly had an episode of loss of consciousness lasting for about 30 minutes. When she awoke she recognized her mother, who had immediately been informed of the event, but could neither speak nor move her right limbs. When admitted to hospital, she was diagnosed with aphasia characterized by an inability to speak, but preserved comprehension, accompanied by right-sided hemiplegia. A CT scan revealed an ischemic lesion (cerebral infarction) in the frontal temporal area and in the basal ganglia of the left hemisphere (cf. Fig. 20.1).

Immediately after the insult, despite her expressive deficit, the child could understand both languages. Her parents continued to address her in Friulian, whereas physicians addressed her in Italian. Two weeks after the onset of the disease, K.B. started to utter a few syllables in Italian. After a month, she started to produce a few sentences, which she articulated very slowly and only in Italian (L2). For a month she continued to express herself in her second language only. After two weeks, K.B. was discharged from hospital. She started speaking Friulian again. She spoke both languages in a

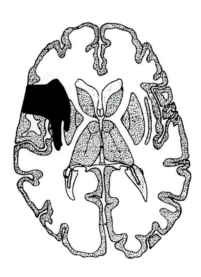

FIG. 20.1.   Site of the lesion in patient K.B.

telegraphic style for more than one year, omitting words and not con-jugating verbs. For one-and-a-half years she attended a speech therapy program in Italian.

Two years after the emergence of the disease the child exhibited good clinical recovery of both languages. Her intellectual functions were pre-served and motor deficits had almost disappeared. However, she used her left hand for writing, whereas before insult she had used her right hand. Neuropsychological tests (dichotic listening, tachistoscopic tests, and tap-ping) showed that her linguistic functions were mainly controlled by the intact hemisphere, namely the right hemisphere. During her school career K.B. continued to exhibit difficulties in written Italian (an example of her written production follows), in arithmetic, and in the foreign language she studied at school. Even though these disorders still persist, nowadays K.B. has achieved what can be considered as good results at school. Only an expert in linguistic disorders can detect mild deficits in her oral expression. At present, the girl sometimes still uses telegraphic expressions, above all when speaking in Friulian.

Two essays by K.B. before and after insult

Before insult (age $7\frac{1}{2}$; second class of primary school)

> There was a goose which laid golden eggs. The farmer fed it a lot. One day he thought he would kill the goose to have more gold. But he found nothing (the farmer thought he would find many golden eggs).

After insult (age 14 years; third class of secondary school)

> Three friends picnic in a woods. The nicest friend lights a fire for the *parbecue*. The other three friends pitch a tent. Once the *sauchages* are ready, the friends eat them. They went away when the fire was still lit. There was a tree next to the fire, the wind blew and the *plame* burnt the tree. Then, the *purnt* plant *purnt* all the woods. A man living nearby decided to cross the path 'cause he had to cross the woods. Then, he saw the burnt woods, he was afraid and took the phone in the car and call the fire brigade, but when they arrived it was too late, because everything was burnt. But the fire had spread, thus after extinguishing the fire, many hectares of the woods were destroyed.

Neurolinguistic assessment

In April 1993, K.B. was administered a series of standardized neuro-psychological tests to assess her verbal and spatial memory, apraxia (inability to perform movements or series of voluntary movements), and agnosia (inability to recognize shapes, objects, etc.). They gave normal results. She was administered the Italian version of the Aachener Aphasie

Test (cf. Chapter 6, pp. 51–3). Her performance was *nonaphasic* (93.1% of the tasks required by the AAT were correctly performed) [with minimal deficits in the token test (48/50), slight minimal deficits in repetition (140/150), slight minimal deficits in written language (88/90), minimal deficits in naming (100/120) and in spontaneous speech (28/30)].

Subsequently, K.B. was administered the BAT in Friulian and in Italian (cf. Chapter 6, pp. 54–6). Her verbal fluency and the average length of sentences were similar in both languages (L1 = 6.1 words per sentence; L2 = 6.5 words per sentence). The patient exhibited the same amount of paraphasias in both languages, for example phonemic paraphasias resulting in nonwords [*cjcjcjche* in place of *cjatât* (found /Friulian/), *lafano* in place of *lavano* (wash /Italian/)]; phonemic paraphasias resulting in words [*sin* (we are) in place of *stin* (we stand /Friulian/), *anca* (hip) in place of *anche* (too /Italian/)]; and semantic paraphasias [*riquadri* (frame) in place of *ritràt* (picture /Friulian/), *madre* (mother) in place of *sorella* (sister /Italian/)]. The most significant feature of her spontaneous speech was the dissociation between her two languages in the number of agrammatisms. Only in Friulian did she significantly omit free grammatical morphemes in bound syntactical contexts (L1 = 16.5% of errors; L2 = 0.8% of errors). K.B. probably made more errors in Friulian because in this language the personal pronoun is not only obligatory, but sometimes it has to be repeated (pleonastic pronoun). The omission of personal and pleonastic pronouns is a serious grammatical error in Friulian as opposed to Italian [for example, "*E se __ soi cun me sûr__ cu le bale*" (correct version: "*E se jo o soi cun me sûr o giuin cu le bale*", literal translation: And if *I I* am with my sister we play with the ball)]. The few agrammatisms made in Italian concerned the omission of articles ["... una persona va a fare _ caffè", "Un giorno ho fatto anch'io _ primo" ("... someone makes _ coffee, one day I made _ pasta, too), where in both cases an article is obligatory in Italian]. In the other tests of the BAT the patient made the same number of errors in both languages, except for the word and nonword acceptability test, the sentence repetition test, and naming, where K.B. obtained lower results in Friulian than in Italian.

Conclusions

The neurolinguistic analysis of this clinical case of acquired aphasia in a bilingual child leads to the following conclusions:

1. Both languages show considerable clinical recovery. In fact, during informal conversations it is very difficult to notice K.B.'s mild linguistic deficits.
2. The second language is better preserved than the mother tongue. This data can be explained on the basis of the following hypotheses: (a) the

mother tongue was affected most because it is organized in the implicit memory systems, whereas the second language, which was learnt and used only at school, is more rooted in the explicit memory systems (cf. Chapter 10); (b) the second language was less affected because it is connected to writing and reading systems (cf. Chapter 13, pp. 120–22), whereas Friulian is an exclusively oral language; (c) the recovery of Italian is likely to depend on the speech therapy program the patient attended and on the fact that the patient attended school in Italian—the patient might thus have been induced to pay more attention to expression in Italian as opposed to Friulian; and (d) the same language disorder may manifest itself in a different manner in two different languages (Menn & Obler, 1990). For example, agrammatisms will be more evident in a language with a more restrictive use of specific syntactic rules (Paradis, 1988, 1998). A recent study of an English-Cantonese bilingual aphasic patient with selective impairment of some syntactic components of his second language (Cantonese) revealed that such impairment cannot be correlated to the structural differences of the two languages only (Yiu & Worrall, 1996).

3. Despite K.B.'s good recovery of her linguistic abilities, mild linguistic deficits still persist seven years after the insult. Therefore, this case corroborates the most recent theory put forward by neurologists that language recovery following acquired childhood aphasia is never complete.

Nevertheless, children with aphasia may have an almost normal life as they do not generally have communicative or intellectual difficulties. Their main cause of frustration remains school, because they generally have written language disorders (agraphia) and calculation disorders (acalculia). Despite their greater effort as opposed to their school mates, they achieve lower results, which is due to greater fatigue, insecurity, and lower self-esteem. If these difficulties are matched by incomprehension, or worse still, incompetence on part of the teachers, school actually becomes an ordeal for these children. What advice can be given to teachers? First of all, greater knowledge of this phenomenon is in order. Second, *tolerance is a virtue*, and constant reward for the results achieved by the child—however modest they may be—is commendable.

CHAPTER TWENTY-ONE

Aphasic syndromes with altered states of consciousness

This chapter describes the clinical history of some bilingual patients who, during altered states of consciousness due to epilepsy or other neurological diseases (cranial trauma, brain infection, etc.), tended to use only some of the languages they knew, or expressed themselves in languages they had apparently lost. During an altered state of consciousness a language that was seemingly lost may be reactivated owing to a temporary reduction of the inhibition that made it unavailable.

ALTERED STATES OF CONSCIOUSNESS DURING EPILEPTIC FITS

In 1896 Eskridge described the linguistic behavior of a bilingual aphasic during an altered state of consciousness (Eskridge, 1896/1983). F.P. was a 23-year-old young man of Bohemian mother tongue who at the age of 13 years had moved to the United States, where he had acquired English as a second language. In September 1895 the young man suffered a severe wound above the left ear. When he was admitted to hospital, the patient was dazed and confused, but answered questions in English relatively well. He was operated on that same day to remove a depressed bone compressing the left frontal lobe. In the evening of the following day (September 22) the patient was no longer able to speak English. He uttered meaningless sentences in Bohemian. Gradually the state of consciousness of the patient worsened, and he suffered convulsive crises. During this period he was in a state of confusion and seemed not to listen to his interlocutors; he replied prevailingly in Bohemian, and only sometimes in English. His verbal production was unintelligible.

On October 5, he underwent another operation to drain a considerable hemorrhage at the level of the first and second left temporal convolutions. Two days after the operation the patient succeeded in reading a few words and in producing correct sentences in English. However, he could not understand English. Five days later, on October 10, he understood simple sentences; for example, when asked "How do you feel?", he answered "Better". "Have you headache?", "Yes, a little". When asked "Where?", he pointed to the left side of his head. The following day he still exhibited poor comprehension, understood only a few questions on his health, and when asked: "What is your name?", "Have you headache? Are you hungry?", he invariably replied with the word "German". On October 22 his spontaneous speech in English was very slow, no appreciable errors in this language were detectable, but the patient complained he had lost Bohemian, which he could no longer speak as well as before the insult. In Eskridge's opinion, the dissociation between the mother tongue and the second language depended on different states of consciousness. His mother tongue, which he had spoken until the age of 13, was linked to old memories and to involuntary and automatic behavior patterns. On the other hand, English—the only language he had spoken over the previous five years—was linked more to his normal state of consciousness and to voluntary expression. The dissociation between Bohemian and English thus depended on the patient's state of consciousness.

In 1949 Minkowski described the clinical case of a patient (G.S.) who was born in a rural community of the Sankt Gallen canton in Switzerland (Minkowski, 1949/1983). His mother tongue was Swiss-German and he had learnt to read, write, and speak in standard German. He had also learnt Italian and French by informal methods. G.S. was a regular reader of books on exotic countries, astronomy, chemistry, and mechanics. At the age of 33, he had a car accident and suffered a cranial trauma with consequent epileptic fits. At the age of 45 (April 1946), while at the workplace, he fell from a ladder that was 8 meters high. This second accident caused a cranial fracture with a lesion to the left frontal lobe. After the accident the patient remained in a coma for a week. In the following three weeks he exhibited right-sided hemiplegia with global aphasia. After a month, G.S. started to understand and speak only standard German, with word-finding difficulties. His family and the patient himself were much surprised by this fact, because before the insult he had spoken only Swiss-German.

After four months (June 1946) he started speaking Swiss-German, too, but in this period he was often euphoric and hyperexcited, and had many epileptiform fits accompanied by loss of consciousness. In October 1946, the patient was visited by Minkowski, who noticed that his speech in Swiss-

German was agrammatic (difficulties in finding the least frequent words, use of the verbs in the infinitive, phonemic and verbal paraphasias). Reading was better preserved than spontaneous speech. When asked what nationality he was, he replied he was born in Paris and that his real father was a French man who had been his mother's fiancé before she got married. He claimed he had attended the first classes of primary school in Paris and that he had subsequently lived in Abyssinia, Iran, Syria, Arabia, India, the Philippines, Australia, and China. In addition, he believed he had acquired the language of some of these countries, i.e. Hindi, Chinese, English, and Spanish, but he had forgotten them as a consequence of the cerebral lesion he had suffered. Over the following years he suffered many epileptic fits of Jacksonian type, accompanied by muscle spasms that started from the right hand and slowly affected the whole arm, generally without a loss of consciousness. During one of these attacks he surprisingly produced some meaningless sentences in French, a language he had neither understood nor spoken for years.

In Minkowski's opinion, this clinical case proved that the patient's representation of mental images of French and Italian had been preserved, despite the fact that he had lost the capacity to understand and speak the two languages. In this case, the lesion had provoked a profound and persistent inhibition of the two languages, which, however, could be overcome during exceptional states of consciousness, such as those provoked by epileptic attacks. During altered states of consciousness the patient could reactivate a seemingly lost language. As in the case described by Eskridge, this case suggests that components of language or even language sets may be suddenly recovered and become manifest in those states of consciousness that deactivate the mechanisms making them inaccessible.

PSYCHIATRIC REACTIONS IN BILINGUAL PATIENTS WITH CEREBRAL LESIONS

In 1955 Krapf described some patients who, subsequent to brain lesions, had episodes of altered states of consciousness during confusional or psychotic crises (Krapf, 1955). The first case concerned a 38-year-old man, of Czech mother tongue and with German as second language, who had acquired Spanish at the age of 24 when he had emigrated to Argentina. The patient was admitted to hospital because of aphasia accompanied by psychomotor seizures and confusional state. Aphasia had been caused by syphilis, which had affected the brain. At hospital his behavior was strange from a linguistic viewpoint. He generally expressed himself in German, but when he was asked about syphilis he used Spanish. In addition, during the treatment for syphilis he spoke only Spanish with his wife, even though she did not understand it.

The second case concerned a patient, aged 33, of English mother tongue and with Spanish as second language. He used to speak English with his wife, and Spanish with his friends. He fell from his horse and suffered a cranial fracture. He had severe episodes of altered states of consciousness, marked by difficulties in recognizing people, and visual hallucinations. After the accident, for a certain period of time, he was irritated by the use of English, and, contrary to his habits, he tended to swear in English. On the other hand, speaking Spanish—also to his wife—relaxed him.

The third case concerned a master mariner who knew only English. Following a cranial trauma accompanied by loss of consciousness for some hours, he used an Oxford-like, highly sophisticated English, particularly with the crew. This phenomenon lasted for some weeks. He spoke with the typical accent of Oxford scholars, using many words of Latin origin and a highly complex syntax. Slowly he recovered the common, highly informal English, with a clear London accent, that he had spoken before insult.

Krapf explained the linguistic behavior of these patients on the basis of Minkowski's theories (cf. Chapter 13, pp. 122–123). Both authors claimed that as a defense reaction the patients they had studied did not speak their mother tongue during acute psychiatric crises. Probably the mother tongue has closer links with the emotional centers of the individual, whereas the use of the second language—generally more detached from the profound emotional sphere—strengthens the psychological defense mechanisms of the subject in situations considered particularly difficult and psycho-emotionally painful.

CHAPTER TWENTY-TWO

Rehabilitation of bilingual aphasics

Language rehabilitation in bilingual aphasics raises problems that differ from those encountered with language rehabilitation in monolinguals. In order to treat bilingual aphasia, the clinician has to decide whether to target one language only—and if so, which—or all the languages known by the patient. At present, the tendency is to treat only one language, i.e. the language chosen by the patient and his relatives. This is due to the fact that, usually, the beneficial effects of rehabilitation may transfer to the untreated languages.

Generally, all monolingual patients with acquired language disorders undergo language rehabilitation. Speech therapy sessions usually begin one month after the emergence of aphasia, take place three times a week for an hour at a time, and last at least six months. The exercises target the patient's specific disorder; for instance, if a patient has phonemic comprehension difficulties, he will be administered appropriate phonemic discrimination tasks. The validity of this kind of language therapy for patients with acquired disorders has not yet been scientifically proved (cf. Paradis, 1993c). However, basically clinicians believe that rehabilitation contributes to avoiding the emergence of incorrect verbal strategies after insult, which might further reduce the patient's linguistic communication abilities.

Speech therapy in bilingual aphasics raises more problems than in monolinguals. Researchers who have become interested in this aspect have attempted to find answers to the main issues concerning language therapy, namely:

1. Is it enough to rehabilitate one language in bilingual aphasics or do all languages known by the patient have to be treated?
2. If the decision is taken to rehabilitate one language only, what are the criteria behind this choice?
3. Does rehabilitation in one language also have beneficial effects on the nontreated languages?
4. Do potential beneficial effects transfer to structurally similar languages (Italian and Spanish) only or also to structurally distant languages (Italian and Japanese)?

Unfortunately, research on language rehabilitation in bilingual aphasics is still at an early stage (Hilton, 1980; Lebrun, 1988; Sasanuma & Park, 1995; Voinescu, Visch, Sirian, & Maretsis, 1977; Watamori & Susanuma, 1976, 1978). So far researchers have mainly analyzed individual cases and, generally, they have not carried out a proper assessment of language disorders before and after rehabilitation. Indeed, very few research studies assessed the patients' linguistic abilities before and after rehabilitation through the Bilingual Aphasia Test, the only existing test battery that can assess about 60 languages in exactly comparable terms. Conclusions drawn from these research studies are thus still speculative, and further studies are in order if more detailed information is to be acquired (Paradis, 1993d; Roberts, 1997). At present, only one language is rehabilitated, especially if the patient shows mixing or switching phenomena, so as not to confuse the patient and to save time. Should two languages be rehabilitated simultaneously, sessions would increase from three to six per week; similarly three languages would require nine sessions, etc.

With regard to the selection criteria, no clear-cut answers are provided: some researchers claim that the mother tongue is preferable, others claim that it is the language that is least impaired, others still claim that the language that is worst impaired should be targeted.

In the case of the bilingual aphasic patients I observed, the selection of the language to be rehabilitated resulted from two parameters: (a) a systematic assessment of the patient's linguistic disorders through the BAT in the languages the patient knew (cf. Chapter 6); and (b) an interview with the patient and relatives during which neurolinguistic data (neurological data, results of the BAT in the languages known by the patient, etc.) and sociolinguistic issues concerning the patient and his family were discussed (which language they preferred to rehabilitate both for affective and for business reasons).

Therefore, except for highly complex neurolinguistic situations, for instance aphasia with paradoxical recovery of one language (cf. Chapter 14), the selection of the language to be rehabilitated depends on the patient and his family's decision, because it has been proven that generally the benefits of rehabilitation in one language tend to extend to the untreated languages (Fredman, 1976; Junqué, Vendrell, Vendrell-Brucet, & Tobeña, 1989). This "mass effect" does not seem to be due to the degree of structural similarity between languages, as it is effective in both structurally similar and structurally different languages (Fabbro, De Luca, & Vorano, 1996).

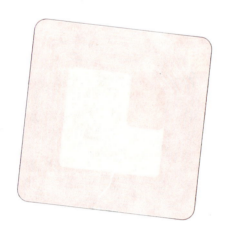

CHAPTER TWENTY-THREE

Electrical stimulation studies in bilinguals

This chapter describes electrical stimulation studies on the cerebral organization of language in bilinguals. Electrical stimulation of specific cortical areas during neurosurgical operations has contributed to the study of cerebral representation of language, and has permitted us to to ascertain that: (a) in all cases of bilingual patients there were cerebral areas common for both languages; (b) at the same time, certain areas, if stimulated, produced interferences only in one language; and (c) the second language tended to have a more diffuse representation in the left hemisphere as opposed to the representation of the mother tongue.

CORTICO-ELECTRICAL STIMULATION IN BILINGUALS

As already stated, patients waiting to undergo neurosurgical operations may be subject to cortico-electrical stimulation and concurrently administered language tests to assess which linguistic functions are inhibited (cf. Chapter 7, pp. 64–67). As this technique permitted the study of the cortical organization of some linguistic components in monolingual subjects, Ojemann and Whitaker decided to apply it to bilinguals, too, in order to study their cerebral organization of language (Ojemann & Whitaker, 1978).

The first patient (case 1) was of Dutch mother tongue. He had moved to the United States at the age of 25, where he had acquired English, even though he preferred to read in Dutch rather than English. At the age of 4, he suffered the onset of psychomotor seizures, a type of epilepsy originating

189

from a focus in the left temporal lobe. At the age of 23, a partial left temporal lobotomy was performed to remove the focus. Unfortunately, at the age of 28, he started suffering epileptic fits again, because a focus had emerged in another area of the left temporal lobe. The patient underwent a second neurosurgical operation. However, before the operation, he was injected with sodium amytal (Wada's test; cf. Chapter 7, p. 64) in order to establish clearly in which hemisphere language was lateralized.

Before the operation the patient was administered a preliminary naming test. He had to name 45 common objects, which were presented visually through slides. Above the picture of the object (for example, a chair) a sentence read "This is a …". The patient had to watch the picture first and then complete the sentence "This is a chair" (cf. Fig. 7.2). The patient named all objects both in Dutch and in English without difficulty. During the operation, while the patient was under local anesthesia, the same naming task was repeated. Once the cerebral cortex of the left hemisphere was exposed, 23 cortical sites were identified with a sterile numbered tag. Subsequently, every single site was electrically stimulated while the patient named all objects in both languages. The stimulation and the presentation of the slide occurred concurrently and lasted 4 seconds. The intensity of the stimulation (cf. Chapter 7, pp. 64–5) did not interfere with the neural activity of the adjacent areas. Six sites out of the 23 stimulated (cf. Fig. 23.1) inhibited naming in both languages (solid circles in Figure 23.1), and seven sites showed differential effects: at some sites only English was inhibited (E in open circles in Fig. 23.1), whereas at others only Dutch was inhibited (D

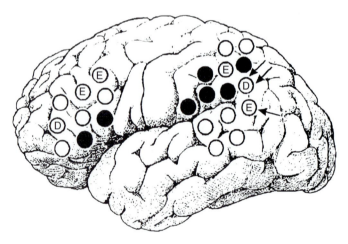

FIG. 23.1. Cortico-electrical stimulation in a bilingual (case 1) (adapted from Ojemann and Whitaker, 1978).

in open circles in Fig. 23.1). With regard to the remaining 10 sites, electrical stimulation did not interfere with the naming task in either language (open circles in Fig. 23.1).

With regard to differential effects, during electrical stimulation of a site localized in the superior temporal gyrus (single arrow in Fig. 23.1), the patient could not correctly name the words *bird*, *apple*, and *flower* in English, whereas electrical stimulation of the same site did not interfere with naming of the words *tree* and *bird* in Dutch. Stimulation at another site, slightly above the previous one (double arrow in Fig. 23.1), provoked the reverse effect: the patient could not name the words *telephone*, *cup*, and *car* in Dutch, whereas electrical stimulation at the same site did not inhibit the correct naming of the words *mountain*, *boat*, and *tree* in English.

The second patient (case 2) studied by Ojemann and Whitaker was a left-handed student, aged 20, of English mother tongue, who had acquired Spanish during her childhood at her grandparents'. At the age of 6, she suffered the onset of psychomotor seizures originating from a right temporal epileptic focus. She underwent a neurosurgical operation to remove it. Wada testing revealed that in the patient language was organized in the right hemisphere. Before the operation she was administered a naming test in both English and Spanish. She had to name 57 common objects presented on slides, as in case 1. The patient performed the task without errors.

The naming test was performed with concurrent electrical stimulation of the 22 sites of the cerebral cortex that had previously been selected. At two sites electrical stimulation inhibited both languages (solid circles in Fig. 23.2), and seven sites showed differential effects: at some sites only English was inhibited (E in open circles in Fig. 23.2), and at others only Spanish was

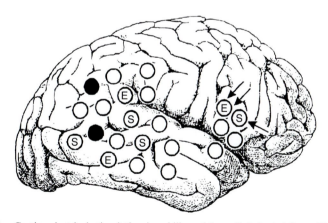

FIG. 23.2. Cortico-electrical stimulation in a bilingual (case 2) (adapted from Ojemann and Whitaker, 1978).

inhibited (S in open circles in Fig. 23.2). At the remaining 13 sites electrical stimulation did not systematically inhibit naming in either of the languages known by the patient. An example of differential effects is provided by two sites situated in the frontal cortex. During electrical stimulation of the first site (single arrow in Fig. 23.2) the patient could not correctly name the words *car*, *key*, *knife*, and *pencil* in Spanish, whereas electrical stimulation of the same site did not interfere with naming of the words *chair*, *coat*, *turtle*, *bed*, and *comb* in English. Stimulation of the second site selected (double arrow in Fig. 23.2) provoked the reverse effect. The patient could not name the words *child*, *bus*, and *lamp* in English, but named the words *child*, *ball*, *boat*, and *house* in Spanish.

A few years later Rapport, Tan, and Whitaker (1983) carried out a similar study on three polyglot patients. Its results corroborated the data of the first experiment. These authors drew three general conclusions:

1. All clinical cases revealed the existence of centers *common* to all languages known by the patients.
2. Centers showing *differential* inhibition effects had also been detected.
3. The second language tended to have a more diffuse representation in the left hemisphere than did the mother tongue. [More recently Berthier, Starkstein, Lylyk, and Leiguarda (1990; cf. Paradis, 1990a) obtained contradictory results by studying a bilingual patient presenting a perisylvian organization of the second language and a more diffuse cortical representation of the mother tongue (Wada's test; cf. Chapter 7, p. 64)].

These interesting studies are not free from methodological criticism. The first objection to be raised concerns the extent of the area to be stimulated, which is almost 1cm in diameter. It is a very large area compared with brain size, and makes electrical stimulation studies extremely imprecise. The second objection concerns the selection of the sites to be stimulated. Their localization is too rough to guarantee that exactly the same sites for both languages have been stimulated (Paradis, 1993a; cf. Chapter 7, p. 67).

UNILATERAL ELECTROCONVULSIVE THERAPY IN BILINGUALS

In 1983, a group of Russian researchers, T. Chernigovskaya, L. Balonov, and V. Deglin, published a study on cerebral organization of languages, which they had carried out using the unilateral electroconvulsive technique. They studied a patient (H.B.), aged 38, of Turkmenian mother tongue, affected by hallucinative-paranoid schizophrenia. At the age of 7, H.B. had acquired Russian, which later became the language he used most. At the end of secondary school he suffered the first episodes of auditory hallucinations and expressed paranoid delusions. During acute crises he was repeatedly admitted to psychiatric clinics and administered unilateral electroconvulsive treatment.

Electrodes are placed on the scalp of the right or left temporal region to induce a unilateral shock. An electrical charge is applied to elicit epileptic fits and to inhibit cortical activities temporarily. Immediately after the application of the electrical charge the patient remembers nothing of what has happened and is highly disoriented. Generally, after few minutes the patient recovers the cognitive functions that had been inhibited by the charge. The electroconvulsive therapy was devised by two Italian physicians, Lucio Bini and Ugo Cerletti, who proposed to use it in the treatment of schizophrenia and severe depression. They claimed that electroconvulsive therapy provoked a temporary loss of consciousness and temporary amnesia and, if repeatedly applied, could destroy the sick personality of the patient and create a new man. Although numerous studies have attempted to assess the therapeutic validity of this technique, it is still unclear whether it can contribute to the treatment of patients with psychological disorders. However, the opinion of patients who underwent this technique is known; it was clearly and succinctly expressed by the first patient who underwent it: "It's hell!" (Valenstein, 1986).

H.B. underwent 10 sessions, 5 for each hemisphere. Before and after the therapy, language tests were administered. Two general aspects of language were assessed: spontaneous speech and repetition of a text in both languages known by the patient. In *spontaneous speech tasks* following inhibition of the left hemisphere, Turkmenian was recovered earlier and faster than Russian. Following inhibition of the right hemisphere the patient answered in Russian even though he was addressed in Turkmenian, and even when asked to speak in Turkmenian, he still answered in Russian. In the *text repetition task* (a short story by Tolstoy) the patient could correctly repeat the story only in Turkmenian following inhibition of the left hemisphere. When the same story was read to him in Russian, he could not repeat it, and if repeatedly requested to, he got angry. Inhibition of the right hemisphere did not seem to affect his ability to repeat the short story in both languages. In this case, the patient was extremely loquacious, but did not really repeat the story. In both languages repetition consisted of the reiterated production of words or chunks without cohesion or coherence. The patient's expressions were perseverations of interrupted chunks. Chernigovskaja et al. concluded that H.B.'s superficial (phonological and syntactic) and semantic functions of Russian were organized in the left hemisphere. Inhibition of this hemisphere impaired spontaneous speech and repetition in Russian. On the other hand, the superficial functions of Turkmenian were organized in the left hemisphere, but the semantic functions were organized in the right hemisphere. Inhibition of the left hemisphere did not impair repetition in Turkmenian.

On the basis of these data a model of the organization of the superficial and semantic linguistic functions in bilinguals was proposed (cf. Fig. 23.3), whereby in monolinguals (I in Fig. 23.3) deep semantic structures (D) of language are mainly organized in the right hemisphere, whereas superficial structures (S) are organized in the left hemisphere. In bilinguals who have acquired the second language only after full acquisition of the mother tongue (II in Fig. 23.3), as in the case of H.B., only the deep structures of the mother tongue (D1) are organized in the right hemisphere, whereas the deep structures of the second language (D2) and the superficial structures of both languages (S1, S2) are organized in the left hemisphere. Lastly, in bilinguals who acquired both languages concurrently (III in Fig. 23.3), the deep structures of both languages are organized in the right hemisphere (D), whereas the superficial structures of both languages (S1, S2) are separate, but organized in the left hemisphere.

Further studies highlighted some general limits of Chernigovskaja et al.'s hypotheses, namely:

1. The model was based on linguistic theories that were later refuted by the very linguists who had advanced them (for example, the distinction between superficial and deep structure proposed by Chomsky is no longer considered valid by Chomsky himself).
2. The model was based on too small a number of experimental observations.
3. The results of an experimental study I carried out with Bruno and Laura Gran on a vast sample of polyglots contradicts this model (Fabbro, Gran, & Gran, 1991).

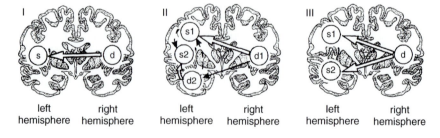

FIG. 23.3. Cerebral organization of some linguistic components (deep and superficial) in different types of bilingualism.

4. Care should be taken in extending data obtained from the study of patients affected by psychiatric disturbances to normal subjects, as some mental diseases are known to bring about a reorganization of hemispheric specialization.

CHAPTER TWENTY-FOUR

A neurolinguistic theory of translation

Translation is one of the most typical verbal behavioral patterns of bilinguals. This chapter describes translation disorders in bilingual aphasics. One of the pathological phenomena in bilinguals with cerebral lesions is the inability to translate. Other patients present spontaneous translation phenomena, namely a compulsive need to translate their own expressions into another language. Others can still translate sentences or words correctly from language to language, but do not understand their meaning. Or they suffer from paradoxical translation, whereby they can only translate into the language they cannot speak spontaneously. The last paragraph of this chapter presents a neuropsychological model of simultaneous interpretation based on recent experimental studies.

The capacity to translate from language to language is one of the most typical verbal behaviors of bilinguals. Even children often act as interpreters for their parents; this phenomenon has frequently been observed in migrant families, where sometimes parents have more difficulties than their children in acquiring the language of the host country. However, translation is not to be considered an exceptional and specific linguistic phenomenon typical only of bilinguals or polyglots, because monolinguals too are able to rephrase or paraphrase sentences or texts in the same language. Encoding and paraphrasing are considered *endolinguistic translations*, namely translations within a language. *Interlinguistic translation* or translation in the proper sense of the word consists—in Roman Jakobson's words—in rendering the linguistic signs of a language through the linguistic signs of another language (Jakobson, 1961). As with all human prerogatives, some subjects—by training or gift—can translate better and more easily than others. However, this capacity is present in all humans, whether monolingual (endolinguistic translation) or bilingual (interlinguistic translation).

This chapter will discuss data concerning the neurolinguistics of oral translation, probably the oldest form of translation, though other forms do exist, written translation being the best known and most widespread. Consider, for example, the amount of poetry, novels, or historical books that have been translated. Numerous linguists and philosophers have acquired an interest in translation and some of them have claimed in large tomes that translation is impossible, and that every translation is a betrayal, especially literary translation. Nevertheless, many of them have insisted that their essays on the unfeasibility of translation be translated into other languages so as to spread their ideas. A more pragmatic stance concerning translation was adopted by French linguist Claude Hagège in his dry statement: "Translation is always possible" (Hagège, 1985). He rightly claimed that any text in any language is translatable into a text in another language, more or less approximately, more or less perfectly. These conclusions hold true for both written and oral translation.

Because translation is one of the most typical verbal behavioral patterns of bilinguals, the study of aphasia in these subjects also has to assess disorders that might impair this specific ability (cf. Chapter 6, pp. 53–6). Numerous cases of bilingual or polyglot aphasics with particular translation disorders have been described. The study of these patients has permitted us to understand better not only the neural organization of this function, but also the linguistic and cognitive aspects involved in the process.

APHASIA WITH INABILITY TO TRANSLATE

One of the most obvious pathological phenomena that bilingual aphasics may exhibit following a brain lesion is the inability to translate. This phenomenon has often been described in neurological literature. One of these cases was reported by Italian neurologist G. Gastaldi in 1951. The patient was a 42-year-old man who had suffered a chronic inflammatory lesion to the left hemisphere that left him with a paralysis of the upper right limb and aphasia. The patient had emigrated to Switzerland at the age of 4, and there he had acquired both Swiss-German and standard German. At the age of 16 he had returned to Italy and had started to speak Italian, especially for business reasons, but he spoke a Lombard dialect with his wife. Aphasia provoked a considerable reduction in his spontaneous speech in both Italian and German. Comprehension of simple orders in both languages was preserved, whereas naming was reduced in both languages. The patient could name objects only in the language in which he was addressed, but could not translate into the other language, in either direction (from Italian into German, or vice versa). Gastaldi interpreted the patient's inability to translate as a fixation phenomenon on a language, which inhibited the switch mechanisms and the translation processes (Gastaldi, 1951).

In a book dated 1971, Jakobson suggested that in polyglot aphasics lesions provoking the loss of any gift for translation, both at intralinguistic and interlinguistic level, affect the posterior areas accounting for language. Lesions in the posterior areas accounting for language organization generally provoke fluent aphasias, with disorders affecting the linguistic level of selection *(paradigmatic level)*. In monolinguals fluent aphasias cause the loss of the ability to find words of corresponding categories (synonyms, heteronyms, etc.), whereas in bilingual aphasics they also affect the mechanisms accounting for translation from language to language. In addition, Jakobson explained *anomia*, a typical symptom of fluent aphasia, as a particular switching disorder between different codes, namely the incapability to switch from the code of the picture describing the object to the linguistic code that is a form of acoustic representation of the object (cf. Jakobson, 1971).

SPONTANEOUS TRANSLATION

Aphasia with spontaneous translation is a pathological phenomenon typical of aphasia in bilinguals, yet not very frequent. It consists of the unsolicited translation of one's own expressions into another language. Kauders was one of the first neurologists who described this phenomenon in 1929. A polyglot patient of his (D.O.), aged 62, suffered a series of strokes, the last of which left him with a lesion in Wernicke's area and in some sections of the left parietal lobe. D.O. was of German mother tongue. He also knew English and French, which he spoke almost as fluently as his mother tongue. The good knowledge of these two languages had permitted him to work for many years as a porter in one of the most prestigious international hotels in Vienna. Immediately after the insult the patient presented a right-sided paralysis accompanied by a complete loss of comprehension in all languages he knew. His spontaneous speech was totally unintelligible, with numerous phonemic paraphasias, some of which were formed by blending syllables from the languages he knew. Slowly the patient recovered his spontaneous speech, frequently mixing French fixed expressions into his German output, i.e. *"Voilà monsieur"*, *"Un beau monsieur"*, *"Oui, très bien"*. Hardly ever did he use complete expressions in French. His wife could only partially understand him, because she only knew German. Moreover, he addressed physicians only in French. In the naming task he could find the correct word only by translating it from other languages. For example, when asked to define the color yellow he first said it in English and French and only later in German. This phenomenon was studied for many months until the death of the patient (Kauders, 1929/1983).

An autobiographical example of automatic translation was provided by linguist Roman Jakobson in 1964. As a result of a car accident, which left him with a cranial trauma and temporary aphasia lasting three hours, Jakobson could no longer inhibit the automatic translation of all sentences he thought into the four or five languages he knew best. In 1984, Perecman described the same phenomenon in a bilingual aphasic patient (H.B.), with German as mother tongue and English as second language, who often spontaneously translated a whole sentence after uttering it, i.e. "*Ich möchte ein Buch haben. I would like to have a book*". These spontaneous translation phenomena were particularly interesting because the patient could not perform the same translation task on request (Perecman, 1984). Often translation is an automatic process that cannot be inhibited and cannot be activated at will or on request.

In a study carried out in 1991, Belgian neurolinguist Yvan Lebrun described a bilingual patient with a particular translation disorder. The patient had suffered a right hemisphere lesion that had not provoked aphasia in oral language, but only a tendency to translate written language spontaneously. In dictation tasks of French words the patient wrote down the words and often unsolicitedly translated them into Flemish. Sometimes he spontaneously translated into Flemish whole texts written in French. In Lebrun's opinion, the lesion to the right hemisphere had provoked a deficit in the control of the sociolinguistic rules of communication, that is, in conversation a subject cannot suddenly switch to another language and does not translate parts of the conversation without reason or without being asked to (Lebrun, 1991).

According to Perecman, in polyglots spontaneous translation is a subconscious process representing one of the several stages during the microgenesis of an utterance. The pathological translation phenomenon is thus the visible stage of normal automatic translation processes, which in multilingual individuals operate at subconscious level (Perecman, 1984).

TRANSLATION WITH COMPREHENSION DEFICITS

This phenomenon was described by Veyrac in 1931. The patient (Ch.) was a woman with English as mother tongue who at the age of 15 had moved to Paris, where a few years later she had married a Frenchman. Since then she had had little occasion to speak English, because she had never returned to England. At the age of 65, she suffered a stroke that left her with aphasia and a right-sided hemiplegia. Three days after insult the patient could not speak, and murmured indistinct sounds and occasionally a stereotyped utterance, "*Mais oui … mais oui*". She did not even understand simple orders in French. However, when her physician addressed her in English and gave her extremely simple orders, she spontaneously translated them and did not carry them out, because she did not seem to understand the sentence she had correctly translated. For example, when asked: "What time is it?" she replied in distinct French *"Quelle heure est-il?"*, without answering the question. When ordered: "Show me your tongue", she answered: *"Montrez-moi la langue"*, yet did not carry out the task. In other words, the patient seemed to be able to translate sentences without understanding them. Over the following days she started uttering a few words and understanding simple sentences in French. After a month, her production and comprehension in French had further improved, whereas her verbal and receptive abilities in English remained unchanged. Only after six months did the patient mildly recover comprehension and production in both languages.

The phenomenon of translation without comprehension was explained by Veyrac (1931/1983) on the basis of three hypotheses:

1. The phenomenon might be explained as an *automatic process*. Aphasics lose the capacity to control their voluntary activities, but can still perform automatic activities. They can sometimes express highly complex automatized sentences, but they cannot voluntarily utter simple syllables.
2. Translation without comprehension might be considered to be an aspect of *articulatory perseveration*. Patients affected by aphasia can correctly repeat words without understanding them and present correct spontaneous, yet incoherent speech. In this case speech is preserved, but separate from the other cognitive functions. These patients can correctly speak without being able to decide and control what they are saying (this specific case was analyzed and described by Geschwind, Quadfasel, and Segarra, 1968, who proposed to define it as the "isolation of the speech areas syndrome"; cf. Chapter 5, p. 46).
3. Lastly, Veyrac proposed to interpret this phenomenon as an aspect of the habit of bilinguals to *translate before understanding*. In his opinion, it is rather usual for individuals knowing a foreign language to translate into their mother tongue what they have just heard before answering the question. This behavior pattern may become highly automatic so that subjects translate the sentence spontaneously before focusing on its meaning. Therefore, in this case, it is not necessary to understand the meaning of the message before translating it.

PARADOXICAL TRANSLATION

This phenomenon was first described by Paradis, Goldblum, and Abidi in 1982. The cases they studied concerned patients who exhibited alternating antagonism with paradoxical translation behavior (cf. Chapter 18, pp. 159–164). Generally, a bilingual finds it easier to translate from the language he masters least well into the language he knows best (L2→L1) as opposed to the reverse (L1→L2). However, in the cases described by Paradis et al. the reverse applied. For example, patient A.D. expressed herself only in Arabic for certain days, conversely other days she spoke French better than Arabic. The day when she understood both languages (December 12) but only expressed herself in Arabic, she paradoxically could translate only from Arabic into French, but not vice versa. The following day the patient could express herself in French, but could translate only from French into Arabic. The second case described by Paradis et al. exhibited alternating antagonism with paradoxical translation behavior as well. For example, during the third week after the operation the patient could express himself in French only. However, he correctly translated everything into English—the language that was unavailable to him—but not into French. This type of translation is defined paradoxical because patients can translate only into the language in which spontaneous expression appears to be inhibited.

In a study of 1984, Paradis analyzed the paradoxical translation phenomenon and the translation without comprehension deficit phenomenon, and presupposed the existence of a series of functionally separate and independent components (Paradis, 1984):

1. a system accounting for comprehension in L1 and in L2;
2. a system accounting for expression in L1 and L2;
3. a system accounting for translation from L1 into L2 (L1→L2);
4. a system accounting for translation from L2 into L1 (L2→L1).

Therefore, a cerebral lesion in a bilingual subject may for a certain period of time selectively inhibit only a component of the translation process, whereas the other component that is functionally independent may continue to perform translation without difficulty. A more schematic representation of translation processes in bilinguals is provided by Fig. 24.1.

A NEUROLINGUISTIC MODEL OF SIMULTANEOUS INTERPRETATION

One of the most complex verbal behavior patterns in bilinguals or polyglots is the concurrent activity of listening to a message in the source language (SL) and translating it into the target language (TL). This process is defined as *simultaneous interpretation*. The term "simultaneous" is obviously to be interpreted *in sensu latu*, because there is always a certain delay of some seconds between the original message in the source language and its translation into the target language on the part of the interpreter. The delay generally corresponds to the duration of a sentence. Therefore, in simul-

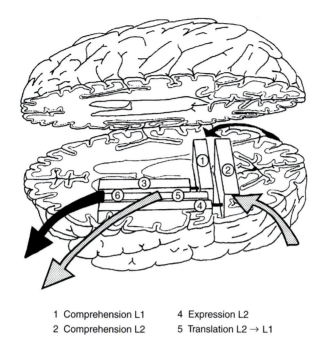

1 Comprehension L1	4 Expression L2
2 Comprehension L2	5 Translation L2 → L1
3 Expression L1	6 Translation L1 → L2

FIG. 24.1.   Neurofunctional systems accounting for translation.

taneous interpreting a sentence is the minimum chunk that is translated by the interpreter. Probably, as the working memory span lasts 10 seconds, it poses a limit to the translation of longer chunks during the process (cf. Chapter 10, pp. 93–6). Studies on chunks of simultaneous interpretation have been carried out to assess the lapse of time during which the speaker and the interpreter speak simultaneously, which happens for 40% of the process; 20% of the time only the speaker speaks, 30% of the time only the interpreter speaks, and for the remaining 10% both speaker and interpreter remain in silence. To carry out the job an interpreter must master at least two languages. The degree of competence is very important because if the interpreter knows both languages at the same level, he can perform the interpretation in both directions equally easily. If, as is often the case, the interpreter knows one language (L1) better than the other (L2), he will find it very easy to translate from L2 into L1 (*passive interpretation*) as opposed to from L1 into L2 (*active interpretation*). Interpreters working for international organizations usually carry out passive interpretation.

Simultaneous interpretation, being a complex cognitive task, is a stressful activity. Interpreters performs this activity in a booth where they listen to a message through earphones and translate it into another language. The output cannot be directly transmitted to the audience by loudspeakers because it would prevent the speaker from giving their speech. The interpreters' translations are transmitted through earphones to the audience, who tune into the channel corresponding to the language they want to listen to. Therefore, if the speech is given in German, part of the audience will listen to the translation into Italian and others to the translation into English or French, simply by connecting to the booths working in the selected language. The working day of an interpreter amounts to seven hours; they work in twos, taking turns of 30 minutes. Professional interpreters know and use a second type of translation, namely *consecutive translation*. In this case the speaker speaks for about 10 minutes, while the interpreter takes notes of the original message by means of a particular system of symbols and words in different languages. The speaker concludes the speech or part of it, and at this juncture the interpreter repeats the speech into the target language by supporting their memory with the notes. This type of interpretation is generally used during negotiations, when the number of participants is very limited, a greater interaction between speaker and interpreter is needed, or if the facilities for carrying out simultaneous interpretation are not available.

During simultaneous interpretation interpreters use strategies of analysis and reproduction of the message into another language that may range between a "semantic translation" and a "word-for-word translation" (rather superficial). In the semantic translation, chunks in the source language are somehow deprived of their linguistic form and only their meaning is stored and reproduced in the target language. With this mode of interpretation it is not necessary to store the SL text into the working memory completely. Interpreters must understand the content of what they are translating but are less prone to syntactic and lexical interferences between the two languages and can thus select the most appropriate expressions in the target language. In the word-for-word translation strategy, interpreters translate the minimal elements at all linguistic levels (phonological, morphological, syntactic, and semantic). The two languages tend to form short circuits and the message can partially be translated without being completely processed by the cognitive system. Interpreters need not understand completely what they are translating. This translation strategy can be used by interpreters only when they are having difficulties or when they have to translate highly specialized and technical speeches, e.g. in mathematics or theoretical physics. In this case, the audience might appreciate the interpretation, even though the interpreters have understood little of what they have translated.

Some years ago, together with a group of colleagues of the University of Trieste, I started a series of experimental studies on the neuropsychological aspects of simultaneous interpretation (Darò & Fabbro, 1994; Fabbro &

Darò, 1994; Fabbro & Gran, 1997; Fabbro, Gran, Basso, & Bava, 1990). These studies showed that the acquisition of the simultaneous interpretation technique elicits modifications in the organization of the linguistic, attentional, and mnestic functions of subjects undergoing an intense training in simultaneous interpretation. For example, after two years of training, right-handed interpreters no longer exhibit the usual superiority of the right ear in the recognition of verbal stimuli (cf. Chapter 7, p. 60). We advanced the hypothesis that this reorganization of acoustic-linguistic functions is probably due to the habit of interpreters to listen to the SL message with their left

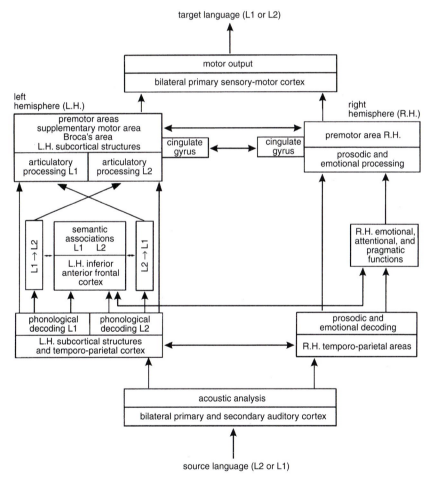

FIG. 24.2. Main functional components involved in the process of simultaneous interpretation.

ear, whereas they control their output with their right ear. In addition, we proved that in students of interpretation the analysis and translation strategies are more oriented towards syntactical (superficial) aspects of the SL message, whereas professional interpreters tend to use semantic translation strategies to a greater extent. Lastly, these studies showed that during interpretation both cerebral hemispheres are activated. The left hemisphere is involved most in the recognition of the SL message and in the processes of translation and reproduction of the TL message. On the other hand, the right hemisphere is involved in emotional-attentive tasks and in the control of the nonverbal and pragmatic features of communication to a larger extent (cf. Fig. 24.2).

By studying professional simultaneous interpreters with aphasia it will probably be possible to shed more light on the cerebral representation of languages in this particular type of polyglot individuals (who are able to keep two different languages active at one point in time, while translating in the so-called "simultaneous" mode) as well as on the processes of oral translation (Paradis, 1994c).

CHAPTER TWENTY-FIVE

The neuropsychology of bilingualism

Numerous clinical and experimental studies on the cerebral organization of language in bilingual subjects have led to the conclusion that different languages are organized partially in the same areas of the brain and partially in specific and separate areas. Hypotheses have been put forward that the languages localized in the same cerebral areas at macroscopic level are represented in distinct neural circuits at microscopic level. At the end of the 1970s some neuropsychologists put forward the idea that language is organized differently in bilinguals and in monolinguals. Subsequent experimental studies, however, have not corroborated this hypothesis. This chapter ends with the description of two models of brain organization in bilinguals based on the latest studies.

CEREBRAL ORGANIZATION OF LANGUAGES

The issue of cerebral organization of language in bilinguals essentially concerns the question of whether two different languages are localized in the same areas or in distinct areas of the brain. Numerous hypotheses have been advanced. I will present some of them in the light of Paradis' recent theory (Paradis & Lebrun, 1983; Paradis, 1985, 1993a, 1996).

The first hypothesis, advanced in the past by many neurologists, suggests that all languages known by a bilingual or a polyglot are localized in the *same cerebral areas*. Sigmund Freud (1891) claimed that languages other than the mother tongue are obviously localized in the same areas that are known to be the centers subserving the mother tongue. In his important study on aphasia in polyglots, Pitres (1895/1983) shared this view, and

Minkowski (1927/1983a), too, claimed that it was not necessary to pre-suppose the existence of separate centers subserving different language sets. In Minkowski's opinion, the disturbances exhibited by polyglot aphasics could be explained by functional factors only, without necessarily postu-lating a separate cerebral organization of languages (cf. Chapters 12 and 13).

The diametrically opposed hypothesis, namely that each language is localized in *separate areas of the brain*, was put forward by Scoresby-Jackson in 1867. In his opinion, if Broca's area is responsible for the acquisition of the mother tongue, each newly acquired language implies the formation of a new center that develops—for reasons of functional adap-tation—in the anterior frontal portions of Broca's area (cf. Chapter 12, p. 112, and Chapter 15, p. 137).

Pötzl (1925, 1930) proposed that bilinguals develop *specialized neuro-anatomical centers*. This third hypothesis was subsequently supported by other German authors. In Pötzl's opinion, bilinguals have specific linguistic behavior patterns, such as the capacity to select a language, the capacity to switch from language to language, the capacity to translate, etc. The left supramarginal gyrus, an area of the parietal lobe, controls these verbal behavior patterns, in particular selection and switching (for data and figures cf. Chapter 17). This area is thus responsible for what is known as "a gift for languages". This hypothesis has been harshly criticized by numerous authors, including Paradis, who claimed that there is no substantial differ-ence between monolinguals and polyglots at a linguistic level. The mech-anisms subserving the use of different linguistic registers and the switching from register to register in monolinguals are similar to the mechanisms subserving the use of different languages and the switching from language to language in polyglots. Moreover, translation processes are present in monolinguals too and make it possible to reproduce a verbal message in the same language—as Jakobson (1961) claimed (cf. Chapter 24).

Proposing hypotheses on the cerebral organization of language in poly-glots by considering macroscopic aspects of the brain only, namely those aspects visible to the naked eye, is a rather naïve way to study higher brain functions. In the past some neurologists had already suggested that lan-guage in bilinguals is organized in the same cortical areas, but in *distinct neural circuits*. In 1889 Adler claimed that distinct cerebral cells subserve different languages (Adler, 1889/1983), whereas Minkowski in 1927 clearly stated that within the same cerebral area the same elements are active, yet in different combinations and interacting differently, according to the different language sets (Minkowski, 1927/1983a).

Finally, a fifth hypothesis has been put forward whereby language is organized *partly in common areas* and *partly in specific and separate areas of the brain*. Numerous scholars support this hypothesis, which is consistent with the classic idea that most of the phenomena accompanying aphasia in bilinguals can be explained from a functional point of view [language recovery (alternating antagonism, paradoxical translation, etc., cf. Chapters 12, 13, 17, and 24), numerous clinical and experimental data (cf. differential aphasia, Chapter 16; electrical stimulation of the cortex, Chapter 23), recent observations on memory organization (role of implicit and explicit memory in the acquisition of mother tongue and second language, cf. Chapters 10 and 14) and fMRI studies showing a different representation of L1 and L2 in Broca's area in fluent bilinguals having acquired L2 after the age of 10, cf. Chapter 10.5]. This hypothesis is thus a synthesis of three previous hypotheses: the first (same areas), the second (separate areas) and the fourth (within the same areas distinct neural circuits independently subserve different language sets) (cf. Fabbro, 1996).

CEREBRAL LATERALIZATION OF LANGUAGES

Neurologist V. Gorlitzer von Mundy (1959/1983) was the first to suggest that in bilinguals the mother tongue and the second language have a different lateralization in the two hemispheres. By studying a bilingual patient in 1959, he claimed that the language acquired only at oral level was represented in both cerebral hemispheres, and that the language acquired both in written and oral form was lateralized in the left hemisphere. J.P., the patient described by Gorlitzer von Mundy, was of Slovenian mother tongue. At the age of 30, he had enlisted in the Austrian infantry, where he had learnt German. The patient was illiterate and ambidextrous, but in the army he learnt to write with the right hand, thus becoming right-handed. At the age of 94, J.P. suffered a stroke to the left hemisphere with consequent aphasia and right-sided hemiplegia. After the insult the patient could no longer speak German, but surprisingly he could speak Slovenian, which he had not used for the previous 40 years. Gorlitzer von Mundy believed that the most plausible explanation for this phenomenon was that the mother tongue, which the patient had acquired when he was still ambidextrous, was represented in both cerebral hemispheres. On the other hand, German had been acquired together with the right-hand preference (for writing), and was thus lateralized in the left hemisphere only. In addition, the author claimed that he had repeatedly observed the same phenomenon in illiterate subjects in the jungle of central Asia.

In 1978, on the basis of Gorlitzer von Mundy's hypothesis, Albert and Obler—in an analysis of the literature on bilingual aphasics—ascertained that almost 10% of bilingual aphasics had suffered a lesion to the right hemisphere, whereas aphasia in right-handed monolinguals following a lesion to the right hemisphere (crossed aphasia) was generally less than 5%. On the basis of these results, Albert and Obler concluded that in bilinguals more often than in monolinguals linguistic functions are represented in the right hemisphere (Albert & Obler, 1978). This hypothesis appealed to the scientific imagery of many researchers, who over the past 15 years have carried out studies on the cerebral lateralization of language in bilinguals and polyglots. These studies have generally been carried out through the most common techniques of experimental neuropsychology (dichotic listening, tachistoscopic technique, finger-tapping, cf. Chapter 7), but their results have been rather controversial. Many factors, such as focusing of attention, the languages used during the test, the subjects' expectancy, etc., influence the results, thus making them less uniform.

The question concerning the possible greater involvement of the right hemisphere in the organization of the linguistic functions in bilinguals can be answered with studies on the cerebral lateralization of languages by means of the intracarotid sodium amytal injection (Wada test; cf. Chapter 7, p. 64), with the systematic study of a suitable number of bilingual aphasics, and with the study using neuroimaging techniques. The only study published on a transient inhibition of one of the two cerebral hemispheres in bilingual subjects (Wada test) was carried out by Rapport, Tan, and Whitaker (1983). The study focused on the subjects' naming capacity after inhibition of both cerebral hemispheres. Four polyglot aphasics waiting to undergo neurosurgical operations participated in the experiment. Retrograde femoral catheterization was performed in the routine fashion, tip position, and one carotid artery was injected with sodium amytal. After two hours the controlateral carotid artery was injected. Immediately after injection the patient was administered a naming test. He had to name 24 common objects in each of the languages he knew. All four patients named over 95% of objects during inhibition of the right hemisphere, whereas the naming percentage was very low during inhibition of the left hemisphere. Importantly, this study did not corroborate the hypothesis that in bilinguals language is represented to a greater extent in the right hemisphere.

In an analysis of the aphasia cases in polyglot patients reported in the literature (where hand preference and site of the lesion were clearly stated) and of other cases I have followed over the years, 81 (92%) right-handed patients out of 88 showed a lesion to the left hemisphere, and 7 (8%) presented with a lesion to the right hemisphere (crossed aphasia). Therefore, in the bilingual or polyglot aphasics included in this analysis, the percentage of crossed aphasia is higher than that in monolinguals. However, this data needs a critical examination, because neurologists generally tend to describe the rarest clinical cases and to omit the so-called common cases. For the same reason, there has been a tendency to describe only, or mainly, crossed aphasia cases in polyglots. For example, at least two cases of aphasia (published by April & Tse, 1977; April & Han, 1980) caused by a right hemisphere lesion were specifically signaled because they were cases of crossed aphasia. The analysis of a suitable number of cases will permit us to establish the extent of this phenomenon. Yet, currently available data—if critically examined—show that the percentage of crossed aphasia in bilinguals is not significantly higher than that of monolingual aphasics (Karanth & Rangamani, 1988; Paradis, 1990b; Solin, 1989).

However, the right hemisphere is known to be crucially involved in the processing of pragmatic aspects of language use (Chantraine et al., 1998). During the first stages of second language learning, or else when L2 is not very well known and is rarely used by the individual, the right hemisphere may be more involved in verbal communication, because "beginners" tend to compensate for their limited implicit linguistic competence (i.e. phonology, morphology, syntax, and the lexicon) in L2 with pragmatic inferences. A stronger participation of the right hemisphere during verbal communication in L2, however, does not mean that language processes *per se*, i.e. the implicit linguistic competence, are represented in the nondominant hemisphere (see Paradis, 1998). It is rather in this light that one should interpret a series of recent studies using PET and fMRI to study the cerebral representation of language in bilinguals having learned L2 at school after the age of 7 and for which they had a moderate proficiency level (Dehaene et al., 1997). These authors have studied the cerebral representation of both languages during listening to stories in L1 and L2. In the listening condition in L2, the subjects presented on average a greater activation of the right hemisphere then in the listening condition in L1.

In the last 20 years, several studies have been carried out in order to evaluate the cerebral lateralization of language in normal bilinguals (cf. Fabbro, 1989; Fabbro & Gran, 1994; Green, Vaid, Schweda-Nicholson, White, & Steiner, 1994; Vaid & Hall, 1991). Although interesting, the results of these studies are rather limited, mainly because of the methods used (prevailingly dichotic listening, finger tapping, and tachistoscopic viewing; cf. Chapter 7, pp. 60–62).

MODELS OF LANGUAGE PRODUCTION IN BILINGUALS

On the basis of current knowledge, provisional models or maps presenting the results obtained have been proposed. In 1986, David Green proposed a general model accounting for verbal expression in bilinguals (cf. Fig. 25.1), which included data and hypotheses derived from psycholinguistics and neurolinguistics. The model is based on a modular principle and presupposes the existence of different mutually independent subsystems (subsystems subserving the analysis of words in L1 and L2, subsystems subserving the expression in L1 and L2), which in turn are formed by an indefinite number of independent, yet constantly interacting modules.

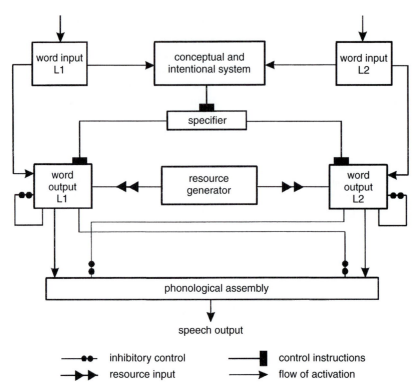

FIG. 25.1.   Green's model of the control of verbal expression in a bilingual (adapted from Green, 1986).

Green's framework postulates three types of relations between the various subsystems: activation, inhibition, and resource. In 1989 Paradis described the features of the *activation* component in detail, claiming that each word and hence each language has a specific activation threshold depending on the frequency of use and on the time elapsed since the last activation. A cerebral lesion can lower the activation threshold of a language, which is thus not lost, but simply inaccessible through the usual activation threshold. Generally, the activation threshold for comprehension is lower than the activation threshold for expression. For this reason, some bilingual aphasics are still able to understand a language, but not speak it (cf. Paradis, 1996).

The *inhibition* component—also present in monolinguals—is also very important. When a word is selected, e.g. "apple", all semantically related words are inhibited (pear, orange, banana, etc.) as are all phonologically similar words (i.e. dapple). In bilinguals, during the selection of a language, inhibitory relations inhibit the deactivated language. Inhibition is generally automatic and avoids interferences between the two languages. Therefore, verbal expression in one language automatically inhibits expression in the other language. A similar inhibition occurs in the patellar myotatic reflex, where agonistic muscles are activated and antagonistic muscles are concurrently inhibited. Similarly, the activation of the word "apple" in L1 inhibits the corresponding word in L2, as well as semantically similar and phonologically similar words in both languages or the translation of the selected word from L1 to L2. A cerebral lesion may impair the capacity to use L1 not only because of an insufficient activation of the language (L1), but above all because of an insufficient inhibition of the other language (L2). Inhibitory relations between languages are probably organized differently in simultaneous interpreting, where both languages are concurrently activated for many hours a day. In this particular profession, the activation thresholds of the two languages are thus quantitatively different to those of the other polyglots (cf. Chapter 24, pp. 202–3).

In addition, Green stressed the importance of a component he defined as the *resource generator*. He drew attention to the mechanical and living systems that need energy to operate. The amount of resources is limited and can be depleted. Therefore, it needs replenishing. In Green's opinion, each language has a certain amount of resources, which decrease each time the language is activated. Once the resources available for verbal expression in L1 are consumed, subjects will have temporary difficulties in expression, whereas they will find it easier to express themselves in another language (L2), as the amount of resources subserving this language is greater. Some typical phenomena of bilingual aphasics, such as alternating antagonism, might be caused by a reduction in the resources subserving a given language and by the impossibility of replenishing them.

Recently, Kees de Bot (1992, 1996), a Dutch linguist, proposed a "bilingual production model" on the basis of a readaptation of the "speaking model" theorized by Levelt (1989, 1993). De Bot decided to use Levelt's model because in his opinion it summarized several decades of experimental researches and observations of speech errors in monolingual speakers. Actually, he has integrated this model by using information and data on bilingual speakers taken from different research domains (applied linguistics, psycholinguistics, neurolinguistics, etc.). In brief, de Bot's bilingual production model hypothesizes the existence of (i) three subsystems for language production (a conceptualizer, a formulator, and an articulator), (ii) a subsystem for comprehension (speech-comprehension system), and (iii) the lexicon, a subsystem that is involved both in production and in comprehension.

1. The *conceptualizer* contains all the information that can be expressed by means of language but that is not linguistic in itself ("preverbal mes-

sages"). In bilingual subjects, this system is also responsible for conventions in conversation, which are language-specific, and for choosing which language should be used in a given utterance. This subsystem has access to information stored in explicit memory systems (cf. Chapter 10) and is probably represented in the most anterior portions of the frontal lobe of both hemispheres and in some parieto-temporal areas of the left hemisphere (cf. Chapter 17).

2. The *formulator* converts the preverbal message into a speech plan (phonetic plan) by selecting the right words or lexical units and applying grammatical and phonological rules. Experimental and clinical studies suggest that bilingual individuals may have (a) a formulator and a separate lexicon for each one of the known languages or else (b) a unique large system that stores all data concerning the different languages. Age and method of acquisition as well as use of a language probably affect the organization of the formulator and the lexicon. In individuals with early acquisition of languages other than L1, the formulator is probably represented in common (cortico-subcortical) cerebral structures; in this case the different languages would be kept separate merely by neurofunctional mechanisms. When languages are learned after the age of 10, however, the neurofunctional systems responsible for grammar and phonology are most likely to be separate also at the neuroanatomical level (Fabbro, 1996; Kim et al., 1997; see also Chapters 10, 14, and 15). On the other hand, in fluent bilinguals the lexicon is probably represented in common neural structures (parieto-temporal areas) and the neurofunctional separation between languages might depend on word use relationships (e.g. elements from one language will be more effectively linked to each other than to elements from another language).

3. The *articulator* converts the speech plan into actual speech. Some authors (cf. Green, 1986) suggested that during verbal expression in bilinguals both the selected language and the dormant language are simultaneously activated at all levels with the exception of the articulation subsystem, which remains inactive for the nonselected language. The articulator transforms the strings of syllables of the selected language into articulatory patterns. It has also been put forward (cf. Flege & Fletcher, 1992) that—with regard to the set of syllables and prosodic aspects—some bilinguals (late bilinguals) may have independent stores for each language, whereas others (early bilinguals) may have only one store containing all elements of both languages.

Thus, the "bilingual production model" has clearly systematized much of the data collected in different domains of the research on bilingualism and has proved to be a very useful stimulus for further psycholinguistic research in the field.

CHAPTER TWENTY-SIX

Forgotten and invented languages

Chapters 26 and 27 require a different approach with respect to the preceding chapters because they deal with issues concerning the knowledge of languages. The author considers them to be of interest, but they need further systematic research before they can be considered part of the so-called scientific knowledge. The first part of this chapter describes cases of bilinguals who will speak a language under hypnotic trance, but deny knowledge of it in the waking state. The second part of the chapter deals with the phenomenon of the conscious and unconscious invention of languages (glossolalia) and presents a neurolinguistic model of glossolalia.

Common sense leads us to think that a language cannot be forgotten if it is still accessible under specific circumstances. Many practical experiences and experimental situations have shown that people can believe they have lost one language or that they do not know it, although that language is still available. One of the most convincing studies proving that forgotten languages are not lost, but are still accessible under specific circumstances, was carried out by Ghilarducci at the end of the last century on patients affected by hysteria (Ghilarducci, 1892/1983). The first case concerned a young woman who, after a severe mental shock, exhibited a hysterical syndrome with total loss of recollection of her past experiences. The patient had completely forgotten English, which she had mastered fluently before the mental shock as she had lived in England for three years. Under hypnosis the patient fully reacquired her command of the English language. The same happened to other patients. A similar case was reported by Breuer, a colleague of Freud's, in 1895. A hysterical patient of his, Fräulein Anna O., ceased to speak her native language, German, and started speaking only English. On the whole, she understood German but insisted on speaking English, even with her servant who did not understand English. At other times, the patient seemed unable even to understand German. Therefore, her relatives were compelled to address her in English. Curiously, under these circumstances, Anna O. was able to read French and Italian, but if she was asked to read aloud in one of these languages, she *sight-translated* the text into English very fluently. However, her mother tongue had neither been lost nor forgotten, because under particular emotional circumstances and hypnosis Anna O. started speaking German fluently again (Freud & Breuer, 1974).

THE COMEBACK OF A FORGOTTEN LANGUAGE

One of the most effective methods of studying some mental "mechanisms" concerning mnestic and emotional functions is hypnosis. This technique, which basically induces a different state of consciousness, has been used in the past in an attempt to distinguish what was called functional (or psychic) from what was known as organic and neurological. One hundred years ago a distinction between hysterical symptoms and real neurological diseases was very difficult; for instance, the incapability to speak one language might be either a hysterical symptom or an aphasic disorder. In uncertain cases the physician made the patient enter hypnosis. If in these circumstances the patient recovered the language, the incapability to speak was considered a psychological functional reaction, rather than an aphasic symptom. At present, neuroimaging techniques permit us to ascertain whether a symptom depends on a neurological illness or, possibly, on a psychological disorder. However, the interpretation of cognitive disorders due to neurological illnesses has become more complex than in the past. Indeed, data show that in neurological illnesses a complex function, i.e. language, can be not so much destroyed as inhibited by the pathological process. The wider knowledge on cognitive and emotional functions is thus contributing to bridging the gap between neurology and psychology.

In 1963 Arvid As described a hypnotic age regression experiment during which a forgotten language was recovered (As, 1963). The subject (S.) was born in Finland. His parents were Finnish and he had been speaking Finnish until he was 5 years old. At that time he followed his mother who moved to the United States to work there. Until the age of 8 S. continued to speak Finnish within his family. Subsequently, this language was abandoned in favor of English. Before the experiment, S.'s competence in Finnish was assessed. The subject stated he had completely lost it, except for a few words. When administered a test consisting of 72 simple questions in Finnish (i.e. "How old are you?", "Have you got brothers or sisters?", "What food do you like?", "Do you know what a horse is?", "Point to your nose", "What color is grass?", etc.), S. only understood 12 (16.6%). In the following two weeks, S. underwent a series of hypnotic sessions during which age regression was suggested to make him relive episodes of his childhood. At the end of the fifth and sixth sessions he was asked in Finnish to relive some episodes when he was 5 years old and still at kindergarten. S. answered in English, saying he had been in the United States for some months then, but he could still remember some Finnish. At this juncture, he was re-tested with the aforementioned 72 questions in Finnish. Under hypnosis S. understood 39 questions, thus showing a significant improvement in his comprehension of Finnish (from 16.6% to 54.2%). On the basis of these results, As concluded that this apparently forgotten language was not lost, but only inhibited.

A few years later, in 1970, North-American psychologist Erika Fromm thoroughly studied some aspects of the mechanisms accounting for the inhibition of a language (Fromm, 1970). Fromm studied Don, a student at the University of Chicago, who was of Japanese origin. His parents were both born in the United States, so his family had always spoken English. When asked, Don claimed he neither understood nor spoke Japanese, except for a few fixed expressions. As Don was highly susceptible to hypnosis and could easily regress to childhood, Fromm asked him to enter hypnosis so as to show a class of university students the effects of this state. Under hypnosis, Don regressed to when he was 8 years old and described a game he liked to play. He later regressed to age 3. He felt good-humored and happy. After a few seconds of silence, with a typical child-like voice, he started— much to the audience's surprise—to speak fluent Japanese. He continued to speak Japanese for almost 20 minutes. Then he was asked to relive an episode when he was 7 years old, and he spontaneously started to speak English again. After termination of the trance Don had spontaneous post-hypnotic amnesia. He was highly astonished to learn that he had spoken fluent Japanese, a language he thought he did not know.

This experience upset Don, who a few months later asked the psychologist to take him on in psychotherapy and help him to find his identity. He thus entered a new hypnotic session with psychotherapeutic aims. Don regressed to when he was 3 years old and started speaking fluent Japanese again. Under hypnosis he was encouraged to remember his experiences before the age of 5 as much as possible. Don gradually relived his infancy in a concentration camp for US citizens of Japanese origin. He was born on December 2, 1941, five days before the Japanese attack on Pearl Harbor. Some time later he had been transferred with his family to a Japanese relocation camp in Minnesota. In these camps, undesirable US citizens, especially old people, very often spoke Japanese and Don, during his first years of life, was exposed only to this language, even though he also learnt English. After the war his parents decided they would only speak English because Don tended to speak Japanese with his schoolmates, who did not understand him. In the following years of his childhood, adolescence, and early adulthood, he did not speak Japanese, which was thus repressed (he still knew Japanese, but probably the activation threshold of this language had become so high that it could be overcome only in an altered state of consciousness, such as hypnosis). In the weeks after his last hypnotic session Don gradually recovered his forgotten language. Owing to these experiences he was able to appreciate the Japanese language and culture.

In Fromm's opinion, the fact that Don no longer used Japanese could only minimally explain his impression that he had lost it; more importantly, inhibitory psychological effects had determined the "repression" of this language. The child, somatically similar to a Japanese, strongly wished to be considered fully American, and not Japanese-American, i.e. a second-class citizen. Therefore, a whole range of emotional and educational factors might have elicited the isolation of Japanese, and hence Don's conviction that he did not know this language.

INVENTED LANGUAGES

Cases in the literature show that languages can be consciously or unconsciously invented (Williams, 1994). The conscious invention of a language is often the result of children's fantasy, whereas in adults it is mostly related to religious reasons (sacred languages of secrete societies) or practical reasons (i.e. auxiliary international languages such as Esperanto). The phenomenon of unconsciously invented languages has been described in some subjects during particular states of religious ecstasy or hypnotic trance, or in patients affected by severe psychopathologies (Fabbro, 1998). This phenomenon is defined as *glossolalia*, a term originating from two Greek words: *glossa* meaning language, and *lalein* meaning to speak.

North-American anthropologists N. Malony and A. Lovekin (1985) described five types of glossolalia:

1. The language of spirits: an esoteric dialect known only by spirits, the god, and the shaman producing it. Its linguistic features are difficult to define.
2. The language of animals: a particular imitation of the sounds uttered by animals. The capacity to speak the language of animals, such as birds and lions, allows the shaman to come to a greater understanding of the secrets of nature.
3. Pre-glossolalic languages are mysterious and strange dialects formed by very rough sounds. In addition, they are characterized by the monotonous repetition of words or melody accompanied by particular gestures and movements that usually ease the state of trance.

4. Ermenoglossy: often glossolalic expressions produced during a religious ceremony by a subject under trance are translated by another subject acting as interpreter so that the whole religious community has the impression to understand what the subject under trance says.
5. Xenoglossy: this type of glossolalia (deriving from the Greek terms *xenos* = foreign, and *glossa* = language) concerns the hypothetical ability of a subject to speak foreign languages without ever having listened to them, or studied them.

Belgian neurolinguist Yvan Lebrun (1983) proposed three types of glossolalia:

1. The glossolalia of the states of religious or hypnotic *trances*, reversible and characterized by monologues.
2. Schizoaphasic glossolalia, which manifests itself in psychiatric patients in the form of monologues and is reversible.
3. Jargonaphasic glossolalia, which manifests itself in patients with lesions to the left temporal lobe, is irreversible, and which also emerges in dialogues.

A neurolinguistic model of glossolalia

North-American researchers V. Shulka and E. Pattison (1983) proposed a neurolinguistic interpretation of a case of glossolalia. A patient underwent a neurosurgical operation to remove an aneurysm in the left middle cerebral artery which was causing epileptic fits. During the attacks the patient became isolated, closed her eyes, and started to perform rhythmic movements with her arms, accompanied by strange sounds that were similar to American-Indian songs. On the basis of this case Shulka and Pattison proposed another cause for glossolalia, and contributed to widen the knowledge of this phenomenon. They maintained that glossolalia could manifest itself:

1. in normal subjects in a religious context during waking states or ecstasy;
2. in normal subjects under experimental hypnotic trance;
3. out of conscious imitation in a linguist;
4. during regression states in psychologically unstable subjects;
5. in subjects affected by severe psychosis; and
6. as a clinical symptom during temporal epileptic fits.

Therefore, they devised a schematic representation of the most important neural centers involved in glossolalic behavior (cf. Figure 26.1). In line with

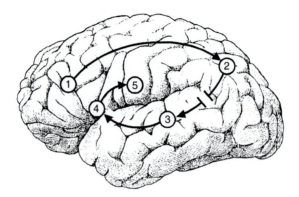

FIG. 26.1.   A neurolinguistic model of glossolalia.

Penfield and Roberts' (1976) views, they identified the main centers subserving verbal expression during episodes of glossolalia:

1. an anterior area of the left frontal lobe where verbal production is
   planned;
2. this center is connected with a center subserving the semantic organization of expression, localized in the temporo-parietal cortex;
3. information is transferred to a lexical representation center localized
   in the temporal lobe;
4. the thought produced is transferred to the motor coordination centers
   of Broca's area;
5. language motor centers send information to the motor cortex of the
   larynx and the vocal tract to guide the movements of the vocal tract in
   the production of language sounds.

Shulka and Pattison concluded that in this case glossolalia was caused by
a paroxysmal epileptic excitation of the lexical center (3), which was dis-
connected from the centers accounting for thought and ideation, as the
patient suffered a functional disorder affecting the temporal lobe. Therefore,
they suggested that all types of glossolalia are probably due to an interruption in the information flow from the semantic center (2) to the lexical
center (3). In glossolalic behavior the lexical center—localized in the temporal lobe—would be excited independently of any connection with
thoughts and ideas.

CHAPTER TWENTY-SEVEN

Languages and biological diversity

This chapter describes the studies that have led to the conclusion that human languages might have been a cultural obstacle to genetic exchange between different peoples, especially in the past. In fact, a language guarantees not only communication between the individuals speaking it, but also determines a separation from the groups not speaking it.

A question that can legitimately be raised by those interested in human biology, hence not only by historians or linguists, is the reason why there are so many different languages. Middle Eastern mythology, for instance, interprets linguistic diversity—in the Biblical tale of the Tower of Babel—as God's wrath against human arrogance (*Genesis* 11,1–9). Another excerpt from Genesis does not consider linguistic diversity as an impoverishment, but as one of the positive aspects of Creation (*Genesis* 10,31).

Two general assumptions on language have echoed from ancient times to the present age. The first assumption concerns the mother tongue and was succinctly expressed by Ferdinand de Saussure (1922) when he stated that every people is satisfied with their own language. The second assumption concerns foreign languages. In the absence of emotional, intellectual, or economic reasons that may determine a certain degree of closeness towards a foreign language, the first impact with unusual sounds—often unintelligible—provokes emotions in the listener ranging from a sense of unfamiliarity to genuine contempt for the seemingly chaotic assemblage of "noise".

In ancient times the Greeks considered Greek the only real language and showed their contempt for foreign languages by maintaining that other people did not speak real languages, they only stuttered. Therefore, they were called barbarians, deriving form the Greek word *barbaros*, which means "incapable of making oneself be understood because of stuttering". This idiosyncrasy towards foreign languages did not even spare Greek people who knew other languages. For instance, Parmenides and his disciple Zeno were looked at with mistrust and contempt because they were bilinguals (apparently, they also knew a Semitic language; cf. Capizzi, 1975).

The reasons for the existence of many languages are usually of historico-geographical nature (Hill, 1985; Laponce, 1987). In fact, languages change over time and geographical distance determines the emergence of new languages in the long term. Furthermore, linguistic mutations in past ages may have been accelerated or even caused by linguistic invention initiatives on the part of individuals with a certain degree of assertiveness within a given linguistic group. A question of crucial importance to a biologist approaching the issue of linguistic diversity is the following: Does language diversity contribute to the evolution of the human species?

LINGUISTIC AND GENETIC DIVERSITY

Answering this question requires the introduction of a number of other issues and the discussion of data and models deriving from the observation of other living species. First of all, let us briefly discuss the functions of a language: a language not only guarantees communication (within a group of speakers) between the people understanding it, but it also contributes to distinguishing those people from other groups speaking different languages (Braitenberg, 1987; Fabbro, 1990, 1992). Evidence has shown that songbird "dialects" (of chaffinches, canaries, etc.; cf. Chapter 3, p. 27) determine genetic isolation within the same species, because these birds show a marked attitude towards mating with individuals who sing the same dialect. Female birds prefer male partners singing the dialect that was sung by their fathers when they were young. Individuals flock into groups that differ from other groups only for cultural reasons (learning of a specific dialect) and individuals of these groups, by mating within the group, create cultural barriers to genetic exchange. This phenomenon is called *cultural pseudo-speciation* and contributes to biological diversity. It is one of the most effective strategies developed by living creatures to guarantee the survival of the species (Baker & Cunningham, 1985).

At this juncture, the following question needs to be answered: Do human languages imply cultural pseudo-speciation phenomena, too? The answer to this question is not yet definitive. First of all, the correctness of this question cannot be assessed with regard to Western cultural lifestyles, because economic, political, and cultural phenomena have wiped out basic steps of human development, such as the marked difference between rather small groups, which is precisely one of the characteristics of the peoples the Western world considers rather "primitive". The study of genetic differences between different peoples of 2000–3000 individuals each who lived in Amazonia in neighboring territories has revealed a close link between linguistic and genetic diversity. In particular, Spielman, Migliazza, and J. Neel (1974) monitored seven Yanomani linguistic groups living in the Venezuelan Amazonian forest, who—in addition to their mother tongue—spoke a lingua franca to communicate and barter. The study of the lexical and syntactical differences between different languages allowed the three researchers to assess the degree of linguistic distance between the seven different groups and to relate it to their separation from a single stock (about 1000 years ago). A given number of individuals belonging to each group had blood taken to analyze important genetic characteristics. On the basis of these results, Spielman and associates concluded that genetic diversity was lower between individuals speaking the same language than between individuals speaking different languages. Furthermore, genetic diversity was higher in individuals speaking languages that had split earlier and, therefore, were linguistically more distant. This study suggests that human languages may indeed be an obstacle to genetic exchange between different peoples.

A number of studies on the genetics of peoples subsequently substantiated the hypothesis that languages and cultural traditions constitute genetic barriers between human groups. Probably for this reason, genetic diversity between individuals belonging to different peoples was determined both by geographical isolation and by linguistic and cultural barriers, especially in the past. However, anthropological studies show that there are exceptions to the rule. Suffice it to mention that the incest taboo, which in many cultural groups forbids sexual intercourse between siblings, was consciously and legitimately ignored in ancient Egypt by members of the Pharaoh family. On the other hand, groups promoting marriage between individuals speaking different languages were monitored in Australia, as were groups in Colombia who consider marriage between individuals of the same linguistic group to be incest.

Future studies will clarify some of these interesting hypotheses. A case in point for the major contributions made to anthropology and historico-scientific sciences by this research line is provided by the studies carried out by L. Cavalli-Sforza, an Italian geneticist who works in the United States (Cavalli-Sforza, Piazza, Menozzi, & Mountain, 1988). On the basis of data resulting from genetic studies of human peoples, he reviewed and sometimes corrected genealogical trees of human languages that had previously been outlined on linguistic grounds only.

CHAPTER TWENTY-EIGHT

Conclusions

This book has attempted to describe and discuss present data and knowledge on the cerebral organization of language in bilinguals. Many questions remain unsolved and will have to be dealt with in the future. In particular, the thorough analysis of numerous cases of bilingual aphasics provided by the Bilingual Aphasia Test will allow a more accurate assessment of the patients' recovery patterns and cerebral lateralization of languages, whether structurally similar or not. Further research on the various types of memory involved in language learning and acquisition is advisable. In addition, greater stress is to be laid on the role played by neural subcortical structures in language as well as on the study of aphasia in bilingual children. An extremely important research line for aphasiologists is that of speech therapy in bilingual aphasics. In this field research studies have just begun. The neurolinguistic study of translation is considered to be at a pioneer stage as well; only a few basic questions have been raised as yet and only a few useful investigation patterns have been detected.

Finally, another field of research concerns a more detailed and reliable study of the cerebral representation of language. Beside neuroimaging and neuropsychological and neurolinguistic investigations on normal subjects and bilingual aphasics, future research studies of language neurophysiology are in order. Linguistic and neuropsychological studies are certainly necessary, but not sufficient, to understand the cerebral organization of languages in bilinguals. As a matter of fact, even though human sciences and medicine consider individual and biographical data to be of fundamental importance, science—to quote E. Rutherford—means physics first. Indeed, what is still lacking in this field is a physics of verbal communication behavior, in other words a *language physiology*.

References

Adler, A. (1983). Contributions to the classification and theory of aphasia. In M. Paradis (Ed.), *Readings on aphasia in bilinguals and polyglots* (p. 23). Montreal: Didier. (Original work published in 1889.)

Aglioti, S., Beltramello, A., Girardi, F., & Fabbro, F. (1996). Neurolinguistic and follow-up study of an unusual pattern of recovery from bilingual subcortical aphasia. *Brain, 119,* 1551–1564.

Aglioti, S., & Fabbro, F. (1993). Paradoxical selective recovery in a bilingual aphasic following subcortical lesions. *NeuroReport, 4,* 1359–1362.

Aitchison, J. (1992). *Linguistics.* Chicago: NTC Publishing Group.

Akmajian, A., Demers, R.A., & Harnish, R.M. (1979). *Linguistics: An introduction to language and communication.* Cambridge, MA: MIT Press.

Albert, M.L., Goodglass, H., Helm, N.A., Rubens, A.B., & Alexander, M.P. (1981). *Clinical aspects of dysphasia.* New York: Springer-Verlag.

Albert, M.L., & Obler, L.K. (1978). *The bilingual brain. Neuropsychological and neurolinguistic aspects of bilingualism.* New York: Academic Press.

Alexander, G.A. (1994). Basal ganglia-thalamocortical circuits: Their role in control of movement. *Journal of Clinical Neurophysiology, 11,* 420–431.

Alexander, M.P. (1989). Clinical-anatomical correlations of aphasia following predominantly subcortical lesions. In F. Boller & F. Grafman (Eds.), *Handbook of neuropsychology* (Vol. 2, pp. 47–66). Amsterdam: Elsevier.

April, R.S., & Han, M. (1980). Crossed aphasia in a right-handed bilingual Chinese man. *Archives of Neurology, 37,* 342–345.

April, R.S., & Tse, P.C. (1977). Crossed aphasia in a Chinese bilingual dextral. *Archives of Neurology, 34,* 766–770.

Aronson, A.E. (1980). *Clinical voice disorders.* New York: Thieme & Stratton.

As, A. (1963). The recovery of forgotten language knowledge through hypnotic age regression: A case report. *American Journal of Clinical Hypnosis, 5,* 24–29.

Asher, R.E. (Ed.) (1994). *The encyclopedia of language and linguistics.* Oxford: Pergamon Press.

Atkinson, R.C., & Shiffrin, R.M. (1968). Human memory: A proposed system and its control processes. In K.W. Spence & J.T. Spence (Eds.), *The psychology of learning and motivation: Advances in research and theory* (Vol. 2, pp. 90–195). New York: Academic Press.

Baddeley, A.D. (1990). *Human memory. Theory and practice.* Hove, UK: Lawrence Erlbaum Associates Ltd.

Baddeley, A.D., Papagno, C., & Vallar, G. (1988). When long-term learning depends on short-term storage. *Journal of Memory and Language, 27,* 586–595.

Baker, M.C., & Cunningham, M.A. (1985). The biology of bird-song dialects. *The Behavioral and Brain Sciences, 8,* 85–133.

Bàlint, A. (1923). Observations in a case of polyglot aphasia. In M. Paradis (Ed.), *Readings on aphasia in bilinguals and polyglots* (pp. 169–175). Montreal: Didier. (Original work published in 1923.)

Bates, E., Thal, D., & Janowsky, J.S. (1992). Early language development and its neural correlates. In F. Boller & J. Grafman (Eds.), *Handbook of neuropsychology, Vol. 7: Child Neuropsychology* (pp. 69–110). Amsterdam: Elsevier.

Békésy, G. von (1960). *Experiments in hearing.* New York: McGraw-Hill.

Benton, A.L. (1969). *Contributions to clinical neuropsychology.* Chicago: Aldine.

Benton, A.L. (1981). Aphasia: Historical perspectives. In M. Taylor Sarno (Ed.), *Acquired aphasia* (pp. 1–21). New York: Academic Press.

Bergson, H. (1911). *Matter and memory.* London: Swan Sonnenschein.

Berthier, M.L., Starkstein, S.E., Lylyk, P., & Leiguarda, R. (1990). Differential recovery of languages in a bilingual patient: A case study using selective amytal test. *Brain and Language, 38,* 449–453.

Bickerstaff, E.R. (1972). Cerebrovascular disease in infancy and childhood. In P.J. Vinken & G.W. Bruyn (Eds.), *Handbook of clinical neurology, vascular diseases of the nervous system* (Vol. 3). Amsterdam: Elsevier.

Bhatia, K.P., & Marsden, D. (1994). The behavioural and motor consequences of focal lesions of the basal ganglia in man. *Brain, 117,* 859–876.

Blanken, G., Dittmann, J., Grimm, H., Marshall, J.C., & Wallesch C.-W. (Eds.) (1993). *Linguistic disorders and pathologies.* Berlin: Walter de Gruyter.

Bonner, J.T. (1980). *The evolution of culture in animals.* Princeton, NJ: Princeton University Press.

Borden, G.J., & Harris, K.S. (1984). *Speech science primer. Physiology, acoustics and perception of speech.* Baltimore, MA, and London: William & Wilkins.

Botez, M.I. (Ed.) (1996). *Neuropsychologie clinique et neurologie du comportement.* Paris: Masson.

Botez, M.I., & Barbeau, A. (1971). Role of subcortical structures, and particularly of the thalamus in the mechanisms of speech and language. *International Journal of Neurology, 8,* 300–320.

Bouillaud, J.B. (1825). *Traité clinique et physiologique de l'encéphalite ou inflammation du cerveau, et de ses suites.* Paris: Baillière.

Bouquet, F., Tuvo, F., & Paci, M. (1981). Afasia traumatica in un bambino bilingue nel 5° anno di vita. *Neuropsichiatria infantile, 236,* 159–169.

Braitenberg, V. (1987). *Gescheit sein und andere unwissenschaftliche Essays.* Tübingen: Haffmans Verlag.

Broca, P.P. (1861). Remarques sur le siège de la faculté du language articulé, suives d'une observation d'aphémie (perte de la parole). *Bulletin de la Société Anatomique, 6,* 330–357.

Broca, P.P. (1865). Du siège de la faculté du langage articulé. *Bulletin de la Société d'Anthropologie, 6,* 337–393.

Brown, J.W. (1977). *Mind, brain, and consciousness.* New York: Academic Press.

Brown, J.W. (1990). *Self and process. Brain states and the conscious present.* New York: Springer-Verlag.

Bruce, L.C. (1895). Notes of a case of dual brain action. *Brain, 18,* 54–65.

Bryden, M.P. (1982). *Laterality. Functional asymmetry in the intact brain.* New York: Academic Press.

Buckingham, H.W., & Hollien, H. (1978). A neural model for language and speech. *Journal of Phonetics, 6,* 283–297.

Bychowsky, Z. (1983). Concerning the restitution of language loss subsequent to a cranial gunshot wound in a poliglot aphasic. In M. Paradis (Ed.), *Readings on aphasia in bilinguals and polyglots* (pp. 130–144). Montreal: Didier. (Original work published in 1919.)

Cabanis, E.A., Iba-Zizen, M.T., Abelanet, R., Monod-Broca, Ph., & Signoret, J.L. (1994). "Tan Tan" the first Paul Broca patient with "aphemia" (1861) CT (1979) and MRI (1994) of the brain. In L. Picard & G. Salamon (Eds.), *4th Refresher Course of the European Society of Neuroradiology "Language and Aphasia"* (pp. 9–22). Udine: Edizioni del Centauro.

Calvet, L.J. (1974). *Linguistique et colonialisme. Petit traité de glottophagie.* Paris: Editions Payot.

Calvin, W.H., & Ojemann, G.A. (1980). *Inside the brain. Mapping the cortex, exploring the neuron.* New York: New American Library.

Calvin, W.H., & Ojemann, G.A. (1994). *Conversations with Neil's brain. The neural nature of thought and language.* New York: Addison Wesley.

Capizzi, A. (1975). *Introduzione a Parmenide.* Bari: Laterza.

Caplan, D. (1990). *Neurolinguistics and linguistic aphasiology. An introduction.* Cambridge: Cambridge University Press.

Cappa, S.F. (1998). Spontaneous recovery from aphasia. In B. Stemmer & H.A. Whitaker (Eds). *Handbook of neurolinguistics* (pp. 536–547). San Diego, CA: Academic Press.

Carrez, M. (1983). *Les langues de la Bible.* Paris: Editons du Centurion.

Cavalli-Sforza, L.L., Piazza, A., Menozzi, P., & Mountain, J. (1988). Reconstruction of human evolution: Bringing together genetic, archaeological, and linguistic data. *Proceedings of the National Academy of Science USA, 85,* 6002–6006.

Chantraine Y., Joanette, Y., & Cardebat, D. (1998). Impairments of discourse-level representations and processes. In B. Stemmer & H.A. Whitaker (Eds.), *Handbook of neurolinguistics* (pp. 262–275). San Diego, CA: Academic Press.

Chernigovskaya, T.V., Balonov, L.J., & Deglin, V.L. (1983). Bilingualism and brain functional asymmetry. *Brain and Language, 23,* 195–216.

Chlenov, L.G. (1983). On aphasia in polyglots. In M. Paradis (Ed.), *Readings on aphasia in bilinguals and polyglots* (pp. 445–454). Montreal: Didier. (Original work published in 1948.)

Chomsky, N. (1977). *Dialogues avec Mitsou Ronat.* Paris: Flammarion.

Chomsky, N. (1980). *Rules and representations.* New York: Columbia University Press.

Claparède, E. (1911). Récognition et moïté. *Archives de Psychologie, Genève, 11,* 79–90.

Code, C. (1987). *Language, aphasia, and the right hemisphere.* Chichester, UK: Wiley.

Cohen, N.J., & Eichenbaum, H. (1994). *Memory, amnesia, and the hyppocampal system.* Cambridge, MA: MIT Press.

Coren, S. (1992). *The left-hander syndrome. The causes and consequences of left-handedness.* New York: Free Press.

Crosson, B. (1992). *Subcortical functions in language and memory.* New York: Guilford Press.

Damasio, H. & Damasio, A.R. (1989). *Lesion analysis in neuropsychology.* New York: Oxford University Press.

Darley, F.L., Aronson, A.E., & Brown, J.R. (1975). *Motor speech disorders.* Philadelphia, PA: W.B. Saunders.

Darò, V., & Fabbro, F. (1994). Verbal memory during simultaneous interpretation: Effects of phonological interference. *Applied Linguistics, 15,* 365–381.

De Bot, K. (1992). A bilingual production model: Levelt's "speaking" model adapted. *Applied Linguistics, 13*, 1–24.

De Bot, K. (1996). The psycholinguistics of the output hypothesis. *Language Learning, 46*, 529–55.

Dehaene, S., Dupoux E., Mehler J., Cohen L., Paulesu E., Perani D., et al. (1997). Anatomical variability in the cortical representation of first and second language. *Neuroreport, 8*, 3809–3815.

De Kerckhove, D., & Lumsden, C.J. (Eds.) (1988). *The alphabet and the brain*. Berlin: Springer-Verlag.

Démonet, J.F. (1998). Tomographic brain imaging of language functions: Prospects for a new brain/language model. In B. Stemmer & H.A. Whitaker (Eds.), *Handbook of neurolinguistics* (pp. 132–143). San Diego, CA: Academic Press.

DeMyer, W. (1988). *Neuroanatomy*. New York: Wiley.

Denès, P. (1983). Contributions to the study of some aphasic phenomena. In M. Paradis (Ed.), *Readings on aphasia in bilinguals and polyglots* (pp. 108–117). Montreal: Didier. (Original work published in 1914.)

Denes, P.B., & Pisoni, E.N. (1973). *The speech chain. The physics and biology of spoken language*. New York: Anchor Press.

De Vreese, L.P., Motta, M., & Toschi, A. (1988). Compulsive and paradoxical translation behaviour in a case of presenile dementia of the Alzheimer type. *Journal of Neurolinguistics, 3*, 233–259.

De Zulueta, F.I. (1984). The implications of bilingualism in the study and treatment of psychiatric disorders: A review. *Psychological Medicine, 14*, 541–557.

Dimitrijevic, D. (1983). On language restitution in polyglot aphasia. In M. Faradis (Ed.), *Readings on aphasia in bilinguals and polyglots* (pp. 391–395). Montreal: Didier. (Original work published in 1940.)

Ellis, N. (1992). Linguistic relativity revisited: The bilingual word-length effect in working memory during counting, remembering numbers, and mental calculation. In R.I. Harris (Ed.), *Cognitive processing in bilinguals* (pp. 137–155). Amsterdam: Elsevier.

Epstein, S.D., Flynn, S., & Martohardjono, G. (1996). Second language acquisition: Theoretical and experimental issues in contemporary research. *Behavioral and Brain Sciences, 21*, 60–99.

Eskridge, J. (1983). Mind and word deafness after depressed fracture of the skull with subcortical hemorrhage-operation; complete recovery. In M. Paradis (Ed.), *Readings on aphasia in bilinguals and polyglots* (pp. 50–57). Montreal: Didier. (original work published in 1896.)

Fabbro, F. (1989). Neurobiological aspects of bilingualism and polyglossia. In L. Gran & J. Dodds (Eds.), *The theoretical and technical aspects of teaching conference interpretation* (pp. 71–82). Udine: Campanotto.

Fabbro, F. (1990). Parcé i popui fevelino plui lenghis al puest di une? *Usmis, 1*, 11.

Fabbro, F. (1992). Fevelâ plui di une lenghe. *Usmis, 3*, 36–37.

Fabbro, F. (1994). Left and right in the Bible from a neuropsychological perspective. *Brain and Cognition, 24*, 161–183.

Fabbro, F. (1995a). *Destra e sinistra nella Bibbia. Uno studio neuropsicologico*. Rimini: Guaraldi.

Fabbro, F. (1995b). Le afasie nei bilingui. *Kos. Rivista di medicina, cultura e scienze umane, 115*, 14–21.

Fabbro, F. (1996). Neurofunctional aspects of bilingual aphasia. *Journal of the Israeli Speech Hearing and Language Association, 19*, 13–15.

Fabbro, F. (1997a). Bilingual aphasia research is not a tabula rasa. *Aphasiology, 12*, 138–141.

Fabbro, F. (1997b). Introduction: Subcortical aphasia. *Journal of Neurolinguistics, 10*, 251–256.

Fabbro, F. (1998). Prospettive d'interpretazione della glossolalia paolina sotto il profilo della neurolinguistica. *Rivista Biblica Italiana, 46*, 89–110.

Fabbro, F., & Darò, V. (1994). Delayed auditory feedback in polyglot simultaneous interpreters. *Brain and Language, 48*, 309–319.

Fabbro, F., & De Luca, G., & Vorano, L. (1996). Assessment of language rehabilitation with the BAT in four multilingual aphasics. *Journal of the Israeli Speech, Hearing and Language Association, 19*, 46–53.

Fabbro, F., & Gran, L. (1994). Neurological and neuropsychological aspects of polyglossia and simultaneous interpretation. In S. Lambert & B. Moser (Eds.), *Bridging the gap: Empirical research on interpretation* (pp. 273–317). Amsterdam: Benjamins.

Fabbro, F., & Gran, L. (1997). Neurolinguistic aspects of simultaneous interpretation. In Y. Gambier et al. (Eds.), *Conference interpreting: Current trends in research* (pp. 9–28). Amsterdam: Benjamins.

Fabbro, F., Gran, L., Basso, G., & Bava, A. (1990). Cerebral lateralization in simultaneous interpretation. *Brain and Language, 39*, 69–89.

Fabbro, F., Gran, B., & Gran, L. (1991). Hemispheric specialization for semantic and syntactic components in simultaneous interpreters. *Brain and Language, 41*, 1–42.

Fabbro, F., & Paradis M. (1995a). Differential impairments in four multilingual patients with subcortical lesions. In M. Paradis (Ed.), *Aspects of bilingual aphasia* (pp. 139–176). Oxford: Pergamon Press.

Fabbro, F., & Paradis, M. (1995b). Acquired aphasia in a bilingual child. In M. Paradis (Ed.), *Aspects of bilingual aphasia* (pp. 67–83). London: Pergamon Press.

Fabbro, F., Peru, A., & Skrap, M. (1996). Bilingual aphasia following thalamic lesions. *Journal of the Israeli Speech Hearing and Language Association, 19*, 68–72.

Fabbro, F., Peru, A., & Skrap, M. (1997). Language disorders in bilingual patients after thalamic lesions. *Journal of Neurolinguistics, 10*, 347–367.

Fant, G. (1970). *Acoustic theory of speech production*. The Hague: Mouton.

Fiez, J.A., Petersen, S.E., Cheney, M.K., & Raichle, M.E. (1992). Impaired non-motor learning and error detection associated with cerebellar damage. *Brain, 115*, 155–178.

Flege, J.E., & Fletcher, K.L. (1992). Talker and listener effects on degree of perceived foreign accent. *Journal of the Acoustical Society of America*, 91, 370–389.

Fodor, J. K. (1983). *The modularity of mind. An essay on faculty psychology*. Cambridge, MA: MIT Press.

Förster, O. (1936). Symptomatologie der Ekrankungen des Gehirns. In O. Blumke & O. Förster (Eds.), *Handbuch der Neurologie* (Vol. 6, pp. 1–357). Berlin: Julius Springer.

Frederiks, J.A.M. (Ed) (1985). *Handbook of neurology, Vol. I (45): Clinical neuropsychology*. Amsterdam: Elsevier.

Fredman, M. (1976). The effect of therapy given in Hebrew on the home language of the bilingual or polyglot adult in Israel. *British Journal of Disorders of Communication, 10*, 61–69.

Freud, S. (1891). *Zur Auffassung der Aphasien. Eine kritische Studie*. Leipzig und Wien: Franz Deutiche.

Freud, S., & Breuer J. (1974). *Studies on hysteria*. London: Penguin.

Fromkin, V., & Rodman, R. (1993). *An introduction to language*. Fort Worth, TX: Harcourt Brace Jovanovich.

Fromm, E. (1970). Age regression with unexpected reappearance of repressed childhood language. *The International Journal of Clinical and Experimental Hypnosis, 18*, 79–88.

Ganschow, L., Sparks, R.L., Javrosky, J., Pohlman, J., & Bishop-Marbury, A. (1991). Identifying native language difficulties among foreign learners in college: A "Foreign language learning disability?". *Journal of Learning Disabilities, 24*, 530–541.

Garrett, M.F. (1984). The organization of processing structure for language production: applications to aphasic speech. In D. Caplan, A.R. Lecours, & A. Smith (Eds.), *Biological perspectives on language* Cambridge, MA: MIT Press.

Gastaldi, G. (1951). Osservazioni su un afasico bilingue. *Sistema Nervoso, 2*, 175–180.

Gathercole, S.E., & Baddeley, A.D. (1993). *Working memory and language*. Hove, UK: Lawrence Erlbaum Associates Ltd.

Gazzaniga, M.S. (1985). *The social brain. Discovering the networks of the mind*. New York: Basic Books.

Gelb, A. (1983). On medical psychology and philosophical anthropology. In M. Paradis (Ed.), *Readings on aphasia in bilinguals and polyglots* (pp. 383–385). Montreal: Didier. (Original work published in 1937.)

Geschwind, N., Quadfasel, F., & Segarra, J. (1968). Isolation of the speech area. *Neuropsychologia, 6*, 327–340.

Ghilarducci, F. (1983). Note to "hysteria and organic disease of the brain". In M. Paradis (Ed.), *Readings on aphasia in bilinguals and polyglots* (p. 25). Montreal: Dider. (Original work published in 1892.)

Goldstein, K. (1983). Disturbances of language in polyglot individuals with aphasia (case summary). In M. Paradis (Ed.), *Readings on aphasia in bilinguals and polyglots* (p. 455). Montreal: Didier. (Original work published in 1948.)

Gomez-Tortosa, E., Martin, E.M, Gaviria, M., Charbel, F., & Ausman J.I. (1995). Selective deficit of one language in a bilingual patient following surgery in the left perysylvian area. *Brain and Language, 48*, 320–325.

Gorlitzer von Mundy, V. (1983). A 94-year-old with one German language center and probably two Slovenian centers. In M. Paradis (Ed.), *Readings on aphasia in bilinguals and polyglots*. Montreal: Didier (pp. 624–625). (Original work published in 1959.)

Gracco, V.L., & Abbs, J.H. (1987). Programming and execution processes of speech movement control: Potential neural correlates. In E. Keller & M. Gopnik (Eds.), *Motor and sensory processes of language* (pp. 163–201). Hillsdale, NJ: Erlbaum.

Grasset, J. (1883). Clinical contribution to the study of aphasias. In M. Paradis (Ed.), *Readings on aphasia in bilinguals and polyglots* (p. 15). Montreal: Didier. (Original work published 1884.)

Green, D. (1986). Control, activation, and resource: A framework and a model for the control of speech in bilinguals. *Brain and Language, 27*, 210–223.

Green, A., Vaid, J., Schweda-Nicholson, N., White, N., & Steiner R. (1994). Lateralization for shadowing vs. interpretation: A comparison of interpreters with bilingual and monolingual controls. In S. Lambert & B. Moser (Eds.), *Bridging the gap: Empirical research on interpretation* (pp. 331–335). Amsterdam: Benjamins.

Grosjean, F. (1982). *Life with two languages. An introduction to bilingualism*. Cambridge, MA: Harvard University Press.

Grosjean, F. (1989). Neurolinguists, beware! The bilingual is not two monolinguals in one person. *Brain and Language, 36*, 3–15.

Grosjean, F. (1992). Another view of bilingualism. R.J. Harris (Ed.), *Cognitive processing in bilingualism* (pp. 51–62). Amsterdam: Elsevier.

Grosjean F. (1994). Individual Bilingualism. In R.E. Asher (Ed.), *The encyclopedia of language and linguistics* (pp. 1656–1660). Oxford: Pergamon Press.

Grosjean, F. (1998). Study in bilinguals: Methodological and conceptual issues. (Manuscript submitted for publication.)

Hagège, C. (1985). *L'homme de paroles. Contribution linguistique aux sciences humaines*. Paris: Arthème Fayard.

Hagège, C. (1996). *L'enfant aux deux langues*. Paris: Odile Jacob.

Haiman, J., & Benincà, P. (1992). *The Rhaeto-Romance languages*. London: Routledge.

Halpern, L. (1983). Restitution in polyglot aphasia with regard to Hebrew. In M. Paradis (Ed.) *Readings on aphasia in bilinguals and polyglots* (pp. 418–422). Montreal: Didier. (Original work published in 1941.)

Hamers, J.F., & Blanc, M.H.A. (1990). *Bilinguality and bilingualism.* Cambridge: Cambridge University Press.

Handel, S. (1989). *Listening. An introduction to the perception of auditory events.* Cambridge, MA: MIT Press.

Harrington, A. (1987). *Medicine, mind, and double brain. A study in nineteenth-century thought.* Princeton, NJ: Princeton University Press.

Hebb, D.O. (1949). *Organization of behavior.* New York: Wiley.

Hebb, D.O. (1980). *Essay on mind.* Hillsdale, N.J.: Erlbaum.

Hécaen, H. (1972). *Introduction à la neuropsychologie.* Paris: Larousse.

Hécaen, H. (1976). Acquired aphasia in children and the ontogenesis of hemispheric functional specialization. *Brain and Language, 3,* 114–134.

Hécaen, H. (1983). Acquired aphasia in children: Revisited. *Neuropsychologia, 21,* 581–587.

Hécaen, H. (1984). *Les gauchers. Etude neuropsychologique.* Paris: Presses Universitaires de France.

Hécaen, H., & Dubois, J. (1971). La neurolinguistique. In G.E. Perren & J.L.M. Trim (Eds.), *Applications of linguistics* (pp. 85–99). Cambridge: Cambridge University Press.

Hickok, G., Bellugi, U., & Klima, E.S. (1996). The neurobiology of sign language and its implications for the neural basis of language. *Nature, 381,* 699–702.

Hikosaka, O. (1991). Basal ganglia—possible role in motor coordination and learning. *Current Opinion in Neurobiology, 1,* 638–643.

Hill, H.J. (1985). Human dialect and language differentiation. *The Behavioral and Brain Sciences, 8,* 107–108.

Hilton, L.M. (1980). Language rehabilitation strategies for bilingual and foreign-speaking aphasics. *Aphasia, Apraxia, Agnosia, 3,* 7–12.

Hinde, R.A. (1972). *Non-verbal communication.* Cambridge: Cambridge University Press.

Hinshelwood, J. (1983). Four cases of word blindness. In M. Paradis (Ed.), *Readings on aphasia in bilinguals and polyglots* (pp. 64–66). Montreal: Didier. (Original work published in 1902.)

Hirst, W., Phelps, E.A., Johnson, M.K., & Volpe, B.T. (1988). Amnesia and second language learning. *Brain and Cognition, 8,* 105–116.

Holmes, G. (1917). The symptoms of acute cerebellar injuries due to gunshot injuries. *Brain, 40,* 461–535.

Huang, S.-Y., & Peng, F.C.C. (1986). Semantic jargonaphasia: A Taiwanese-Japanese bilingual case. *Journal of Neurolinguistics, 2,* 261–276.

Huber, W., Poeck, K., Weniger, D., & Willmes, K. (1983). *Der Aachener Aphasie Test (AAT).* Gottingen: Hogrefe.

Ingvar, D.H. (1983). Serial aspects of language and speech related to prefrontal cortical activity. A selective review. *Human Neurobiology, 2,* 105–114.

Ingvar, D.H. (1985). "Memory of the future": An essay on the temporal organization of conscious awareness. *Human Neurobiology, 4,* 127–136.

Ito, M. (1994). La plasticité des synapses. *La Recherche, 267,* 778–785.

Jackendoff, R. (1994). *Patterns in the mind. Language and human nature.* New York: Basic Books.

Jackson, J.H. (1958). On the nature of the duality of the brain. In J. Taylor (Ed.), *Selected writings of John Hughlings Jackson* (Vol. 2, pp. 129–145). New York: Basic Books. (Original work published 1874.)

Jacobs, B., & Schumann, J. (1992). Language acquisition and the neurosciences: Towards a more integrate perspective. *Applied Linguistics, 13,* 282–301.

Jakobson, R. (1961). *Essais de linguistique générale.* Paris: Minuit.

Jakobson, R. (1971). *Studies on child Language and aphasia.* The Hague: Mouton.

Jakobson, R., & Waugh, L. (1987). *The sound shape of language.* Berlin: de Gruyter.

James, W. (1890). *The principles of psychology*. New York: Holt.

Joanette, Y., Goulet, P., & Hannequin, D. (1990). *Right hemisphere and verbal communication*. New York: Springer-Verlag.

Johnson, J.S., & Newport, E.L. (1989). Critical period effects in second language learning: The influence of maturational state on the acquisition of English as a second language. *Cognitive Psychology*, 21, 60–99.

Junqué, C., Vendrell, P., Vendrell-Brucet, J.M., & Tobeña, A. (1989). Differential recovery in naming in bilingual aphasia. *Brain and Language*, *36*, 16–22.

Jürgens, U. (1979). Anatomical and functional cerebral organization of phonation in animals. In O. Creutzfeld et al. (Eds.), *Hearing mechanisms and speech* (pp. 171–182). Berlin: Springer-Verlag.

Jürgens, U., & von Carmon, D. (1982). On the role of the anterior cingulate cortex in phonation: A case report. *Brain and Language*, *15*, 234–248.

Kainz, F. (1983). Speech pathology I: Aphasic speech. In M. Paradis (Ed.), *Readings on aphasia in bilinguals and polyglots* (pp. 636–640). Montreal: Didier. (Original work published in 1960.)

Kandel, E.R., Schwartz, J.H., & Jessell, T.M. (Eds.) (1991). *Principles of neural science*. Amsterdam: Elsevier.

Karanth, P., & Rangamani, G.N. (1988). Crossed aphasia in multilinguals. *Brain and Language*, *34*, 169–180.

Kauders, O. (1983). On polyglot responses in a sensory aphasia. In M. Paradis (Ed.), *Readings on aphasia in bilinguals and polyglots* (pp. 286–300). Montreal: Didier. (Original work published in 1929.)

Kim, K.H.S., Relkin, N.R., Lee, K.-M., & Hirsch J. (1997). Distinct cortical areas associated with native and second languages: *Nature, 388*, 171–174.

Klein, D., Milner, B., Zatorre, R., Evans, A., & Meyer, E. (1994). Functional anatomy of bilingual processing: A neuroimaging study. *Brain and Language*, *47*, 464–466.

Klein, D., Zatorre, R.J., Milner, B., Meyer, E. & Evans, A.C. (1995). The neural substrates of bilingual language processing: Evidence from positron emission tomography. In M. Paradis (Ed.), *Aspects of bilingual aphasia* (pp. 23–36). London: Pergamon.

Kolb, B., & Whishaw, I.Q. (1990). *Fundamentals of human neuropsychology*. New York: Freeman.

Konishi, M. (1985). Birdsong: from behaviour to neuron. *Annual Review of Neuroscience, 8*, 125–170.

Kosslyn, S.M. (1983). *Ghosts in the mind's machine. Creating and using images in the brain*. New York: W.W. Norton.

Kraetschmer, K. (1982). Forgotten cases of bilingual aphasics. *Brain and Language*, *15*, 92–94.

Krapf, E.E. (1955). On the linguistic behaviour of brain damaged patients. In M. Paradis (Ed.), *Readings on aphasia in bilinguals and polyglots* (pp. 552–562). Montreal: Didier. (Original work published in 1955.)

Krapf, E.E. (1983). On aphasia in polyglots. In M.Paradis (Ed.), *Readings on aphasia in bilinguals and polyglots* (pp. 569–574). Montreal: Didier. (Original work published in 1957.)

Kuehn, D.P., Lemme, M.L., & Baumgartner, J.M. (Eds.) (1989). *Neural bases of speech, hearing, and language*. Boston: College-Hill Press.

Kuhl, P.K. (1994). Learning and representation in speech and language. *Current Opinion in Neurobiology, 4*, 812–822.

Kuypers, H.G. (1958). Corticobulbar connections to the pons and the lower brain-stem in man. *Brain, 81*, 364–388.

Laborit, H. (1976). *Eloge de la fuite*. Paris: Laffont.

Laborit, H. (1983). *La colombe assassineé*. Paris: Grasset & Fasquelle.

Lambert, W.L. (1992). Challenging established views on social issues. The power and limitations of research. *American Psychologist, 47*, 533–542.

Lambert, W.L., Genesee, F., Holobow N., & Chartrand L. (1993). Bilingual education for majority English-speaking children. *European Journal of Psychology of Education, 1*, 3–22.

Lamendella, J.T. (1977a). General principles of neurofunctional organization and their manifestation in primary and nonprimary language acquisition. *Language Learning, 27*, 155–196.

Lamendella, J.T. (1977b). The limbic system in human communication. In H. Whitaker & H.A. Whitaker (Eds.), *Studies in neurolinguistics* (Vol. 3, pp. 157–222). New York: Academic Press.

Laponce, J.A. (1987). *Languages and their territories.* Toronto: Toronto University Press.

Lebrun, Y. (1975). Early bilingualism. In A. van Essen & J. Menting (Eds.), *The context of foreign-language learning* (pp. 61–66). Assen, The Netherlands: Van Gorcum.

Lebrun, Y. (1983). La glossolalie. In J.P. Van Noppen & G. Deburscher (Eds.), *Communicating and translating* (pp. 227–239). Bruxelles: Editions de l'Université de Bruxelles.

Lebrun, Y. (1988). Multilinguisme et aphasie. *Revue de Laryngologie, 109*, 299–306.

Lebrun, Y. (1991). Polyglotte Reaktionen. *Neurolinguistik, 5*, 1–9.

Lebrun, Y. (1995). The study of bilingual aphasia: Pitres'' legacy. In M. Paradis (Ed.), *Aspects of bilingual aphasia* (pp. 11–22). London: Pergamon.

Lecours, A.R., & Lhermitte, F. (Eds.) (1979). *L'aphasie.* Paris: Flammarion.

LeDoux, J.E. (1996). *The emotional brain.* New York: Simon & Schuster.

Leiner, C.H., Leiner, A.L., & Down, R.S. (1991). The human cerebro-cerebellar system: its computing, cognitive, and language skills. *Behavioural Brain Research, 44*, 113–128.

Leischner, A. (1983a). Aphasia of deaf-mutes. In Paradis, M. (Ed.), *Readings on aphasia in bilinguals and polyglots* (pp.; 423–444). Montreal: Didier. (Original work published in 1943.)

Leischner, A. (1983b). On the aphasia of multilinguals. In M. Paradis (Ed.), *Readings on aphasia in bilinguals and polyglots* (pp. 456–502). Montreal: Didier. (Original work published in 1948.)

Lenneberg, E.H. (1967). *Biological foundations of language.* New York: Wiley.

Lesser, R. (1978). *Linguistic investigations of aphasia.* London: Arnold.

Levelt, W.J. (1989) *Speaking: From intention to articulation.* Cambridge, MA: MIT Press.

Levelt, W.J. (1993) Language use in normal speakers and its disorders. In G. Blanken et al. (Eds.), *Linguistic disorders and pathologies* (pp. 1–15). Berlin: de Gruyter.

Liberman, A.M. (1996). *Speech: A special code.* Cambridge, MA: MIT Press.

Lichtheim, L. (1885). On aphasia. *Brain, 7*, 433–485.

Lieberman, P. (1967). *Intonation, perception and language.* Cambridge, MA: MIT Press.

Lieberman, P. (1975). *On the origins of language: An introduction to the evolution of human speech.* New York: Macmillan.

Lieberman, P., & Blumstein, S.H. (1988). *Speech physiology, speech perception, and acoustic phonetics.* Cambridge: Cambridge University Press.

Locke, J.L. (1993). *The child's path to spoken language.* Cambridge, MA: Harvard University Press.

Luria, A.R. (1973). *The working brain. An introduction to neuropsychology.* New York: Basic Books.

Luria, A.R. (1976a). *The man with a shattered world.* Chicago: Regnery.

Luria, A.R. (1976b). *Basic problems in neurolinguistics.* The Hague: Mouton.

Luria, A.R. (1980). *Higher cortical functions in man.* New York: Basic Books.

Luzzatti, C., Willmes, K., & De Bleser R. (1992). *Aachener Aphasie Test (AAT). Versione italiana.* Firenze: Organizzazioni Speciali.

MacLean, P.D. (1973). *A triune concept of the brain and behaviour.* Toronto: University of Toronto Press.

MacNeilage, P., & Ladefoged, P. (1976). The production of speech and language. In E.C. Carterette & M.P. Friedman (Eds.), *Handbook of perception* (Vol. VII, pp. 75–120). New York: Academic Press.

Malberg, B. (1974). *Manuel de phonétique générale*. Paris: Editions A. & J. Picard.

Malony, H.N., & Lovekin, A.A. (1985). *Glossolalia. Behavioral science perspectives on speaking in tongues*. New York: Oxford University Press.

Marler, P. (1981). Birdsong: the acquisition of a learned motor skill. *Trends of Neuroscience, 4*, 88–94.

Marsden, C.D., & Obeso, J.A. (1994). The function of the basal ganglia and the paradox of stereotaxic surgery in Parkinson's disease. *Brain, 117*, 877–897.

Marshall, J.C. (1983). How could you tell how are grammars represented? *The Behavioral and Brain Sciences, 6*, 411–412.

Martinet, A. (1985). *Syntaxe générale*. Paris: Armand Colin.

Maruszewski, M. (1975). *Language communication and the brain. A neuropsychological study*. The Hague: Mouton.

Masutto, C., Bravar, L., & Fabbro, F. (1993). A neurolinguistic differentiation of subtyped dyslexic children. *Journal of Learning Disabilities, 27*, 520–526.

McCarthy, R.A., & Warrington, E.K. (1990). *Cognitive neuropsychology. A clinical introduction*. Orlando, FL: Academic Press.

McCawley, J.D. (1983). Execute criminals, not rules of grammar. *The Behavioral and Brain Sciences, 6*, 410–411.

McEwen, B.S., & Sapolsky, R.M. (1995). Stress and cognitive function. *Current Opinion in Neurobiology, 5*, 205–216.

Menn, L., & Obler, L.K. (Eds.) (1990). *Agrammatic aphasia. A cross-language narrative sourcebook*. Amsterdam: Benjamins.

Meunier, M., Bachevalier, J., & Mishkin, M. (1994). L'anatomie de la mémoire. *La Recherche, 25*, 760–766.

Miceli, G., Silveri, M.C., Romani, C., & Caramazza, A. (1989). Variation in the pattern of omissions and substitutions of grammatical morphemes in the spontaneous speech of so-called agrammatic patients. *Brain and Language, 36*, 447–492.

Miller, G.A. (1951). *Language and communication*. New York: McGraw-Hill.

Miller, G. A. (1981). *Language and speech*. San Francisco: W.H. Freeman.

Milner, B., Corkin, S., & Teuber, H.L. (1968). Further analysis of the hippocampal amnesic syndrome: Fourteen year follow-up study of H.M. *Neuropsychologia, 6*, 215–234.

Mimouni, Z., Béland, R., Danault, S., & Idrissi, A. (1995). Similar language disorders in Arabic and French in an early bilingual aphasic patient. *Brain and Language, 51*, 132–134.

Mingazzini G. (1913). Über den Verlauf einiger Hirnbahnen und besonders der motorischen Sprachbahnen. *Archiv für Psychiatrie und Nervenkrankheiten, 51*, 256–321.

Minkowski, M. (1983a). A clinical contribution to the study of polyglot aphasia especially with respect to Swiss-German. In M. Paradis (Ed.), *Readings on aphasia in bilinguals and polyglots* (pp. 205–232). Montreal: Didier. (Original work published in 1927.)

Minkowski M. (1983b). On a case of aphasia in a polyglot. In M. Paradis (Ed.), *Readings on aphasia in bilinguals and polyglots* (pp. 274–279). Montreal: Didier. (Original work published in 1928.)

Minkowski, M. (1983c). A particular case of aphasia with polyglot reactions, confabulation, and other disorders after cranio-cerebral trauma. In M. Paradis (Ed.), *Readings on aphasia in bilinguals and polyglots* (pp. 524–534). Montreal: Didier. (Original work published in 1949.)

Minkowski, M. (1963). On aphasia in polyglots. In L. Halpern (Ed.), *Problems of dynamic neurology*. Jerusalem: Hebrew University.

Murdoch, B.E. (1990). *Acquired speech and language disorders. A neuroanatomical and functional neurological approach*. London: Chapman & Hall.

Murdoch, B.C. (1992). *Acquired neurological speech-language disorders in childhood.* London: Taylor & Francis.

Nadeau, S.E., & Crosson B. (1997). Subcortical aphasia. *Brain and Language, 58,* 355–403.

Neville, H.J., Coffey, S.A., Lawson, D.S., Fischer, A., Emmorey, K., & Bellugi, U. (1997). Neural systems mediating American Sign Language: Effects of sensory experiences and age of acquisition. *Brain and Language, 57,* 285–308.

Neville, H.J., Mills, D.L., & Lawson, D.S. (1992). Fractionating language: different neural subsystems with different sensitive periods. *Cerebral Cortex, 2,* 244–258.

Newman, J.D. (Ed.) (1988). *The physiological control of mammalian vocalization.* New York: Plenum.

Nilipour, R., & Ashayeri, H. (1989). Alternating antagonism between two languages with successive recovery of a third in a trilingual aphasic patient. *Brain and Language, 36,* 23–48.

Nottebohm, F. (1970). Ontogeny of bird song. *Science, 167,* 950–956.

Ojemann, G.A. (1991). Cortical organization of language. *The Journal of Neuroscience, 11,* 2281–2287.

Ojemann, G.A., & Whitaker, H.A. (1978). The bilingual brain. *Archives of Neurology, 35,* 409–412.

O'Neill, Y.V. (1980). *Speech and speech disorders in Western thought before 1600.* Westport, CT: Greenwood Press.

Paivio, A. (1986). Bilingual cognitive representation. In A. Paivio (Ed.), *Mental representations. A dual coding approach.* New York: Oxford University Press.

Papagno, C., & Vallar, G. (1995). Verbal short-term memory and vocabulary learning in polyglots. *Quarterly Journal of Experimental Psychology, 48A,* 98–107.

Paradis, M. (1977). Bilingualism and aphasia. In H. Whitaker & H.A. Whitaker (Eds.), *Studies in neurolinguistics* (Vol. 3, pp. 65–121). New York: Academic Press.

Paradis, M. (1984). Aphasie et traduction. *Meta Translators' Journal, 24,* 57–67.

Paradis, M. (1985). On the representation of two languages in one brain. *Language Sciences, 7,* 1–39.

Paradis, M. (1986). Henry Hécaen and neurolinguistics. *Journal of Neurolinguistics, 2,* 1–14.

Paradis, M. (1987a). *The assessment of bilingual aphasia.* Hillsdale, NJ: Erlbaum.

Paradis, M. (1987b). The neurofunctional modularity of cognitive skills: Evidence from Japanese alexia and polyglot aphasia. In E. Keller & M. Gopnik (Eds.), *Motor and sensory processes of language* (pp. 277–289). Hillsdale, NJ: Erlbaum.

Paradis, M. (1988). Recent developments in the study of agrammatisms: Their import for the assessment of bilingual aphasia. *Journal of Neurolinguistics, 3,* 127–160.

Paradis, M. (1989). Bilingual and polyglot aphasia. In F. Boller & J. Grafman (Eds.), *Handbook of neuropsychology* (Vol. 2, pp. 117–140). Oxford: Elsevier.

Paradis, M. (1990a). Differential recovery of languages in a bilingual patient following selective amytal injection: A comment on Berthier et al. (1990). *Brain and Language, 39,* 469–470.

Paradis, M. (1990b). Language lateralization in bilinguals: Enough already! *Brain and Language, 39,* 576–586.

Paradis, M. (1993a). Multilingualism and aphasia. In G. Blanken et al. (Eds.), *Linguistics disorders and pathologies* (pp. 278–288). Berlin: de Gruyter.

Paradis, M. (1993b). Linguistic, psycholinguistic, and neurolinguistic aspects of "interference" in bilingual speakers: The activation threshhold hypothesis. *International Journal of Psycholinguistics, 9,* 133–145.

Paradis, M. (Ed.) (1993c). *Foundations of aphasia rehabilitation.* Oxford: Pergamon Press.

Paradis, M. (1993d). Bilingual aphasia rehabilitation. In M. Paradis (Ed.), *Foundations of aphasia rehabilitation* (pp. 413–419). Oxford: Pergamon Press.

Paradis, M. (1994a). Neurolinguistic aspects of implicit and explicit memory: implications for bilingualism and second language acquisition. In N. Ellis (Ed.), *Implicit and explicit language learning* (pp. 393–419). London: Academic Press.

Paradis, M. (1994b). Neurolinguistic aspects of "native speaker". In R. Singh (Ed.), *The native speaker*. Newbury, CA: Sage.

Paradis, M. (1994c). Toward a neurolinguistic theory of simultaneous translation: The framework. *International Journal of Psycholinguistics, 10*, 319–335.

Paradis, M. (1995a). Bilingual aphasia 100 years later: Consensus and controversies. In M. Paradis (Ed.), *Aspects of bilingual aphasia* (pp. 211–223). Oxford: Pergamon.

Paradis, M. (1995b). Selective deficit in one language is not a demonstration of a different anatomical representation: Comments on Gomez-Tortosa et al. (1995). *Brain and Language, 54*, 170–173.

Paradis, M. (1996). The cognitive neuropsychology of bilingualism. In A. De Groot & J. Kroll (Eds.), *Tutorials in bilingualism: Psycholinguistic perspectives*. Hillsdale, NJ: Erlbaum.

Paradis M. (1998). Language and communication in multilinguals. In B. Stemmer & H.A. Whitaker (Eds.). *Handbook of Neurolinguistics* (pp. 418–431). San Diego, CA: Academic Press.

Paradis, M., & Goldblum, M.C. (1989). Selective crossed aphasia in a trilingual aphasic patient followed by reciprocal antagonism. *Brain and Language, 36*, 62–75.

Paradis, M., Goldblum, M.C., & Abidi R. (1982). Alternate antagonism with paradoxical translation behavior in two bilingual aphasic patients. *Brain and Language, 15*, 55–69.

Paradis, M., Hagiwara, H., & Hildebrandt, N. (1985). *Neurolinguistic aspects of the Japanese writing system*. Orlando, FL: Academic Press.

Paradis, M., & Lebrun, Y. (1983). La neurolinguistique du bilinguisme: représentation et traitment de deux languages dans un même cerveau. *Languages, 72*, 7–13.

Paradis, M., & Lebrun, Y. (Eds.) (1984). *Early bilingualism and child development*. Lisse: Swets & Zeitlinger.

Parkin, A.J. (1997). The development of procedural and declarative memory. In N. Cowan & C. Hulme (Eds.), *The development of memory in childhood* (pp. 113–137). Hove, UK: Psychology Press.

Penfield, W. (1959). The learning of languages. In W. Penfield & L. Roberts (Eds.), *Speech and brain mechanisms* (pp. 235–257). New York: Atheneum (fourth Atheneum printing 1976).

Penfield, W., & Roberts L. (1976). *Speech and brain-mechanisms*. New York: Atheneum.

Perani, D., Bressi, S., Cappa, S.F., Vallar, G., et al. (1993). Evidence of multiple memory systems in the human brain. A [18F]FDG PET metabolic study. *Brain, 116*, 903–919.

Perani, D., Dehaene, S., Grassi, F., Cohen L., Cappa, S.F., Dupoux, E., Fazio, F., & Mehler, J. (1996). Brain processing of native and foreign languages. *NeuroReport, 7*, 2439–2444.

Perecman, E. (1984). Spontaneous translation and language mixing in a polyglot aphasic. *Brain and Language, 23*, 43–63.

Perecman, E. (1989). Language processing in the bilingual: evidence from language mixing. In K. Hyltenstam & K.L. Obler (Eds.), *Bilingualism across the lifespan. Aspects of acquisition, maturity, and loss* (pp. 227–244). Cambridge: Cambridge University Press.

Perkell, J.S. (1969). *Physiology of speech production: Results and implications of a quantitative cineradiographic study*. Cambridge, MA: MIT Press.

Peru, A., & Fabbro, F. (1997). Thalamic amnesia following venous infarction. Evidence from a single case study. *Brain and Cognition, 33*, 278–294.

Pick, A. (1983). Cured tuberculosis meningitis: at the same time a contribution to the study of aphasia in polyglots. In M. Paradis (Ed.), *Readings on aphasia in bilinguals and polyglots* (pp. 102–107). Montreal: Didier. (Original work published in 1913.)

Pinker, S. (1994). *The language instinct. The new science of language and mind*. London: Penguin.

Pitres A. (1983). Aphasia in polyglots. In M. Paradis (Ed.), *Readings on aphasia in bilinguals and polyglots* (pp. 26–49). Montreal: Didier. (Original work published in 1885.)

Poeck, K. (1982). *Klinische Neuropsychologie*. New York: Thieme.

Pötzl, O. (1925). Über die parietal bedingte Aphasie und ihren Einfluß auf das Sprechen mehrerer Sprachen. *Zeitschrift für die gesamte Neurologie und Psychiatrie, 96*, 100–124.

Pötzl, O. (1930). Aphasie und Mehrsprachigkeit. *Zeitschrift für die gesamte Neurologie und Psychiatrie, 12*, 145–162.

Pulvermüller, F., & Schumann, J.H. (1994). Neurobiological mechanisms of language acquisition. *Language Learning, 44*, 681–734.

Rapport, R.L., Tan, C.T., & Whitaker, H.A. (1983). Language function and dysfunction among Chinese—and English-speaking polyglots: Cortical stimulation, Wada testing, and clinical studies. *Brain and Language, 18*, 342–366.

Reynolds, A.F., Turner, P.T., Harris, A.B., Ojemann, G.A., & Davis, L.E. (1979). Left thalamic hemorrhage with dysphasia: A report of five cases. *Brain and Language, 7*, 62–73.

Roberts, P.M. (1997). Clinical research needs and issues in bilingual aphasia. *Aphasiology, 12*, 119–146.

Saint-Cyr, J.A., Taylor, A.E., & Lang, A.E. (1988). Procedural learning and neostriatal dysfunction in man. *Brain, 111*, 941–959.

Salmon, D.P., & Butters, N. (1995). Neurobiology of skill and habit learning. *Current Opinion in Neurobiology, 5*, 184–190.

Sapir, E. (1921). *Language. An introduction to the study of speech*. New York: Harcourt, Brace & World.

Sasanuma, S., & Park, H.S. (1995). Patterns of language deficits in two Korean-Japanese bilingual aphasic patients. A clinical report. In M. Paradis (Ed.), *Aspects of bilingual aphasia* (pp. 111–122). Oxford: Pergamon Press.

Satz, P., & Lewis, R. (1993). Acquired aphasia in children. In G. Blanken et al. (Eds.), *Linguistic disorders and pathologies* (pp. 646–659). Berlin: de Gruyter.

Saussure, F. de (1922). *Cours de linguistique générale*. Paris: Editions Payot.

Schacter, D.L. (1996). *Searching for memory. The brain, the mind, and the past*. New York: Basic Books.

Schwalbe, J. (1983). About the aphasia in polyglots. In M. Paradis (Ed.), *Readings on aphasia in bilinguals and polyglots* (p. 155). Montreal: Didier. (Original work published in 1920.)

Schwartz, M. (1994). Ictal language shift in a polyglot. *Journal of Neurology, Neurosurgery, and Psychiatry, 57*, 121.

Scoresby-Jackson, R.E. (1867). Case of aphasia with right hemiplegia. *Edinburgh Medical Journal, 12*, 696–706.

Segalowitz, S.J., & Chevalier H. (1998). Event-related potential (ERP) research in neurolinguistics. Parts I and II. In B. Stemmer & H.A. Whitaker (Eds.), *Handbook of neurolinguistics* (pp. 96–125). San Diego, CA: Academic Press.

Shallice, T. (1988). *From neuropsychology to mental structure*. Cambridge: Cambridge University Press.

Sharwood Smith, M. (1981). Consciousness-raising and the second language learner. *Applied Linguistics, 11*, 159–168.

Sheehan, P. (1993). The phenomenology of hypnosis and the experiential analysis tecnique. In E. Fromm & M.R. Nash (Eds.), *Contemporary hypnosis research* (pp. 364–389). New York: Guilford Press.

Shulka, V.R., & Pattison, E.M. (1983). *Organically induced glossolalia*. Augusta: Medical College of Georgia.

Silverberg, R., & Gordon, H.W. (1979). Differential aphasia in two bilingual individuals. *Neurology, 29*, 51–55.

Smirnov, B.L., & Factorovich, N.Y. (1983). Concerning aphasia in polyglots. In M. Paradis (Ed.), *Readings on aphasia in bilinguals and polyglots* (pp. 535–538). Montreal: Didier. (Original work published in 1949.)

Solin, D. (1989). The systematic misrepresentation of bilingual-crossed aphasia data and its consequences. *Brain and Language, 36*, 92–116.

Speedie, L.J., Wertman, E., Ta'ir, J., & Heilman, K.M. (1993). Disruption of automatic speech following a right basal ganglia lesion. *Neurology, 43*, 1768–1774.

Spielman, R.S., Migliazza, E.C., & Neel, J.V. (1974). Regional linguistic and genetic differences among Yanomana Indians. *Science, 184*, 637–644.

Squire, L.S. (1987). *Memory and brain*. New York: Oxford University Press.

Squire, L.R., & Zola-Morgan, S. (1991). The medial temporal lobe memory system. *Science, 253*, 1380–1385.

Stager, C.L., & Werker, J.F. (1997). Infants listen for more phonetic detail in speech perception than in word-learning tasks. *Nature, 388*, 381–382.

Stemmer, B., & Whitaker, H.A. (Eds.) (1998). *Handbook of neurolinguistics*. San Diego, CA: Academic Press.

Stengel, E., & Zelmanowicz, J. (1933). Über polyglotte motorische Aphasie. *Zeitschrift für die gesamte Neurologie und Psychiatrie, 149*, 292–311.

Sutton, D., Larson, C., & Lindeman R.C. (1974). Neocortical and limbic lesions effects on primate phonation. *Brain Research, 71*, 61–75.

Taylor, J. (1958). *Selected writings of John Hughlings Jakson*. New York: Basic Books.

Taylor Sarno, M. (Ed) (1981). *Acquired aphasia*. New York: Academic Press.

Trevarthen, C. (1984). Hemispheric specialization. In J.M. Brookhart & V.B. Mounctastle (Eds.), *Handbook of physiology. Section 1: The Nervous System* (Vol. III, pp. 1129–1190). Bethesda, MD: American Physiological Society.

Tulvig, E. (1987). Multiple memory systems and consciousness. *Human Neurobiology, 6*, 667–680.

Uexküll, J. von (1956). *Streifzüge durch Umwelten von Tieren und Menschen*. Reinbeck bei Hamburg: Rowohlt.

Vaid, J. (Ed.) (1986). *Language processing in bilinguals: Psycholinguistic and neuropsychological perspectives*. Hillsdale, NJ: Erlbaum.

Vaid, J., & Hall, D.G. (1991). Neuropsychological perspectives on bilingualism: Right, left, and center. In A.G. Reynolds (Ed.), *Bilingualism, multiculturalism, and second language learning* (pp. 81–112). Hillsdale, NJ: Erlbaum.

Valenstein, E.S. (1986). *Great and desperate cures*. New York: Basic Books.

Vallar, G., Cappa, S.F., & Wallesch, C.-W. (Eds.) (1992). *Neuropsychological disorders associated with subcortical lesion*. Oxford: Oxford University Press.

Veyrac, G.J. (1983). A study of aphasia in polyglot subjects. In M. Paradis (Ed.), *Readings on aphasia in bilinguals and polyglots* (pp. 320–338). Montreal: Didier. (Original work published in 1931.)

Voinescu, I., Visch, E., Sirian, S., & Maretsis, M. (1977). Aphasia in a polyglot. *Brain and Language, 4*, 165–176.

Vygotsky, L.S. (1986). *Thought and language*. Cambridge, MA: MIT Press.

Wallesch, C.W., & Papagno, C. (1988). Subcortical aphasia. In F. Clifford Rose, R. Whurr, & M.A. Wyke (Eds.) *Aphasia* (pp. 257–287). London: Whurr.

Walsh, K. (1994). *Neuropsychology: A clinical approach*. Edimburgh: Churchill Livingstone.

Warrington, E.K., & Shallice, T. (1969). The selective impairment of auditory short-term memory. *Brain, 92*, 432–444.

Watamori, T., & Sasanuma, S. (1976). The recovery process of bilingual aphasia. *Journal of Communication Disorders, 9*, 157–166.

Watamori, T., & Sasanuma, S. (1978). The recovery process of two English-Japanese bilingual aphasics. *Brain and Language, 6*, 127–140.

Weber-Fox, C.M., & Neville, H.J. (1996). Maturational constraints on functional specializations for language processing: ERP and behavioral evidence in bilingual speakers. *Journal of Cognitive Neuroscience, 8*, 231–256.

Wernicke, C. (1874). *Der aphasische Symptomencomplex. Eine psychologische Studie auf anatomischer Basis.* Berlin: Springer-Verlag. (Original work published in 1874.)

Whitaker, H.A. (1998). Neurolinguistics from the Middle Ages to the pre-modern era: Historical vignettes. In B. Stemmer & H.A. Whitaker (Eds.), *Handbook of neurolinguistics* (pp. 27–54). San Diego, CA: Academic Press.

Whitaker, H.A., & Etlinger, S.C. (1993). Theodor Meynert's contribution to classical 19th century aphasia studies. *Brain and Language, 45*, 560–571.

Williams, C.G. (1994). Glossolalia. In R. E. Asher (Ed.), *The Encyclopedia of language and linguistics* (Vol. 3, pp. 1444–1445). Oxford: Pergamon Press.

Woll, B., & Kyle, J.G. (1994). Sign language. In R.E. Asher (Ed.), *The Encyclopedia of language and linguistics* (Vol. 7, pp. 3890–3912). Oxford: Pergamon Press.

Yiu, E. M-L., & Worrall, L.E. (1996). Sentence production ability of a bilingual Cantonese-English agrammatic speaker. *Aphasiology, 10*, 505–522.

Zatorre, R.J. (1989). On the representation of multiple languages in the brain: Old problems and new directions. *Brain and Language, 36*, 127–147.

Author index

Subject index